DISPATCHES

Michael J. Totten

Michael J. Totten is a novelist and foreign correspondent who has reported from all over the world.

His first book, *The Road to Fatima Gate*, won the Washington Institute Book Prize in 2011, and his novel, *Resurrection*, was optioned for film in 2014.

His work has appeared in the *New York Times,* the *Wall Street Journal,* the *Los Angeles Times* and numerous other publications.

He lives with his wife in Oregon and is a former resident of Beirut.

Visit his blog at www.MichaelTotten.com

ALSO BY MICHAEL J. TOTTEN

The Road to Fatima Gate
In the Wake of the Surge
Where the West Ends
Taken: A Novel
Resurrection: A Zombie Novel
Tower of the Sun

DISPATCHES

MICHAEL J. TOTTEN

Copyright © 2016 by Michael J. Totten

All rights reserved. No part of this publication may be reproduced in any form or by any means without the prior written permission of Michael J. Totten

First American edition published in 2016 by Belmont Estate Books

Cover design by Kathleen Lynch
Cover photo by Zoriah Miller, www.zoriah.com
Edited by Elissa Englund

Manufactured in the United States on acid-free paper

FIRST AMERICAN EDITION

Totten, Michael J.
Dispatches
ISBN-13: 978-0692616864
ISBN-10: 0692616861

*For all my colleagues who risked their lives
to get the story and lost*

Contents

1. ISRAEL - The July War   11
2. IRAQ - Raid Night   38
3. CUBA - The Last Communist City   47
4. ITALY - The Worst Airline in the World   79
5. LEBANON - The Battle of Beirut   99
6. PALESTINIAN TERRITORIES - Darkness in Palestine   111
7. UKRAINE - Where the West Ends   124
8. EGYPT - The Slow Rot of Hosni Mubarak   162
9. IRAQ - The Road Up IED Alley   200
10. VIETNAM - Ho Chi Minh's Nightmare   213
11. LIBYA - In the Land of the Brother Leader   237

One

The July War

Lebanese/Israeli border 2006

Early in the morning on July 12, 2006, Ehud Goldwasser and Eldad Regev were on patrol near the Northern Israeli town of Zar'it, just south of the border with Lebanon, when unseen guerrillas ambushed their Humvee. Three of their fellow soldiers were killed in the attack, but Goldwasser and Regev fared even worse; they were captured by Hezbollah and dragged over the border fence into the wilds of South Lebanon.

The Israeli response was formidable. Another Israel Defense Forces soldier, Gilad Shalit, had been snatched just two weeks before by Palestinians and smuggled through a tunnel into Gaza. Israelis were in no mood to tolerate cross-border attacks on two fronts at once. Prime Minister Ehud Olmert promised "a very painful and far-reaching response." He launched artillery and air strikes at Hezbollah's positions in South Lebanon, at the command and control centers in the suburbs south of Beirut, and at infrastructure throughout the country, including roads, bridges, and Beirut's international airport.

Hezbollah's response was likewise ferocious. Its fighters fired thousands of World War II-era Katyusha rockets at Israeli civilian population areas in the cities of Haifa, Kiryat Shmona, Nazareth, and Tiberias. The entire northern sixth of the country—including Arab-majority areas—was blanketed with constant daily rocket attacks. Hezbollah wanted a brief border skirmish and an exchange of prisoners but instead found itself in a full-scale war that produced millions of refugees and devastated parts of both countries.

I was in Iraq when it started and could not get into Lebanon—the Israeli Air Force had put holes in the runway at the airport to prevent Hezbollah from flying the captured soldiers out to Iran. So I teamed up with my friend and colleague Noah Pollak, then-assistant editor at *Azure* magazine in Jerusalem, and took a rental car from Tel Aviv to the Israeli side of the front.

By then the war had been blazing for weeks. The Israeli government was proposing a cease-fire to end it even though Israel had so far gained practically nothing. It wasn't yet over, but it was already widely seen as a debacle. There was talk in the local newspapers about removing Olmert from the prime minister's office immediately. But the farther north we drove, the less relevant any talk of cease-fires and parliaments seemed. The fighting raged on, and we were approaching Hezbollah's shooting gallery.

Haifa, Israel's third-largest city, was empty and burning, as was every other city in the country near the Lebanese border.

Traffic thinned as we drove, but we hadn't yet seen overt signs of war. At some point we would cross an invisible boundary between the "safe" part of Israel, supposedly beyond the range of Hezbollah's rockets, and the kill zone. Neither Noah nor I knew exactly where that boundary was, but every mile we traveled brought us closer.

When we arrived at the resort town of Tiberias on the shore of the Sea of Galilee, it looked like a city at the end of the world. The streets were entirely empty of people and cars. More than a million civilians had packed up their valuables and fled south in their vehicles. Only a handful of brave, elderly, sick, poor, stubborn, and possibly suicidal people remained. It would have made a terrific set for a zombie movie.

"Stop the car," I said to Noah. "I want to get out."

Noah stopped the car in the middle of a major intersection. There was no need to pull over or park because there was no traffic.

I stepped out of the car. It was the middle of summer, and we were well below sea level. The air was unbearably hot, humid, heavy, and still. Nothing moved. Nothing seemed real. I heard no sound at all except the chirping of birds in the middle of a major city at noon. *We shouldn't be here*, I thought. I expected an explosion at any moment, but I couldn't see any damage and wasn't sure whether we were actually inside, or just near, Hezbollah's rocket range.

I got back in the car and we continued to drive. Just past the city and beyond the shores of the sea, we saw hillsides scorched from Katyusha fire. We were inside the zone now and could be killed at any time without warning.

As we approached the city of Kiryat Shmona, I braced for hell. It seemed to be Hezbollah's target of choice. It was so close to the border—less than two miles away—that there was no time to warn civilians to head to the bomb shelters when incoming rockets were detected on radar. They often exploded at the same instant the air-raid sirens turned on, and sometimes even before.

My colleague Lisa Goldman had been up there just a few days earlier with a colleague, and she described the scene as a horror.

"The nearly abandoned city reminded us of scenes in Hollywood movies set in Grozny," she wrote, "or Sarajevo, circa 1992. Brush fires set off by Hezbollah rockets blazed everywhere, creating a thick pall of smoke that dimmed the usually bright Levantine sunlight. Bits of ash floated about like snowflakes, the smell of smoke permeated the air and was absorbed in my clothes and hair. And the constant booms, explosions and sirens provided loud background music—a live, postmodern version of Albinoni's *Adagio in G Minor* for this long shot of *Apocalypse Now: The Middle Eastern Version*." Lisa and her journalist colleague drove as fast as physically possible through burning streets, walls of fire just feet from each side of the car.

Noah and I heard air-raid sirens wailing even out in the countryside as we closed in on the city.

Israeli civil defense instructed everyone to pull over and get out of and away from their cars when they heard the sirens. A nearby explosion could startle drivers and cause them to crash. That wasn't all. Katyusha shrapnel punctured vehicles as though they were made of paper, and direct hits to gas tanks instantly turned cars and trucks into fireballs.

When we finally reached the city, it looked surprisingly okay from the main road. Although we drove fast through the streets and the nonfunctioning traffic signals, I saw no fires, no smoke, and no serious damage.

It was a good day to drive through. Storms of incoming rockets moved through the north like malevolent weather.

I unfolded our map and looked for the turnoff to Kibbutz Misgav Am. Military historian Michael Oren, author of *Six Days of War*, spokesman for the IDF Northern Command waited for us there. (He would later be appointed Israel's ambassador to the United States.) It wasn't clear which road we should take, so after we passed Kiryat Shmona, we pulled off to the side of the road and asked directions from two officers in an idle police car.

I stepped out into the road and nearly jumped out of my skin as I heard and felt a loud *BOOM* from just on the other side of a nearby hill.

"Outgoing," Noah said to put me at ease. I laughed and said "of course," although to me at the time there was no such thing as *of course*. Noah had visited the border just a few days before and was much more comfortable in that environment. I hadn't yet learned to distinguish the sounds of incoming and outgoing.

The officers told us how to get to Kibbutz Misgav Am, which was not really a kibbutz. It was a military base on the border. They didn't ask us who we were, what we were doing, or why on earth we wanted to go there. War creates a crazily "libertarian" environment where, as was said in the time of the Roman Empire, the law falls silent.

Once we knew where we were going, Noah and I drove through an increasingly dodgy-looking environment where tents, tanks, and heavy artillery pieces were set up in fields burned away by incoming fire.

We turned left past Kiryat Shmona and drove up the steep hill toward the base. Thick smoke boiled off the top of a ridge. Israel was on fire. I did not want to be there.

Concrete bomb-blast walls lined the road. In a few short minutes we reached Misgav Am overlooking the snaking fence on the Lebanese border. Noah parked next to the remains of a car that had taken a direct hit and was utterly blown apart. The largest piece remaining was a hubcap. A thick black oil spot pooled in the center of the former car's wreckage.

I stepped out of our car and braced for an explosion. The Israelis fired artillery shells over our heads every couple of moments toward points unknown on the other side of the horizon. I jumped every time and tried in vain to get used to it.

Noah approached a reservist sitting next to a bomb-blast wall and asked if he knew where we could find IDF Spokesman Michael Oren. The reservist had never heard of him.

"It's quiet today compared with yesterday," he said. "A rocket fell thirty meters from me yesterday. But I just kept reading the newspaper."

"How can you *do* that?" I said. I felt raw and exposed, horribly vulnerable to Hezbollah's random destruction. Even the thunderous sound of outgoing ordnance made me want to dive into the dirt.

"I have to keep myself normal and clear," he said. "I have been here for three weeks. There have been lots of rockets in Haifa today. But none here."

Earsplitting outgoing artillery shells exploded from cannons just a few dozen yards from where I stood. Car alarms went off everywhere. Ten thousand volts of adrenaline instantly kicked into my system. I instinctively ducked my head and wondered, for a split second, whether I should take cover behind the wall. For the uninitiated, even the sounds of nonthreatening outgoing fire trigger every urgent survival mechanism in the human body.

Three Katyusha rockets slammed into the side of the Golan Heights on the other side of the valley. Rockets often landed in clusters. Hezbollah usually fired several rockets at once in the same direction. If one hit anywhere even vaguely near you, watch out. More were probably coming.

I didn't know what the Israeli army was shooting at when they fired their shells into Lebanon. Those who fired the shells didn't know either. Unlike Hezbollah, though, they were shooting at actual targets. They were not just firing at random toward Lebanese farmland and towns. IDF soldiers on the other side of the border marked specific targets and called in coordinates.

Michael Oren still hadn't arrived. Where was he? Noah and I got back in the car and drove down the hill toward Kiryat Shmona. Noah punched Oren's number into his cell phone.

"Where are you guys?" he said and paused. "Okay, we'll wait for you at the bottom of the hill."

So we drove to the bottom of the hill and got out of the car next to an open field arrayed with tanks and gigantic guns.

Bang, followed by an arcing tear in the atmosphere.

Bang, followed by the sound of ripping sky.

A mile or so in front of us, a series of glowing surface-to-surface missiles hurtled toward Lebanon at impossible speeds and somehow got faster as they flew farther.

Jets screamed overhead on their way into Lebanon. The Israeli Air Force scrambled their fighters to take out Katyusha launchers and rain down hell from the sky onto Hezbollah's critical infrastructure—especially in the town of Bint Jbail and in the *dahiyeh*.

The air-raid sirens wailed. Rockets were detected crossing the border, which was less than a mile from where we were standing. Noah and I moved into a bus stop fitted with bomb-blast walls and hoped the rockets would hit the fortified side, not the open side, if they landed anywhere near us.

Bang. Bang. More outgoing artillery. Shells tore menacingly across the sky in an arc over my head.

The air-raid siren kept wailing. It sounded like World War II outside.

Hurry up and get here, Michael Oren, I thought. *I can't take much more of this.*

Whump. An incoming Katyusha landed somewhere off in the

distance. The air-raid siren winded down.

"Man, this is intense," I said to Noah. "Are we crazy to be here?"

"Probably," he said.

We finally found Michael Oren back up top where we had looked for him before, standing on a ridge next to some bushes and squinting through binoculars at Lebanon in the distance.

Noah knew Oren from the Shalem Center in Jerusalem and introduced me to him. Oren greeted both of us warmly.

The Israeli government was proposing a cease-fire. I wanted to know what Oren thought of it, although I suspected already he wasn't thrilled. Israel had accomplished very few of its objectives in Lebanon.

"It's probably the best we could get under the circumstances," he said. "We don't have a lot of leverage right now."

Israel's Second Lebanon War looked, to me anyway, like a disaster in the making almost from the very beginning. Successful foreign interventions are nearly impossible to pull off in Lebanon without either massive public support from the Lebanese—something the Israelis were extremely unlikely to ever receive—or a massive deployment of ruthless brute force of the sort only the Syrians had recently been comfortable using.

The war almost looked as though it might have gone differently during the first couple of hours. Many Lebanese initially shrugged at Israel's opening counterstrike. Everyone knew Hezbollah started it, and the Party of God wasn't well liked by the majority of Lebanese anyway. Some even welcomed and cheered Israel's bloody-minded reaction. The Lebanese army wasn't strong or cohesive enough to give Iran's private militia a thrashing, so if the Israelis didn't fight Hezbollah, nobody would fight Hezbollah.

That sentiment didn't last long. Olmert blamed the Lebanese government, not just Hezbollah, for the attack. It didn't matter to most Israelis that the Lebanese government had nothing to do with the killing and kidnapping of their soldiers—the attack came from inside Lebanese territory. So the Israeli Air Force destroyed targets even in areas outside Hezbollah's control. Hezbollah was a Shia militia, but even some Christian and Sunni regions where the overwhelming majority despised Hezbollah were hit by Israeli air strikes.

Sympathy inside Lebanon for the Israeli "enemy of my enemy" plunged after that happened. Hezbollah briefly managed to rebrand itself as a national fighting force. Israel's air strikes overwhelmingly landed in Hezbollah-controlled areas, but not all of them did, so almost everyone in Lebanon felt like they could be killed. The Lebanese army—as usual during Israel's wars—sat out the fighting. If Hezbollah didn't fight the Israelis, nobody would fight the Israelis.

Temporarily lost in all this was the fact that Israelis wouldn't be shooting at Lebanon in the first place if it weren't for Hezbollah.

On July 30, 2006, Lebanese rage against Israel reached its apogee when history eerily repeated itself. The Israeli Air Force destroyed a three-story building in the village of al-Khuraybah near the larger town of Qana. Twenty-eight people, many of them children, were killed. IDF Chief of Staff Dan Halutz apologized for the deaths of civilians and blamed Hezbollah for using them as human shields. Lebanese Prime Minister Fouad Siniora accused Israel of committing a war crime.

Killing civilians near Qana—and it didn't matter whether or not the Israelis did it on purpose—was bound to send the Lebanese over the edge. Qana was where a nearly identical incident took place ten years earlier. On April 18, 1996, the IDF shelled a United Nations compound while Hezbollah fired Katyusha rockets into Northern Israel from a few hundred yards away. One hundred six people were killed. The incident is known inside Lebanon as the Qana Massacre, and it is infamous.

Whatever remaining scrap of sympathy or understanding some Lebanese had for Israel's point of view vaporized after "Qana" was repeated. The Israelis knew they screwed up, and they knew they screwed up badly. Air strikes were halted for forty-eight hours even as the Katyusha rockets kept flying.

I told Michael Oren that I'm not normally pessimistic about the performance of Western armies in wars but that this one didn't look good. Cities, towns, villages, roads, bridges, and houses in Lebanon had been bombed. Hundreds of civilians had been killed. Hezbollah fighters had also been killed, but the Katyushas were still flying just as fast and as often as they were at the beginning. It didn't look like much had been accomplished. Hezbollah, astonishingly, was popular in Lebanon all over again, yet another civil war could easily ignite once the inevitable postwar backlash kicked in.

"Talk me out of it," I said. "Tell me if I'm wrong."

He didn't want to say much. I could tell from the look on his face that he was not happy either, but he was an official spokesman and had to be careful with what he said on the record.

"Has anything been permanently accomplished up there?" I said.

"Some things, yes," he said. "We destroyed a lot of their infrastructure. They had more weapons and more underground bunkers and tunnels than we had any idea. People coming out of there say it's vast."

"What do you think about the proposal for an international force on the border?" I said. The United Nations would, in fact, soon put more troops on the Lebanese side of the border ostensibly to prevent Hezbollah from controlling that part of the country again.

"The problem with that," he said, "is that the force could act as a shield for Hezbollah. Hezbollah could fire missiles right over the tops of their heads and make it very difficult for us to go in there and stop them. It needs to be a combat force in Lebanon, not a peacekeeping force."

"Hassan Nasrallah declared victory today," I said.

Oren laughed. Of course he would laugh. It was obvious well in advance that Hezbollah's secretary general would declare victory no matter what happened as long as he wasn't captured or killed. The Arab bar for military victory had been set low for decades. All their side had to do was survive. They "won" even if their country was torn to pieces. The very idea of a Pyrrhic victory, where losses exceed paltry gains, seemed not to occur to leaders incapable of defeating the State of Israel in battle.

"Look at Nasrallah today," Oren said. "In 2000 he did his victory dance in Bint Jbail. He can't do that this time. His command and control south of Beirut is completely gone. We killed 550 Hezbollah fighters south of the Litani River out of an active force of 1,250. Nasrallah claimed South Lebanon would be the graveyard of the IDF, but we only lost one tenth of 1 percent of our soldiers in South Lebanon. The only thing that went according to his plan was their ability to keep firing rockets. If he has enough victories like this one, he's dead."

"Have Hezbollah's fighting techniques evolved or degraded since 2000?" I said.

"They're the same," he said. "They're good. These guys are very experienced. They have been fighting for a long time. But we've killed more than 25 percent of their fighting force. I think they'll break. All armies break. Killing even 1 percent of a Western army is a disaster. It's prohibitive."

Another IDF spokesman stood at Oren's side. I was surprised to see this guy. He was the famous Hollywood screenwriter Dan Gordon, and he volunteered for the job. Credits to his name include *The Hurricane* with Denzel Washington and 1994's *Wyatt Earp*. I thought it was crazy that an American civilian would volunteer to work in a Middle Eastern war zone until I remembered that I was doing exactly the same thing myself.

Gordon walked me to another lookout point just at the top of another ridge over Lebanon. A village with apparently intact buildings lay just below. We had no cover. The windows of the buildings looked threatening. I had stood on that border just a few months earlier, when everything was still quiet, and yet was warned by an Israeli military commander that Hezbollah might be watching us through a sniper scope.

"Have you had any sniper attacks?" I asked Gordon.

"Yes, actually we have," he said and stepped back. "This is probably not a good place for us to be standing."

I thought it strange that I was more sensitive to the danger than he was. That, I suppose, was an advantage of being unaccustomed to war zones. My extreme discomfort kept me from feeling like I was invincible. That would come later after I adapted.

"Hardly any journalists have mentioned this," he said, "but at the very beginning of this thing, when Hezbollah captured our soldiers, they also tried to invade, conquer, and hold the town of Metula along with two other towns. And they were repulsed."

Of course Hezbollah was repulsed. It was a guerrilla army. It didn't have standard infantry troops.

"We do have one serious asset from this war," he said. "Hassan Nasrallah got his ass kicked. And he knows it."

"Did he really get his ass kicked?" I said. "The IDF fought Hezbollah for years to a standstill before. What made you think it would be easy to get rid of them this time?"

"This time it's different," he said. "This time we're going in there to kill them. We are not trying to hold on to territory. This is actually working. We are not stuck in the mud. Oh, and here's another tangible: Hezbollah-occupied Lebanon no longer exists."

Later I received a phone call from my friend and colleague Allison Kaplan Sommer in Tel Aviv. "Have you heard the news?" she said.

I hadn't.

Neither had Dan Gordon. Neither had Michael Oren.

"The cease-fire is dead," she said. "The ground invasion is starting."

Individual ground units had been making brief jaunts into Lebanon from the beginning, but Olmert had just decided to launch the real thing.

Noah and I lost access to our spokesmen. The war was ramping up and they were summoned to meetings. So we drove to the border town of Metula, the one Hezbollah had tried to invade, and watched Israel's invasion of Lebanon from the roof of the Alaska Inn.

War does strange things to the mind. The first time you hear the loud *boom*, *bang*, and *crash* of incoming and outgoing artillery, you will jump. You will twitch. You will want to take cover. You will want to hide. You will feel like you could die at any second, like the air around you is drenched with gasoline, like the universe is gearing up to smash you to pieces.

It's amazing how fast you get used to it, even if you have no military training and grew up in tranquil suburban America.

It took me four hours.

Any given location in Northern Israel and South Lebanon would almost certainly never be hit with a missile, bullet, bomb, or artillery shell. Lebanon was hit more frequently, and Israel was hit more randomly, but the vast majority of people in both places weren't even scratched, let alone killed.

Explosions jack your survival instinct up to eleven, but after a while straight math kicks in. You run numbers in your head, even subconsciously. Most places aren't ever hit, so what were the odds, really, that you would be standing in one of the few places that were hit at the precise moment it happened?

Being under fire in Northern Israel was not like, say, walking around loose by myself in Baghdad. No one was out to get *me*. Only Hezbollah fighters and its leaders in Lebanon were targeted as individuals. All of Northern Israel was a collective target, but a very large one that I vanished into almost completely.

The odds that any given place in Northern Israel would be hit were the same as the odds that any other given place in Northern Israel would be hit. Hezbollah's rockets landed almost at random. They were pathetic military weapons, but perfect terrorist weapons.

There were a few exceptions. Kiryat Shmona was hit quite a lot. Metula was hit hardly at all, although Hezbollah did fire a mortar round into the side of the Alaska Inn two hours before Noah and I arrived. Still, anywhere out in the open was just as dangerous as anywhere else out in the open.

This is logical, but the mind doesn't always work like that when sensing danger from the environment.

Driving on an empty road and looking at an impact site up ahead was unsettling. Kibbutz HaGoshrim put me at ease because it was idyllic and sheltered by shade trees. Yet neither location was safer or more dangerous than the other.

The trees at the kibbutz blocked out the sky and made me feel protected. Obviously, the branches of trees could do nothing to stop or slow a Katyusha rocket, but when you're under fire from above, the sky feels like a gigantic malevolent eyeball. When you're underneath trees, the gigantic malevolent eyeball can't see you. Therefore a rocket won't hit you. That's not how it was, but that's what it felt like.

During my first several hours in the war zone I constantly tried to figure out what I could do to make myself safer. Should I stand here instead of there? How about if I crouch down a little bit? Maybe if I sit on the ground, a rocket will miss my head? I figured it was better to stand near things than away from things, as long as those things were not cars.

All this thinking was useless. I would either be hit or I wouldn't. Walking or driving faster could get me away from an incoming rocket, or it could get me closer. It was all totally random.

Fear has a purpose. It forces you to think hard and fast about what you can or must do to protect yourself. As soon as you realize there is nothing more you can do, fear loses its purpose and vanishes. It really does.

New York City immediately after September 11, 2001, was a much scarier place than Northern Israel during the war once I got used to it. It wasn't *safer*, not even remotely, but there is only so much adrenaline in the human body.

This is the fatal weakness of terrorism. What's a terrorist to do once the terror wears off?

While Noah and I sat on the roof of Metula's Alaska Inn watching Israel gear up for the ground invasion, a voice below blared something in Hebrew over a loudspeaker.

"What was that?" Noah asked an Israeli woman standing next to us.

"He said, 'Go to the shelters because a rocket is about to hit the roof of the hotel,'" she said.

"Seriously?" I said.

"No," she said and laughed. "But a rocket really is coming. It really is time to go to the shelters."

We waited for the elevator. It seemed to take forever.

"Where is the shelter, anyway?" I said.

"I don't know," the Israeli woman said.

The elevator doors opened. We all got in. It took ages to get down to the lobby.

When the doors opened on the main floor, none of the people in the lobby or restaurant were moving. They were all perfectly calm as though nothing out of the ordinary was happening. All of us, though, heard the sirens.

Everyone knows fear is contagious. What I think is less understood is that calm is also contagious.

I walked up to the front desk and asked the young man standing next to the register whether they had a bomb shelter.

"Of course," he said.

"Should we go down there or does nobody care?" I said.

"Nobody cares," he said.

"Let's get a Coke," Noah said.

So we grabbed two seats in the restaurant and asked the waiter for two Cokes.

I heard a faint *whump* somewhere off in the distance. The rocket had landed. Nobody moved. Nobody cared.

The Israel Defense Forces wanted to snap up as much territory as possible between the border fence and the Litani River before agreeing to the cease-fire that ended the war. It didn't take long to reach the Litani.

From our perch on the roof, Noah and I watched as much as we could. All day long, outgoing artillery shells tore through the sky on their way to Hezbollah targets. As soon as the ground invasion was set to start, all fell eerily quiet.

For a brief period, the only visible evidence of war was a fire burning in a Lebanese field off to our right.

Just south of Metula, the war was a little more obvious, even though it was quiet there too. Tanks and heavy artillery were set up in an idyllic field. It was a jarring sight. The scenery was lovely in Northern Israel. Lots of Israelis and foreigners liked to visit on holiday because it was so picturesque and serene, yet war machinery was scattered all over the place. War, in my mind, was supposed to occur in ugly places.

The Israeli invasion of Lebanon didn't look like an American invasion of any place. When Americans go to war, they fly to the other side of the world and spend weeks or even months preparing, then push hundreds of miles through enemy territory on the way to their targets. Israeli soldiers just took out some wire cutters, snipped holes in the fence, and *walked* into Lebanon.

Tanks rolled into Lebanon, too. From the top of the Alaska, Noah and I saw a whole line of them getting ready to blast through a long-closed border checkpoint called Fatima Gate into Hezbollah's territory.

The scene was ominous, but it felt perfectly calm. Birds chirped. You could have put the sunset on a postcard. The streets of Metula were clean and well ordered. A man in sweatpants, a T-shirt, and running shoes jogged down the sidewalk with his dog alongside him, its tongue lolling out the side of its mouth. I waved hello to an elderly grandmother in her gardening hat drinking from a tall slender glass on her front porch. Why on earth hadn't these people left with everyone else?

Noah ordered ravioli in a restaurant and I ordered pizza. I asked a woman behind the counter whether she was being paid extra wages for serving food in a war zone. "No," she said and shrugged, as if to say *why should they pay me more money*?

Shepard Smith from Fox News broadcasted live from the roof of the Alaska, although I doubt he had much to report. Little was going on at the time. Metula was a nice little town with restaurants and bed-and-breakfasts. And that's what it looked and felt like, at least while the war lulled for a few hours.

Shortly after the sunset, Noah and I walked down the street to the line of tanks just outside town so we could interview some of the soldiers.

A young soldier with sunglasses and a pierced eyebrow asked me to take his picture. "Put me in your magazine," he said, "next to the hot models in swimsuits and lingerie."

"I'll see what I can do," I said and laughed.

I raised my camera to take another soldier's picture.

"No, no, no!" he said and held up his hand. "Last time I went into Lebanon, every guy with me who had his picture taken earlier that day was injured. None of us who didn't have our pictures taken were injured. I know it's superstitious and stupid, but I need to feel good before I go in there."

"What's it like fighting Hezbollah?" I said.

"It depends," he said.

"On what?" I said.

"On the place and on the day," he said. "Sometimes when we go into Lebanon, nothing happens. We can't find the Hezbollah. Other times they are everywhere and it's hard."

"Do you ever see civilians?" I said.

"No," he said. "Not in the towns. Only in the villages."

"What do they do when they see you?" I said.

"They go inside," he said.

"Do they say anything to you?" I said.

"No," he said. "They don't say anything, they don't wave, they don't throw rocks. They just go in their houses."

Noah chatted with two young men who were getting ready to push into Lebanon ahead of the tanks to clear mines. They didn't seem nervous at all, although their work must have been extraordinarily stressful.

That was about all we could get out of the soldiers. They seemed happy to see us, not at all suspicious that we might be hostile journalists or even anything *other* than journalists. No one asked us to show credentials, but they didn't want to say much specific. I got the impression they enjoyed having us around as a distraction from the grim work ahead.

"Can we go with you guys into Lebanon?" Noah asked one of the soldiers.

"Do you *want* to?" the soldier said.

"Yeah," Noah said.

The soldier didn't know if it was possible. Maybe it was, and maybe it wasn't.

I didn't want to. I would later embed with American soldiers and Marines in Iraq, but I felt queasy about hitching a ride with an army on its way into Lebanon. I wasn't Lebanese, and I didn't like Hezbollah any more than the Israelis did, but I had *lived* in Lebanon until just three months earlier. The country was the closest thing I had in the world to a second home.

One Israeli soldier I spoke to whom I'll call Eli spent the entire war in and out of South Lebanon. He and his unit worked in some villages nine or so miles in from Metula. His job was to go in and mark artillery targets.

"These whole villages," he said, "they were empty, just filled with Hezbollah terrorists. No civilians were walking around South Lebanon. I know. I was in their villages. In their houses. Anyone who was there was definitely working for the Hezbollah or working as a Hezbollah fighter."

"You didn't see any women?" I said. "It was mostly men and no children?"

"I never saw one woman or any children in Lebanon," he said. "I was going in and out for the whole time since the day the soldiers were kidnapped. We flew from my unit straight to the north in helicopters."

Houses all over South Lebanon were destroyed, sometimes by

Hezbollah, mostly by Israelis. It's not clear, though, that Israelis deserved most of the blame. Not only did Hezbollah build houses explicitly for use during a war, but they used civilians and their strictly residential houses as shields. They hid behind private homes and fired rockets from inside populated areas. The Israeli Air Force took out every rocket launcher it could, thus destroying much of the civilian infrastructure next to the launchers.

"Did they use populated areas to fire?" Eli said. "It was clear that they did. Except Israel also dispersed fliers ordering all the civilian population of South Lebanon to leave. Anyone who was in those villages was probably helping Hezbollah fighters. Hezbollah could take any house they wanted because the whole place was empty. Everyone left. When we were fighting, we were fighting from house to house. They would just skip houses and go to a different house. We would detonate one house; they would fire a few from another house and skip to yet another one. They would go wherever they wanted. It was their area in South Lebanon. It's not like *they* thought about them as civilian houses."

Australian reporter Chris Link published revealing photographs in the *Herald Sun* newspaper on July 30, 2006, that showed Hezbollah fighters wearing civilian clothes and operating an antiaircraft gun in a suburban neighborhood. Perhaps Hezbollah neither knew nor cared, but installing military targets like antiaircraft guns in residential neighborhoods is against the laws of war. It recklessly endangers the civilians who live there. Meanwhile, destroying an antiaircraft gun in a residential neighborhood with an air strike *isn't* a war crime. The laws and conventions of war are absolutely clear about this, and they squarely said Hezbollah was at fault for turning those areas into targets.

"If there was a full-out war," Eli said, "you know, tanks against tanks, combat units against combat units, and everything done out in the open—Israel would definitely, *totally* defeat and win. Guerrilla warfare is extremely hard. It's stressful because it's not a real army; it's not an army. It's like cells. You're fighting against cells that are operated by bigger cells."

The Americans were fighting the same kind of war at the same time just a few hundred miles away in Iraq. It wasn't going much better for the U.S. than it was for Israel. The Americans were just as bewildered in Iraq as the Israelis were in Lebanon. Both fought invisible enemies in the alleyways of an alien society where they had little leverage. American soldiers and Marines weren't strictly limited to one- or two-day little jaunts into Iraq followed by hasty withdrawals, and at least they weren't trying to fight a counterinsurgency primarily with the Air Force, but the wars in both Lebanon and Iraq were going badly for similar reasons. Guerrilla fighters and terrorists were humbling two of the most powerful and sophisticated armed forces in history. Whatever institutional knowledge about effective counterinsurgency strategies that once existed within the ranks of Western military officers seemed, in the middle of 2006, to have been lost.

"There are people walking around towns," Eli said, "with weapons who aren't wearing uniforms. They look like civilians. I mean, in every civilian house in Lebanon, there is a shotgun. And that's not because they're against the IDF or because they're against Israel; it's that most people in the small villages, they're hunters. They hunt for food. But we also saw people walking around with AK-47s and handguns. Those are definitely Hezbollah people in civilian clothes."

Arabs were once among the most militarily powerful people on earth. Shortly after the founding of Islam in what today is Saudi Arabia, they surged north into Mesopotamia and the Levant and west across North Africa in a massive and rapid expansion of power. It had been a long time, though, since the Arab world fielded competent armies capable of conquering territory. Some Israelis thought that was the only reason they could even survive in the Middle East while surrounded and greatly outnumbered by enemies. When legendary war hero Moshe Dayan was asked about Israel's secret to success in modern warfare after defeating three armies in six days in 1967, he said, "Fight Arabs."

Hezbollah fighters, though, were the most formidable enemies Israelis had ever faced. "We think of Hezbollah as the Iranian army," IDF

Spokesman Jonathan Davis told me, and they were not entirely wrong in doing so.

"The chief of the military in Israel did not come from the army," Eli said. He came from the Air Force. "He did not use the ground troops as well as he should have. He would send ground troops one kilometer in, they would stay for a few days, and walk out. And every time we went in and went out, people got killed."

Night fell. The Israeli soldiers were gearing up for a real ground invasion this time instead of just a quick hop over the border, and they were getting twitchy.

There's something about darkness in war, even during the quiet times. All were less talkative than before, and there was clearly no way Noah and I could get any useful or interesting information out of them at that point.

So we walked the line of tanks.

"Don't be here," a soldier said.

"We're journalists," I said.

"I know," he said. "But this is a war zone. Don't be here."

So we went back to the hotel in the dark and sat on the roof.

The view north into Lebanon was an ominous sight. The Lebanese town of Kfar Kila directly faced Metula across a small patch of farmland. There wasn't any no-man's-land in between.

The two towns were in different countries, but they were almost in the exact same location. If it weren't for the border, I could have walked from one to the other in less than ten minutes.

But that night all of Lebanon was black. It was as if Lebanon did not exist. The lights of emptied Israeli ghost cities twinkled behind me, but Lebanon was enveloped in a vast darkness.

A fire burning in a Lebanese field off to my right grew bigger and brighter. No fire department existed on the other side that could douse it. South Lebanon, always lawless and beyond the control of the state, was a truly anarchic and perilous place on the night of August 11.

Distant flashes lit up the horizon. A low rumble of war in the distance sounded like thunder. It sounded like the physical breaking of Lebanon.

The next morning Noah and I heard loud machine-gun fire coming from the other side of fence in Kfar Kila. No one seemed to be guarding either side of the border. No one could have stopped us from walking to our doom had we been dumb enough to cross over.

We did not dare. Most of the violence was on Lebanon's side. We were near enough to hear it and could walk to it in just minutes, but we were just out of range as long as we stayed in Israel.

Far more dangerous were the Hezbollah fighters themselves. If we were caught and questioned, and if they found no recent Lebanese entry stamps in our passports, they would know we had crossed illegally from the Israeli side. We had no good reason to think we would be released unharmed under such circumstances. It's possible, and perhaps even likely, that Hezbollah would assume, if they found us, that we were Israeli intelligence agents. Risking *that* would not have been brave; it would have been stupid.

The most surprising thing about looking into Kfar Kila from Metula was how little damage was visible. I had expected to see serious destruction in the Lebanese border towns, but the towns I could see didn't appear damaged at all.

Noah scanned the buildings from the roof of the Alaska with a pair of binoculars borrowed from another reporter. He couldn't locate a single damaged building or house, not even among those that were right on the border and easiest for Israelis to hit.

Obviously, there was damage in South Lebanon. Those thousands of outgoing artillery shells weren't landing on nothing. For all I knew at the time, Hezbollah's de facto southern capital Bint Jbail was a pile of rubble. I would soon visit Bint Jbail and find that much of it really *was* a pile of rubble, but Lebanon's towns in the vicinity of Metula seemed to be more or less intact.

The war was just about over. IDF spokesmen were given gag orders and couldn't say anything to me, Noah, or anyone else. Military police shooed us away from the soldiers and told us to stay in the hotel or get out of the area. We decided it was time to head back to Tel Aviv.

Our fuel was running low, so we stopped to fill up the gas tank just south of Kiryat Shmona.

Israeli gas stations could be incredibly frustrating for foreigners. After Noah swiped his credit card at the pump, the computer asked for his Israeli national ID number. Noah lived in Israel at the time, but he's American. He didn't have a national ID number to enter. Obviously, I didn't either. So we asked an IDF soldier who happened to pull up in a truck if he would use his credit card and ID number to get us some gas if we gave him cash.

"Of course," he said and swiped his card into the machine. "Where are you guys from?" he said as he punched in his number.

"We're both Americans," Noah said.

"Are you tourists?" he said.

I laughed. "*Here*?" I said. "No, we're not tourists. We're journalists."

"There are adrenaline tourists up here," he said. "There are agents in Tel Aviv and Jerusalem who set up the tours."

It couldn't be *too* dangerous in Northern Israel if this sort of thing was going on, I thought. Surely there were no "adrenaline tours" in South Lebanon at the time.

Just then a Katyusha rocket exploded inside a residential neighborhood in Kiryat Shmona a few hundred yards from where we were standing.

"Wow," Noah said. "Let's go take pictures of that."

"No," said the soldier. "Don't go there."

More rockets often followed the first. They arrived in pairs and in threes. So we didn't go. We went kinda sorta near it, but kept a prudent distance. We drove to a place where we could take pictures without actually standing where another rocket was likely to explode at any moment.

On the way back to Tel Aviv, we passed once again through entire towns eerily emptied of people. Very few houses or stores had been looted. It would have been easy to steal just about anything in cities depopulated of even police officers, but hardly anyone did. War brings people together with a shared sense of purpose. While the laws fell silent in the north of the country, common human decency didn't.

Common human decency held up on the Lebanese side, too, for the most part. Despite the fact that large numbers of Christians and Sunnis feared and loathed Lebanon's Shias and blamed them for starting the war, many provided shelter in their own homes for refugees fleeing the south.

Hezbollah didn't behave nearly as well.

On July 16, 2008, Hezbollah agreed to return the bodies of captured soldiers Ehud Goldwasser and Eldad Regev in exchange for Israel releasing captured Hezbollah fighters and the infamous child murderer Samir Kuntar. On April 22, 1979, in the northern Israeli town of Nahariya, Kuntar killed policeman Eliyahu Shahar, civilian Danny Haran, and Haran's four-year-old daughter, Einat, by placing her head on a rock and smashing her skull with the butt of his rifle.

When the bodies of Goldwasser and Regev were returned to Israel, former Chief Rabbi of the IDF Yisrael Weiss said, "If we thought the enemy was cruel to the living and the dead," he said, "we were surprised, when we opened the caskets, to discover just how cruel. And I'll leave it at that."

What Israelis call the Second Lebanon War, and what Lebanese call the July War, created hundreds of thousands of refugees on each side of the border. That's where proportion ended. Israel had a real army and a real air force and was able to inflict severe damage on its enemies. Hezbollah, meanwhile, was only strong enough to inflict light damage and a relatively small number of casualties.

he so-called Party of God could sabotage Lebanon and terrorize

Israel, but Hassan Nasrallah's "martyrs" could not repel or even slow an invading army. They could only harass that army and kill a minuscule percentage of its soldiers.

While most foreign journalists packed up and left Israel as soon as each side stopped shooting, I drove back to Kiryat Shmona to do a little postwar inspection of what had just happened.

Israel's most targeted city looked intact from a distance, and even up close the damage wasn't all that severe. Rockets landed all day in the city for weeks, so I expected to see destroyed homes. There may well have been some, but I drove all over town and couldn't find any.

The worst damage I saw was relatively minor under the circumstances. A Katyusha had hit the roof of a carport. A parked van was torched. The nearby kitchen window was blown in by shrapnel. A portion of the side of the house was damaged. Anyone standing at the kitchen sink when the window blew in certainly would have been killed, but the house itself could be fixed without too much difficulty.

Katyusha rockets are pip-squeaks. They don't feel like pip-squeaks when they're flying in your direction, but they are. They can't be aimed worth a damn, and they'll only do serious damage if they ignite something else after impact, such as a fuel station or the gas tank of a car. Forget trying to use Katyushas against a properly outfitted and trained Western army. They have little military value unless they're fired in barrages at close range. From a distance, they can be counted on only to break a few things at random in the general direction they're aimed.

They did break a few things in Kiryat Shmona, especially because Hezbollah was clever enough to pack them with ball bearings. Buildings and houses all over the city were riddled with pockmarks from shrapnel that looked, when I squinted, like bullet holes from automatic weapons fire. Broken glass crunched under my feet when I walked. Kiryat Shmona looked like a city that had suffered massive firefights in almost every neighborhood.

Anyone who spent any significant amount of time walking those streets during the war would have been in extreme danger. The city itself, while scarred on the surface, may have been otherwise almost intact, but it was an extraordinarily lethal environment for humans while the rockets were falling.

Katyusha shrapnel kills people who aren't wearing body armor and wounds those who are. Believe me: You don't want to be hit with this stuff. The rockets may be nearly useless against an army or infrastructure, but they're devastatingly effective as terrorist weapons against civilian population centers. Shrapnel may not hurt an apartment building too badly or even slow down a tank, but it will tear *you* to pieces if you're in the way.

There was a lot of talk in the media about Hezbollah's targets in Israel. Some insisted Hezbollah aimed its Katyushas at the Israeli military. The fact that twelve soldiers were killed by a rocket just before I arrived on the border was used as evidence for that claim.

But Hezbollah hit a little of everything in Northern Israel: houses, trees, streams, grass, apartments, roads, vineyards, and cows. Thousands of rockets exploded in that part of the country. The odds that none of the rockets would hit a *single* IDF soldier were minuscule.

The truth is, I was far safer on military bases, in open fields, and on tiny kibbutzim than in cities during Hezbollah's rocket war. A disproportionate number of their rockets landed in urban areas.

Rockets rained down on Kiryat Shmona almost constantly even though there were no soldiers, no tanks, no artillery pieces, no bases, nothing of military value in the city at all. None of the journalists I met were willing to risk their lives by lingering there, but we were all relatively relaxed on IDF bases. The odds of us being hit there by a rocket were merely random, the same as if we were out among cows in the fields. The city of Haifa, which was almost twenty miles from the border, was hit more often than bases that were right on the border and which were therefore easier targets. The odds of being hit in Kiryat Shmona were fantastically higher than the odds of being hit anywhere else. Our lives depended on correctly computing the odds.

If Hezbollah really did the best they could to avoid killing civilians with their inaccurate rockets, as they and their apologists claimed, I would have set up shop in Kiryat Shmona and stayed away from Israeli soldiers for my own protection. But the situation was exactly reversed.

What happened in Israel and Lebanon in July and August of 2006 was a radical break from the past. Arab armies couldn't invade Israel without being quickly repelled or demolished. Even terrifying waves of suicide bombers could be beaten back with separation barriers and human intelligence. But Hezbollah was able to fire barrages of rockets throughout the conflict all the way up to the cease-fire. The IDF defeated three armies in six days in 1967 but couldn't even slow the rocket war down in a month.

Israeli intelligence agents at the Ministry of Defense told me they feared missile war was replacing terrorist war. It seems they were right. Hamas later replicated Hezbollah's strategy and ramped up its own relatively low-key rocket war out of Gaza against the Israeli cities of Sderot and Ashkelon. Only missile war could force hundreds of thousands of Israelis to flee their homes, and both Hamas and Hezbollah threatened to one day blanket the entire country with barrages of missiles and make Israel uninhabitable once and for all.

Feelings of existential dread increased markedly after the Second Lebanon War. Israel is a small country, haunted by horrors past. "Daytime Israel makes a tremendous effort to create the impression of the determined, tough, simple, uncomplicated society ready to fight back, ready to hit back twice as hard, courageous, and so on," Israeli novelist Amos Oz once said. "Nocturnal Israel is a refugee camp with more nightmares per square mile I guess than any other place in the world. Almost everyone has seen the devil."

This war was a transition, the testing of a new doctrine. It was a potential disaster for Israel, but in the end an even bigger disaster for those who thought it was a terrific idea. I wouldn't want to be anywhere near Lebanon or the Palestinian territories of the West Bank and Gaza if sophisticated Iranian-made Zelzal missiles were crashing into the sides of Tel Aviv apartment towers and skyscrapers.

When I left Israel and made plans to return to Lebanon, I could feel it: War was coming again, and it was coming like Christmas.

Two

Raid Night

Baghdad, Iraq 2007

"We want to use you as bait," Sergeant Eduardo Ojeda told me when I embedded with his unit on what was shaping up to be a night raid in Baghdad.

"Excellent," I said. "That's why I'm here."

That's what passed for black Army humor in Iraq.

"Our TST [time-sensitive target] blew up a vehicle and killed four soldiers and an interpreter in the next AO [area of operations]," he said. "He's somewhere in our AO now."

He could tell by the frozen and dubious look on my face that I wasn't sure I wanted to go.

"Don't worry," he said. "These guys hardly ever fight back when we nail them. And they *always* lose when they do. Come on. Let's go fuck 'em up."

I donned my armor and helmet, slung my Nikon around my neck and jumped in the back of one of the Humvees.

"I need your full name and blood type," First Sergeant Ray Fisher said. "In case something happens."

"Stay close to me," said Sergeant Ojeda as he plugged his mouth with tobacco. "In the dark, just look for the short guy. And call me Eddie."

The military intelligence officers at the War Eagle outpost knew the target was somewhere in their area, but they didn't know precisely where or how long he'd be there. My unit's job was to go out and patrol the neighborhood known as Tunis until they could pinpoint his location.

We drove in the dark. The soldiers used night-vision goggles. I had to rely on my eyes.

"How long are you in Iraq, sir?" Sergeant Fisher asked me.

"As long as I feel like it," I said. "A month and a half, maybe."

"You're lucky, sir," he said. "We're here for 18. I just got back from leave and missed the birth of my baby boy by two days. At least I got to see him."

"You don't have to call me sir," I said.

"Okay, sir," he said and laughed.

"What's the situation in Tunis?" I said.

"It's not too bad anymore," said Lieutenant Evan Wolf. "It's a rich neighborhood. Lots of educated and cultured people live there, doctors and lawyers, people like that. It was infested with al-Qaeda a while ago, so the neighborhood formed a protectionist militia. They set up roadblocks, gates around the mosque, and they drove al-Qaeda out. But now the militia harasses and extorts the residents. They follow us from house to house and intimidate whoever we talk to."

Our convoy of Humvees crossed an overpass and stopped on a dark road among trees just outside the neighborhood. Half the soldiers dismounted the vehicles and set out to patrol the streets on foot. The other half stayed with the Humvees.

I joined those who went out on foot.

"How long will we be out?" I said to Eddie.

"Could be a while," he said and plugged his mouth with more smokeless tobacco. "Last time we had a raid night, we were out for more than 12 hours." He spit on the sidewalk. "We chased a guy from house to house to house. Didn't catch him that night, but he was caught somewhere else three days later."

Baghdad gets only one hour of electricity every day. Some parts of the city at night are almost as dark as the wilderness. The soldiers I was with could see everything, but I could barely see anything. It was next to impossible to tell who was who in the dark.

Eddie was obvious, though. He was the short guy. He told me to stay next to him, so I did.

It was 100 degrees outside even at midnight. My shirt felt disgustingly hot and close under my body armor. I heard choppers roaming low in the sky over the city.

"This country would be beautiful if it were not for the invention of the plastic bag," somebody said. "That bag is everywhere—in the trees, stuck in barbed wire, on the sidewalks, crammed in every corner. Man, when this war is over, I'm coming back to open a recycling factory. I'll be raking it in."

The area did appear to be nice, billowing plastic bags notwithstanding. I couldn't make out many details, but I could see the shapes of the houses. Most were considerably larger than the average American home.

"I suppose I shouldn't smoke," I said to Eddie.

"You got that right," Eddie said. "Snipers wearing night vision can see the tip of your cigarette from a mile away. They'll watch as you lift the cigarette to your mouth and figure out where your head is. Then BLAMMO. They're really good shots."

I kept the cigarettes in my pocket.

"We're being followed," said Sergeant Fisher.

Eddie, the rest of the soldiers and I turned around.

"Four of 'em," Eddie said.

I couldn't see anyone without night-vision goggles but the soldiers standing right next to me. "Where are they?" I said.

"In the shadows two blocks behind us," Eddie said. "They weren't there a minute ago."

Curfew enforcement in Tunis was total. In some areas of Baghdad, only military-age males driving cars are stopped by Army patrols after 10 p.m. Tunis, though, is infested with a militia. No one is allowed on the streets after dark except licensed generator repairmen.

We kept walking. Half the soldiers walked backward so they could keep an eye on the men following us.

Some of the soldiers stood in the light from a storefront lit by generator power.

I tried to stick to the shadows. Presumably the men following us were militia. If they didn't have night-vision goggles—and they probably didn't—they wouldn't be able to see me any better than I could see them. And I couldn't see them.

"Five of 'em now," somebody said. "They're still following."

The soldiers took up positions, crouched on one knee and pointed their rifles down the street in the direction of our stalkers. I ducked behind a wall separating two driveways and checked the windows and the roofs of the houses to make sure nobody saw me.

"Why don't you send the Humvees after them?" I said to the nearest soldier.

"We're sending them now," he said.

"More are out now," said another. "Seven or eight of them."

No one knew how many were coming out of their houses on side streets. No one knew who they were, either. They could have been local militia, or they could have been the al-Qaeda cell the army was hunting. Perhaps they found us before we found them. I no longer thought "We want to use you as bait" sounded funny.

An old man speaking on a cell phone walked toward us from the direction of our stalkers.

"Turn that phone off right now!" yelled one of the soldiers. "Right now!" He ran toward the man. "You turn it off *now!*" The man kept talking in Arabic.

Our interpreter told him to shut it off. He shut it off. Perhaps he was giving information to the militia. Perhaps he was talking to his wife. Nobody knew. Either way he was violating the curfew.

"Go home," somebody told him.

Suddenly the soldiers started walking back in the direction we came from—toward the men who were following us and who hid in the shadows.

"We're walking toward them?" I said to the soldier next to me. I still couldn't tell who was who. "Are they still there?" I still couldn't see them.

"They're still there," he said. "We're pushing back to see what they do."

For the first time since I'd arrived in Iraq, I wished I had a weapon. When I couldn't stay in the shadows, I zigzagged at random to make myself a more difficult target.

Eddie sidled up beside me.

"Stay right next to me," he said. "If there's shooting, I'll get you in the safest possible place." The safest possible place, I thought, was *outside* Iraq. "If it escalates ..." He trailed off.

"If it escalates ... what?" I said.

"We'll deal with it," he said.

"Four more to the west," said a soldier. "They're running."

This time I could see them—four men rounding a corner and running away down a street. They were more afraid of us than we were of them.

"Does this kind of thing happen around here a lot?" I said to Eddie.

"It happens," he said.

The Humvees finally pulled up to the area where the hidden men lurked. When our foot patrol caught up with them, I saw that two had been caught.

The rule for properly building suspense in horror movies is based on how fear works in real life. Faceless and invisible enemies are scary. Real human beings with faces and fears of their own aren't so much.

Our two busted stalkers looked a lot less intimidating in person. They seemed rather pathetic, actually, and they were not armed.

"My air conditioner's broken," said the first through our interpreter. "I was just going to a friend's house to get another one. I can show you the broken one now."

I've been on patrol with soldiers after curfew a number of times. Most Iraqis out after dark don't appear to be threatening or up to no good. This guy stood out, though. I didn't believe he was only trying to borrow an air conditioner. He was twitchy and much more nervous than anyone I had seen questioned before.

And anyway, aside from the twitchiness, why was he following soldiers around in the dark?

Our Iraqi interpreter wore a mask over his face to avoid being recognized by the locals. He checked the suspect's identification.

The man did live in the area. ID cards, though, don't say "militia man" on them.

Two soldiers guarded the second suspect while the rest of us walked to the first suspect's house and knocked hard on the door.

No one came to the door. A soldier banged on the door with his fist. "Open up!" he yelled.

The residents of the house finally stirred.

"There are lots of people in there," someone said.

I stepped back, having no idea what to expect.

A large man wearing shorts and no shirt opened the door. An old man in a dishdasha stood behind him. They weren't armed and didn't seem threatening.

"*Salam aleikum*," said the shirtless man.

"Can we come in?" said the soldier who knocked.

The shirtless man beckoned us in, and so we went in.

Soldiers dispersed throughout the house and rounded up everyone—four men, three women and two children—into one room. Everybody, soldiers and Iraqis alike, was mellow and cool. No one seemed to be angry at anyone. Our shirtless host seemed to be the head of the household, so the soldiers spoke mainly to him instead of to the suspect they had captured outside.

"You're right, he was bad," the man said.

"The curfew is for your safety," said a soldier through the interpreter. "We're hot too, okay? Finding an air conditioner isn't a good enough reason to go outside after dark."

"Sorry," the man aid. "Please forgive us. Anything you want, we are with you."

"There are bad guys out after dark."

"I understand, very sorry."

We said goodnight and left the house. There was no interrogation. All the soldiers did was drop the guy off at home to get him off the street. Whether he really was trying to borrow an air conditioner or whether he belonged to the neighborhood militia, I'll never know.

The second captured man was still being detained.

"I work at the mosque," he said through our masked interpreter. "I work there at night. I was just out getting some dinner."

We had walked past the neighborhood mosque earlier and there were no lights on inside. It didn't look like anyone worked there at night, at least not in any normal capacity.

All of us started walking toward the mosque.

"What are you going to do with him?" I said to Eddie.

"We're going to take him to the mosque and see if he really works there," he said.

When we arrived outside the mosque, some of the soldiers squatted in driveways across the street and scanned the roof. I joined them as Eddie and the others took the suspect to the gate.

"There are four men on the roof," a soldier said. "You can't see them anymore. They just ducked away as we got here." I crouched near the ground. "They have a little bunker up there. You can't see it from here, but it has sandbags and sniper netting around it."

"What are you going to do?" I said.

"Nothing," he said. "It's a mosque."

"They're violating curfew," I said, "and stalking us in the dark from a militarized mosque. And you aren't going to do anything?"

"Our rules of engagement say we can't interfere in any way with a mosque unless they're shooting at us," he said.

So we dropped off our stalker with his "co-workers" and left.

We walked the streets of Baghdad at midnight while waiting for the call from intelligence officers back at the outpost. If they could determine which exact house the al-Qaeda target was in, the soldiers

I patrolled with would be first on the scene. All he had to do was make one more phone call on his cell phone and he'd be located. Then he'd be quietly surrounded by two dozen infantry soldiers, along with me with my notepad and camera, before he had any idea what was happening.

In the meantime, we chased shadows and silhouettes and dark vehicles on blacked-out streets without any headlights.

We chased a car so far from our starting point, I wondered if anybody still even knew where we were. We sure as hell weren't in Tunis anymore. Eventually, the driver pulled over and stopped. I got out of my Humvee and followed Eddie to the driver's-side door. Vicious dogs snarled at us from behind a gate.

Three men were inside. All were told to get out of the vehicle and were questioned and patted down.

It's possible the three young men in the car didn't even know we were trying to catch them. Humvees are driven in Iraq in the dark without headlights. They're almost invisible. And they don't go very fast.

None of the young men were armed. Soldiers searched the vehicle, didn't find anything and sent everyone home.

This is what it is like most nights during counterinsurgency warfare. "It's like we're Baghdad P.D.," as one soldier put it. It's not open war and constant explosions and bang-bang. Much of it entails patient police work and the chasing of ghosts.

We never did get the call from the intelligence officers. The insurgent commander, whose name I know but was asked not to reveal, was almost, but not quite, captured that night. His capture would have saved lives, and it would have been something to see.

This isn't the movies, however. The Iraqi counterinsurgency would be a hard war to film accurately. Most of the time it's so quiet. But it's the quiet of an Alfred Hitchcock movie, not of rural Middle America. Explosions, mortars, bullets, rockets … these things can come flying at you at any time.

We drove. I watched the dark city through bulletproof glass. Most homes were blacked out. Very few families stayed up late and ran their generators past midnight. Most Iraqis—and I knew this even though I could not see it—slept on the roofs of their houses, where it's cooler at night.

The dark shapes of palm trees somehow looked menacing and benign at the same time. They looked slightly more ominous as we drove into a dense grove bathed in an eerie glow from starlight shining through dust.

Anything could have been waiting for us on the road up ahead. Anyone could have been watching and waiting, perhaps even with the same night-vision goggles the soldiers themselves wore.

Suddenly the trees were gone and the sky opened up. I couldn't see anything.

"We're in the slum now," Lieutenant Evan Wolf said. "It's a nasty one too. Some houses are literally made out of cardboard. I would kill myself before I lived here."

I have no idea how these people survive without air conditioning and clean water. The environment here in the summer is unrelentingly hostile.

"How did you get into this job?" Eddie said.

"I needed to get out of the office," I said.

"You're way out now," Eddie said and laughed.

"I can't wait to get in the office," Lieutenant Wolf said.

"Do you like your job?" Eddie said.

"I love my job," I said. "It's the best I've ever had. Do you like yours?"

"I wouldn't say it's the worst decision I ever made," he said. "It's hard for soldiers. We all want to go home, of course. But we also want to stay and make sure our buddies did not die for nothing."

There were no streetlights. All I could see was absolute darkness and the faint outlines of hovels against a backdrop of stars.

"It's always interesting, though," Eddie said. "No one gets to see places like this. Only Iraqis. And you. And us."

Three

The Last Communist City

Havana, Cuba 2013

Fidel Castro made a liar out of me. Okay, I didn't *have* to lie to immigration, customs and security officials at Havana's José Martí International Airport. I could have just applied for a journalist visa and hoped they'd approve me. But colleagues warned that I'd have to wait months for an affirmative, and the authorities wouldn't tell me if the answer was *no*. They'd simply toss my application into the trash if they thought I'd write anything "negative." Six months, nine months, a year would finally pass, and I'd still be waiting and wondering if I'd ever hear from them.

I had a job to do. I couldn't wait six to 12 months in bureaucracy hell. So I lied.

"Tourism," I said when the nice woman at Passport Control asked what I was doing there.

The Cubans knew I was coming. My name was on the flight manifest. If anyone googled me, they'd find out at once that I worked as a journalist. And if they checked their records, they'd know I didn't have the right visa. Reporters who worked in Cuba on tourist visas were arrested, interrogated and deported. It made no difference whether or not off-the-books journalists were friendly to the government. They were required to register with and—more important—get *permission* from the proper officials.

I had to stay off their radar. Freedom House ranked Cuba as the sixth most oppressive country in the world for journalists. The Castro government created a more hostile working environment than even the Syrian and Iranian governments. The only countries on earth that repressed reporters more ruthlessly were, in order: North Korea, Turkmenistan, Uzbekistan, Eritrea and Belarus. All are either communist or postcommunist in name only.

Some of my colleagues in the media weren't sure I'd get away with it. "You're pretty high-profile," said one. "And it's not like you can hide."

Several who had worked in Cuba in the past warned me not to bring a laptop.

"That alone will be a red flag," said one. "They'll put you under surveillance."

I'd also have to hide my notebook.

"Cuban security agents from the Ministry of Interior will sweep through your hotel room," warned a veteran American visitor to Cuba, "so lock all your note-taking materials up in your room safe."

"The Castro government already knows who you are and what you'll be doing," said Valentin Prieto, a Cuban exile in Miami and founder of the blog *Babalú*. "And make no bones about it, the KGB, Stasi et al have nothing—and I mean nothing—on the Cuban security apparatus. It may seem primitive, but it is highly effective. You will be monitored from the moment you step on the tarmac. You will never be alone while on the island, even in your hotel room, if not especially so. Be careful and keep in mind that you are in a very closed society whose fuel is fear."

So I tensed up a bit when the nice woman at Passport Control typed my name into her computer. Something appeared on her screen. Her eyes tracked back and forth as she read.

What did it say? What did they know about me? Had they looked me up in advance? Prieto's concerns to the contrary, I figured they probably hadn't, but I couldn't know for sure that they'd let me in unless they actually let me in.

It was an absurd moment. I was standing there sweating while trying to sneak into a police state that hundreds of thousands of people risked their lives to escape from.

"Stand back, please," the Passport Control lady said. "And look into the camera."

A webcam dropped down from the ceiling. I grinned at the thing like a stupid tourist on holiday. It clicked.

She finally stamped my passport and smiled. "Welcome to Cuba."

I smiled back. *Suckers.*

Wait. I was not yet in the clear. While I waited for my suitcase to arrive on the baggage-claim belt, a young policeman seized my passport and would not give it back. "I need you to answer some questions."

Shit.

"What are you doing here?"

I lied.

"Where are you staying?"

But told him the truth about that.

"Which parts of Cuba will you be visiting?"

Havana, of course.

"What do you do for a living?" No choice but to lie.

"What's the name of the company you work for?" I had to lie about that one as well. I hated having to do it, but overcontrolled police states make liars of everyone.

"Are you planning to visit any schools or medical facilities?" he said.

"I *hope* I don't have to visit a medical facility," I said, to lighten the mood.

He smiled and laughed. "Yes. Let's hope not."

He was so unfailingly friendly and polite that I didn't worry he'd catch me. And he didn't drill down into granular details or ask any follow-up questions. He just dutifully wrote down my answers.

They had no idea I was a journalist or that I intended to write about Cuba, and they weren't going to find out. That was clear. And when the policeman finished questioning me, he did something unprecedented in all my years of crossing borders.

He returned my passport and said "Sorry about that" with a sheepish look on his face.

He was *sorry*? Really?

"I hope you have a nice time in Cuba."

Fidel Castro and Che Guevara overthrew the squalid and bloody dictatorship of Fulgencio Batista in 1959 with support from a broad swath of Cuban society. I would have supported the revolution too, if I'd lived there at the time. Castro described himself as a freedom fighter and promised not communism but political liberalism.

"Democracy is my ideal, really," he said in 1959. "There is no doubt for me between democracy and communism." That first sentence was a lie, but the second sentence sure wasn't.

Even after he took power and formed a new government, even as Guevara lined men and boys against the blood-soaked walls of La Cabaña and had them executed by firing squad, Castro kept his communist designs to himself. Later, however, he boasted about it with a terrifying ferocity.

"They corrupt the morals of young girls!" he shouted in 1968 against Cuba's hippies, "*and destroy posters of Che!* What do they think? That this is a bourgeois liberal regime? NO! There is nothing liberal in us! We are collectivists! We are communists! There will be no Prague Spring here!"

I visited a year and a half before the United States and Cuba had restored diplomatic relations. No kind of "spring," Prague-like or otherwise, had yet to appear, so I felt a bit apprehensive about showing up there under false pretenses. But Cuba's hard illiberal nature was softened somewhat by three things—by the warmth of its people, by the beauty of its architecture and setting and by ideological tiredness.

"Cuba is gorgeous," said my journalist pal Terry Glavin. up in

British Columbia when I told him where I was going. "Although I expect it's gone to shit in some respects since I was there. The regime is that much more decrepit with the absence of Daddy Warbucks in Moscow. The things you will most love about Cuba, I bet, are the Cubans and the ravaged beauty of the place. I can't imagine any people on earth putting up with such bullshit with as much grace and humor and decency as the Cubans have managed, God love 'em. Were it not for the regime, I'd happily live in Havana."

The Cubans did seem to handle it well, though I have no idea how. "You would make a fortune," wrote Havana-based journalist Marc Frank in his book *Cuban Revelations*, "if you could patent as an antidepressant whatever brain chemical kept the Cubans' spirits up through the hard times."

I wondered, though, how much of it was real. Prieto warned me that to an extent, it was not. "You will most likely see many smiling faces while you're there," he said. "Lots of laughter and dancing too. But there will always be something much more profound behind all the smiles and laughter. Every Cuban, regardless of how content they may appear, lives with two underlying things—sadness and fear, the latter being more prevalent. Most Cubans will not openly display it, as you are a foreigner, but read between the lines when they speak to you."

I know what it's like to wear a false face. Not only did I have to lie at the airport, I also had to conceal my identity from every single person I met in the country, including other Americans, lest someone say the wrong thing about me in public in front of the wrong person at the wrong time. I had vowed to myself before I even left the United States that I wouldn't tell a single human being in Cuba who I was or what I was doing, no matter how much I felt like I trusted them. I hated having to do that, and I felt a little self-loathing because of it, but I had to be careful and consoled myself with the fact that I could be honest about everything later in writing.

The first thing I had to do was get into Havana. The international airport is located outside the city, and the ride in was a little unusual.

There is no product advertising in Cuba. Every billboard in the entire country is plastered with propaganda from the Communist Party.

The first one I saw featured a hangman's noose and said "BLOQUEO—*El genocidio mas largo de la historia.*" "BLOCKADE—The longest genocide in history."

The government was referring to the embargo, or sanctions, put in place against Cuba in 1962 after Castro nationalized U.S. property. But the sanctions were not a blockade—which is an act of war—and they certainly did not constitute genocide.

Another billboard showed the logo of the UJC, the Union of Communist Youth, which was composed of the faces of three communist leaders—Che Guevara, Camilo Cienfuegos and Julio Antonio Mella—men who were dubbed "the protagonists of our time." The UJC's motto was "Study, work, rifle."

I groaned to myself at these absurd slogans and images but was delighted when I later heard Cubans dismiss it all as "state propaganda."

Aside from the billboards on the way in, Havana didn't look like a communist city. It had not been transformed into a sullen drabscape of gray concrete towers like so many capitals in the former Soviet bloc. Small one-story homes in a state of mild disrepair appeared through junglelike foliage. Hundreds of people stood on the side of the road waiting for buses or to be picked up by one of the cars that passed periodically. Once I reached the city proper, all I saw—aside from a few faded high-rises—was European architecture in every direction. Most of Havana was built before the communist era, when Cuba was still a rich country, and hardly anything else had been built in the meantime.

I grinned like a kid when I first saw the classic American Chevys and Fords from the 1940s and 1950s that Cubans manage to keep working even though they no longer have parts.

"You wouldn't believe what they have under the hoods of those things," said one Cuban, who was clearly not a backyard mechanic himself. "They use pieces from old Russian washing machines."

I felt more like I was driving into a time warp than into a tropical version of the Soviet Union. But I *had* just entered a tropical version of the Soviet Union. And much to my surprise, some people grumbled about it in public, at least in English.

"Is there *any* private enterprise in Cuba?" I heard an American man in my hotel lobby say to his Cuban tour guide.

"No," said the tour guide—which was not strictly true, but it might as well have been.

I couldn't resist butting into their conversation.

"How do people here feel about that?" I said. "Honestly."

"We hate it, of course," she said. "But there's nothing we can do about it but leave."

Like the rest of the country, Havana's hotels were time warps. I stayed at two. The more interesting of the pair was the Habana Libre, or Free Havana, which had been a five-star Hilton before Fidel Castro seized it and turned it into his headquarters. It had been under communist management ever since and had been downgraded to three stars.

It wasn't a *bad* hotel. Like the classic cars out on the streets, it just hadn't been updated since the '50s. It was a modern-day throwback to the era of *Mad Men*.

The lights worked, the air conditioning didn't crap out, and the hot-water heater never ran cold, but I woke every morning in pain. The mattress, like the rest of the furniture, also dated back to the 1950s and was at least half as firm as the floor.

And I felt like I was being spied on the minute I stepped into my room.

I knew I wouldn't find any surveillance equipment, but I couldn't help looking. I didn't look hard, though. I didn't want anyone to *see* me looking for bugs, wires or cameras if they were watching. A colleague told me they place cameras as well as microphones in the rooms and that the cameras point at the bed. I had no idea if it was true. Perhaps it was just a paranoid rumor. Maybe the regime itself started the rumor to make people paranoid.

At the end of the day, it didn't matter if it was true, because I had little choice but to behave as though it were true. And it affected my job. Not only did I have to leave my laptop at home, but I also couldn't sit on the bed and take notes with pen and paper. I had to look and behave exactly like a tourist even in the "privacy" of my hotel room, and tourists don't generally sit down and write for long stretches.

I had no laptop and no notebook, but I had to take notes. *How?*

I could have typed something up in the business center and emailed it to myself, but incoming and outgoing Internet traffic was heavily monitored, so that solution was out. I know of two people who got in trouble doing that sort of thing, and one of them really was just a tourist. All he did was criticize Fidel Castro on Facebook.

But there are other ways to take notes. If you know a month in advance that you're heading into a situation like this, you'll think of something. I did. And I figured out how to do it in such a way that no one would know what I was doing even if they watched me do it on a video feed, nor would I be caught if my belongings, including the images on my camera, were thoroughly searched.

I may be the only person in the history of journalism who has used this particular method, partly because it's bizarre, partly because I used a product designed for a different purpose entirely and partly because that product didn't even exist until recently. (I'd love to tell you how, but it's my own personal trade secret that I may use again in the future.)

Even if the business center downstairs had been a viable option, the experience was miserable by design.

Private Internet was banned. You could only get online in hotels, Internet cafés and government offices. The price effectively prohibited regular citizens from accessing the Web. It cost me seven dollars an hour to use a dial-up connection. The government capped Cuban salaries at 20 dollars a month, so it costs a citizen ten days of income just to get online for an hour. Once they do get online, the connection will be so slow that surfing around is impossible. It took me the better part of my hour to get connected, to open my inbox and to send a single email to my wife telling her I had arrived safely and without incident.

The government strangled the Internet because it feared free information. There can be no other reason. That's also why they vetted journalists in advance and required special visas. Information could barely get in and barely get out. There could be no Twitter or Facebook revolution in Cuba's near future.

And there were apparently no real newspapers or magazines, at least none that I saw. No *International Herald Tribune*. No *Newsweek* and *Time* in the dentist's office. No Google News, since there was no Google. Certainly not the *Wall Street Journal* or the *Economist*.

I hadn't even been there a full day, and I already felt umbilically severed from the rest of the planet. My awareness of the world narrowed to what I could see right in front of me. I felt as though I had lost one of my senses. I had no real access to the Internet. No CNN, no *New York Times*. No blogs, not even my own. Nothing at all. I could not use my iPhone. I may as well have been at the bottom of the ocean.

The only newspaper I saw was *Granma*, the official organ of the Communist Party. *Juventud Rebelde* supposedly existed somewhere as well, but I didn't see any copies.

That, by the way, was an outrageously named newspaper. The English translation of *Juventud Rebelde* is *Rebel Youth*—as if it was Cuba's version of *Rolling Stone*. But God, no. It was not that at all. *Rebel Youth* indoctrinated young people with the zombie ideology of walking dead men. Youthful and rebellious it wasn't. It was the most tired, stale, old and establishment "newspaper" in the hemisphere.

Here's an excerpt from a recent interview with Raúl Castro, who took over from his ailing brother Fidel in 2008. It reads like an interview with the secretary general of Hezbollah. "These 50 years have been ones of resistance," Raúl said to the journalist, who didn't even merit a name, "years of survival, years of the determination of the people, in which we have maintained our strength, and that refers to the vast majority of the country." He goes on and on like that for pages. "We have not had peace, we have not had tranquility. The enemy says that socialism has been a failure. Why don't they leave us in peace to fight on equal terms? But it has not been a failure, not even under these conditions. It has been an incessant battle."

I never heard a single human being speak that way in Cuba. I doubted it even happened at Communist Party meetings anymore.

Granma, the newspaper aimed at adults, was sold by men standing on street corners. I never saw anyone buy it or read it.

I smiled the first time I stepped out for a walk. I was not supposed to be there, but nobody stopped me.

The air was warm and humid but not oppressive, as long as I walked in the shade. Direct sunlight, however, made me feel like I was standing next to an oven on a blazing-hot afternoon. Tropical sunshine is a force to be reckoned with, especially for someone like me whose ancestors hail from the North Atlantic and who lives now in the Pacific Northwest. The Spaniards who first settled the place without sunscreen must have looked like angry red lobsters before their bodies adjusted and their skin started producing additional melanin.

The city was reportedly safe, especially for visitors. Crimes against tourists were punished with tremendous severity. I felt secure everywhere. Not a single person looked or felt sketchy. Individuals approached and spoke to me once in a while, but they never seemed to want anything. They did not ask for money. They weren't trying to lure me into their shop like touts in the Middle East often do. (Cuba didn't really have any shops.) With a single exception, they weren't pimping prostitutes.

What struck me most while walking around Havana for the first time was how dead and quiet it was. This was unexpected, though in hindsight I should have known. Where has communism ever been lively?

Michael Frayn visited Cuba on the 10th anniversary of its revolution and wrote an essay at the time titled "Farewell to Money."

"No representation—but, then, no taxation. No bars—but then, no drunks. No news, no institutions to protect the rights of the individual, nothing in the shops. Often no water in the pipes, occasionally no electricity in the wires. 'No liberalism whatsoever! No softening whatsoever!' (Castro.) … Havana is the saddest sight—shabby, blank, full of nothingness."

Little had changed in 2014. That had been the defining characteristic of Cuba since 1959. It didn't change. The water and electricity seemed to work better, and parts of Old Havana had been fixed up for tourists, but otherwise Frayn's description was spot-on almost a half-century later.

The city felt languid, slow, inert. It was eerily quiet all the time, as if it had been partly depopulated. You hardly had to look before crossing the street, because there was so little traffic. Every day felt like Sunday used to feel in the United States, when more people went to church and fewer establishments were open.

But Havana's establishments were not closed. There just weren't very many of them. You could not go shopping. There was nothing to buy. If you had millions of dollars, you would not be able to spend it. The city would be horrifying if were in a cold climate with dismal architecture, like much of the former Soviet Union, but it didn't strike me as horrifying. It was just static.

Nobody hurried. They had all the time in the world. And it's a good thing too, because, as one Cuban said, "our national sport is standing in lines."

It reminded me a bit of Libya under Muammar Qaddafi, which I visited for the first time 10 years earlier, only Cuba was better educated, more advanced culturally and—even though much of its architecture was thoroughly ravaged—more pleasing aesthetically.

But there's a reason I'm comparing it to Libya under Qaddafi and to the Soviet Union. Qaddafi modeled his government on Nicolae Ceausescu's communist regime in Romania. The Brother Leader of the al-Fateh Revolution never called himself a communist; he insisted his Libyan brand of socialism was the "third way" between liberal capitalism and Soviet-style collectivism. But he was effectively a communist in all but name, and Libya at the time looked even more the part than Havana.

"Cuba looks exactly like its photos," wrote writer and translator M.J. Porter in 2011, "and yet it feels *different*. I fell in love with Cuba and Cubans. Something felt like home. Completely unforeseen, however, was the weight of the totalitarian state."

She wrote those words for the introduction to the outstanding book *Havana Real*, by Cuban dissident Yoani Sanchez. I read it before I went to Cuba, and I had to wonder: How on earth could the weight of the totalitarian state not be foreseen, especially if Porter had read Yoani Sanchez? Cuba had been totalitarian for more than 50 years. Raúl Castro was liberalizing the economy slightly, but it was still more like North Korea's than anyone else's, and there had been no political opening whatsoever.

I understand now. The totalitarian state did weigh heavier than expected. At least it did for me and for M.J. Porter, despite having read Yoani Sanchez and so many others. Which is strange, because the totalitarian state was all in the shadows.

After the revolution, the State Security Department, known locally by some at the time as the Red Gestapo, recruited thousands of *chivatos* (rats), internal secret police who operated more or less like the Stasi did in East Germany. Repression was out in the open back then. Thousands were murdered and tens of thousands thrown into prison for political reasons.

In an essay titled "Interminable Totalitarianism in the Tropics," collected in *The Black Book of Communism* by Harvard University Press, French historian Pascal Fontaine described the Committees for the Defense of the Revolution, Castro's ruthless enforcers of ideological correctness. One was set up on each block in urban areas to keep watch on everybody. Everything about them intimidated. Next to the front door of one CDR office, I saw the image of a faceless man wielding a sword above the words "Always in combat."

Always in combat against whom, you might ask?

The neighbors.

"The surveillance and denunciation system is so rigorous," Fontaine wrote, "that family intimacy is almost nonexistent."

Family intimacy is almost nonexistent.

Aside from the slave-labor camps and the staggering body counts, I can think of no more devastating an indictment of totalitarian government than that sentence. Something broke inside me when I read it.

I certainly wasn't intimate with anybody in Cuba—and I don't mean physically any more than Fontaine did. I had to lie by omission every minute of every hour of every day, just like the Cubans. A person could get used to this sort of thing, I suppose, but that does not make it less alienating. That's the counterintuitive thing about totalitarian systems. They herd people into Borg-like collectives, yet every individual is savagely atomized.

I'd never felt so alone in my life.

I couldn't help feeling watched in that kind of environment, especially since so many people insisted the hotels were bugged.

I wasn't paranoid about it. Security personnel weren't going to bust into my room and take me away. There was not much to fear, really. People weren't getting shot in the streets. No one pointed a gun at anybody in my presence, nor did I see anyone get hauled off to prison. Cuba was not a war zone. It was not the Cambodian Killing Fields. Nor was it North Korea, which Christopher Hitchens once described as a place "where everything that is not absolutely compulsory is absolutely forbidden." It wasn't *that* bad.

But it was a total-surveillance police state.

And so I felt watched, not by thugs but by yawning functionaries who probably would rather do something else, like the policeman who questioned me in the airport. Maybe they were watching or listening some of the time and maybe they weren't. I'll never know.

Since I couldn't see anyone watching or following me, the tingling sense of being observed was self-generated. In a way, it was all in my head. I wasn't imagining things—the hotels really were bugged—but I still don't know if anyone ever actually spied on me. It took me a while to figure out what to make of that, and my blood ran cold when I finally did.

British philosopher Jeremy Bentham devised an ingenious low-tech system of total surveillance 200 years ago. It would work in hospitals, schools and psychiatric institutions, he argued, but it would work even better in prisons.

The idea was straightforward: Build a circular prison with a tower in the center so the guards can see inside any and every cell from a single location. The watchtower could even be obscured so that prisoners would have no idea if the guards were looking at them or not. Since prisoners would know they might be watched at any given moment, they'd act as though they were being watched at all moments.

"Morals reformed," Bentham wrote, "health preserved, industry invigorated, instruction diffused, public burdens lightened, economy seated—as it were—upon a rock, the Gordian knot of the poor-law not cut but untied, all by a simple idea in architecture!" He touted his prison as "a mill for grinding rogues honest" and "a new mode of obtaining power of mind over mind, in a quantity hitherto without example."

He called it Panopticon.

French philosopher Michel Foucault assailed it as a cruel, ingenious cage. "The panoptic schema makes any apparatus of power more intense," he wrote. "Its strength is that it never intervenes, it is exercised spontaneously and without noise."

Prisoners collaborated in their own surveillance because their heads were haunted by the thought of an all-seeing eye.

No prison was ever designed to all of Bentham's specifications, but dozens were constructed around the world that met most of them. The one that most closely resembled Bentham's Panoptic regime was in Cuba.

Fidel Castro didn't build it. The Presidio Modelo complex was built in the mid-1920s, when Gerardo Machado was still president.

Castro and his brother Raúl were incarcerated there for a few years after attacking the Moncada military barracks in 1953 in their first botched uprising against the Batista regime. Fidel gleefully turned things around in the 1960s and used the Presidio complex to warehouse political prisoners, gays, dissidents and those who promoted the counterculture.

Today it's no longer a prison. It stands now as a national monument and, like almost everything else on the island, is in a state of decay.

Why did Castro close the Presidio complex?

Because, why not? *It was superfluous.*

An oblivious tourist could be blissfully unaware of all this and have a nice time in Cuba, I guess, but I was not an oblivious tourist and knew perfectly well that Fidel Castro and Che Guevara turned the entire island nation into Bentham's Panopticon.

I visited a small art gallery inside the home of famous photographer José Figueroa and his wife, Cristina Vives. When I first stepped into the living room, I thought I might have made a mistake, that I was not where I wanted to be, because the first photographs I saw on the wall by the front door featured Castro's chief executioner, Che Guevara. The most prominent wasn't actually a photo of Che Guevara, per se. Rather, it showed a cigarette lighter embossed with the famous chic image of Che taken by Alberto Korda.

Figueroa himself seemed a shy man, but Cristina was happy to show tourists around.

"José was visiting the United States on 9/11," she said. "He was in New York City. It was a frightening time, and he had that lighter with him." She pointed at her husband's photograph on the wall, the one with the Che lighter. "Because of what had just happened, the lighter was confiscated in the security line at the airport. That famous lighter with that famous image is gone forever because of Osama bin Laden. It's a shame, but it's a great story, isn't it? Think about it."

Wait. Why, exactly, is that a great story, and why was she telling me to think about it? What did she mean? That the United States had a heavy-handed government too? That the Americans got in one last swipe at Che Guevara before moving on to the war on terror? That the ripple effects from al-Qaeda's assault on New York City reached as far as Havana? That an object showing the face of one mass-murdering sonofabitch was indirectly destroyed by another mass-murdering sonofabitch?

I don't know what she was trying to say, but she made one thing loud and clear: She wanted me to think about what she was telling me, and she was leaving some things unsaid. That's often how people talk to each other in totalitarian countries. Foreigners who aren't used to it need to know and pay close attention.

Most of Figueroa's pictures on the wall were taken in the 1960s and 1970s. They featured bourgeois middle-class people doing bourgeois middle-class things during a time of proletarian collectivism. His photos were in black and white, which suggested a bygone era even at the time they were taken.

"I'm sure you've seen other pictures from Cuba at that time," Cristina said. "They probably showed bearded revolutionaries with guns. But most Cubans were not bearded revolutionaries with guns. Most of us were middle class. And we were here too."

Figueroa's black-and-white images of Cuba's vanished middle class were as sad as they were arresting. An entire class of people—my class— was murdered, imprisoned, forced into exile or forced into poverty. Fidel Castro didn't only destroy Havana's buildings. He also destroyed the lives of the people who lived in them.

Many of Figueroa's pictures seem to me quietly subversive in the most subtle of ways, not because they were anticommunist but because they were *non*communist. That's my take, anyway. Neither he nor his wife said a single word critical of the regime. Maybe I'm wrong. This is my interpretation. I own it.

But listen to what Cristina said next.

"You should go to the art museum," she said, "the Museo Nacional de Bellas Artes. Everyone who goes there is struck by a Flavio Garciandía painting from 1975. You have to realize that everything was political then. Cuban art was required to serve socialist principles. The Beatles were banned. Yet Garciandía painted a picture of a pretty girl lying in a field of grass and called it *All You Need is Love,* after the Beatles song. The museum immediately bought the painting for a small sum and prominently displayed it. Things started to change after that."

So Garciandía the painter and the art-museum curators mounted a protest. Not only did they get away with it, but it had the desired effect.

Only in a communist country or an Islamist theocracy would such acts be considered rebellious. Few in Europe or the United States would even notice that painting. It certainly wouldn't be a political lightning bolt. Only in a totalitarian country where every damn thing under the sun has to be ideological can such a blatantly apolitical painting be considered political.

Is that what José Figueroa was doing with his photographs in the '60s and '70s? Being anticommunist by being noncommunist at a time when everything had to be communist? Did he get away with it because he used a camera instead of a canvas and because he covered his ass once in a while by including Korda's image of Che?

I don't know. Nobody said that to me. He certainly didn't, nor did his wife. Maybe I only saw what I wanted to see. It happens.

Displaying noncommunist art was allowed now, and they said nothing "negative" about the revolution or government, so nothing they did in that gallery was technically subversive at all, nor was anything either of them said to me. For all I really know, they're both regime sympathizers.

But there was more to see in their gallery. Figueroa and his wife had mounted a television screen on the wall above a doorway into one of the back rooms. On the screen played a video shot from a handheld camera at the window of a commercial airplane at cruising altitude. I could see the wing jutting out the side of the plane above clouds far below, and I could hear the roar of the engine, but that was it. Nothing was actually happening on-screen.

"What am I looking at here?" I said. The film, if I could call it that, seemed incredibly dull, but there had to be a point I wasn't seeing.

"That," Cristina said, "is a film of the entire flight in real time from Havana to Miami."

Oh. Well. *That* was certainly interesting.

"The flight takes less than an hour," she said. "It feels like a long time if you stand here and watch it, but it's no time at all if you're on the plane. We are so close and yet so far. It all depends on your perspective."

Most photographs on the wall in their home were black and white, but I'll never forget one color photograph in the very last room. The image struck me with great force before I even knew what it was.

It showed a man inside what appeared to be a Cuban house. The main room was sparsely furnished. Paint peeled off the walls. The man was opening his front door just the tiniest crack and carefully peering outside. The image conveyed to me a feeling of fear and hope at the same time.

"Do you know what that is?" Cristina said. "On his television screen?"

I hadn't really noticed that inside the man's house in the photograph was a small black-and-white television set. The image on the screen was grainy and vague.

"No," I said. "I can't tell what's on the screen."

"It is the fall of the Berlin Wall," she said, "broadcast on Cuban television."

I felt a jolt of adrenaline. It was my body's way of telling me I was seeing and hearing something important, something I'd have to remember and later write down.

"But there's something wrong with the picture," Cristina said. "Do you know what it is?"

I looked intently at it again. What was wrong with the photo? All I saw was a Cuban man peering with tremendous caution outside his front door while communism self-destructed in Europe.

"Tell me," I said.

"The picture is fake," she said. "The fall of the Berlin Wall was never broadcast on television in Cuba."

Neill Blomkamp's 2013 science-fiction film *Elysium* depicts a world where the wealthy have moved off-planet into an orbiting luxury satellite while the wretched majority remain in squalor on earth. Blomkamp is South African, and the film works passably as an allegory to the apartheid regime he grew up under, but it takes place in Los Angeles two centuries from now. It's a rather cartoonish vision of the future for the United States, and it has been panned by some critics for pushing a socialist message, but the dystopian world Blomkamp depicts is a near perfect metaphor for a then actually existing socialist nation just 90 miles from Florida.

In Cuba, as in *Elysium*, a small economic and political elite lived in a rarefied world above the impoverished masses below. Karl Marx and Friedrich Engels, authors of *The Communist Manifesto*, would be appalled by the misery ordinary citizens were required by law to put up with and by the relatively luxurious lifestyles of those who kept the poor down by force. Cuba was stricken with some of the same problems as capitalist nations, the kind that should be instantly recognizable to the Occupy Wall Street crowd—only in Cuba, they were more grotesque and bizarre.

Many tourists returned home convinced that the Cuban model had succeeded where the Soviet model failed. But that's because they never left Cuba's Elysium.

Havana has a delightful little tourist sector, but the rest of the city looks like it had suffered a catastrophe on the scale of Hurricane Katrina or the Indonesian tsunami. Roofs had collapsed. Walls were splitting apart. Window glass was missing. Paint had long vanished. It was almost entirely free of automobile traffic and felt postapocalyptic.

I walked for miles through an enormous swath of destruction

without seeing a single tourist. Most foreigners didn't know this other Havana even existed, though it made up most of the city. Tourist buses avoided it, as did taxi drivers bringing people in from the airport. It looked like a dead civilization that was somehow still populated by people struggling to eke out a life for themselves in the ruins. As Anthony Daniels once wrote, "Havana is like Pompeii and Castro is its Vesuvius."

Yet the bones of Cuba's capital are unmatched in our hemisphere. "The Cubans of successive centuries created a harmonious architectural whole almost without equal in the world," he added. "There is hardly a building that is wrong, a detail that is superfluous or tasteless. The tiled multicoloration of the Bacardi building, for example, which might be garish elsewhere, is perfectly adapted—natural, one might say—to the Cuban light, climate and temper. Cuban architects understood the need for air and shade in a climate such as Cuba's, and they proportioned buildings and rooms accordingly. They created an urban environment that, with its arcades, columns, verandas, and balconies, was elegant, sophisticated, convenient, and joyful."

Cuba was indeed relatively wealthy before Castro flattened the country with a Marxist-Leninist battering ram. "Contrary to the myth spread by the revolution," wrote Dr. Alfred Cuzán, a professor of political science at the University of West Florida, "Cuba's wealth before 1959 was not the purview of a privileged few. ... Cuban society was as much of a middle-class society as Argentina and Chile." But rather than raise the poor up, Castro and Guevara shoved the rich and the middle class down. The result was collapse. "Between 1960 and 1976," Cuzán continued, "Cuba's per capita GNP in constant dollars declined at an average annual rate of almost half a percent (.04%). The country thus has the tragic distinction of being the only one in Latin America to have experienced a drop in living standards over the period."

It was obvious at a glance that Havana used to be prosperous. Poor nations do not—cannot—build such grand or elegant cities. Its wealth was not ancient history. Cuba, and Havana especially, flourished well into the postwar period of the 20th century.

Castro created one of the largest refugee crises in the history of the Western Hemisphere, but Europeans were almost as desperate to get in before 1959 as Cubans later were to leave. Back then, more Europeans moved to Cuba as a percentage of population than moved to the United States.

Cuban exile Humberto Fontova, the author of a series of books about Castro and Guevara, put it into perspective. "More Americans lived in Cuba prior to Castro than Cubans lived in the United States," he told me. "This was at a time when Cubans were perfectly free to leave the country with all their property. In the 1940s and 1950s, my parents could get a visa for the United States just by asking. They visited the United States and voluntarily returned to Cuba. More Cubans vacationed in the U.S. in 1955 than Americans vacationed in Cuba. Americans considered Cuba a tourist playground, but even more Cubans considered the U.S. a tourist playground."

In 1958, Cuba had a higher per capita income than much of Europe did. In the early 21st century, it was a wreck of a place that only looked "good" next to North Korea and emergency-room cases like Somalia. "Who jumped on rafts to escape Batista?" Fontova said. "Nobody. Back then, people jumped on rafts to get *into* Cuba, primarily from Haiti and Jamaica. Haiti is only 60 miles away, and Haitians used to cross the water because the living conditions were better. We sure don't see that anymore."

Cuba cratered during the communist period, but unprecedented pain and deprivation slammed into the country when Moscow cut off its subsidies after the fall of the Soviet Union. Frank wrote about it in chilling terms in his book, *Cuban Revelations*. "I landed in a world that resembled the aftermath of a natural disaster or war. The lights were off more than they were on, and so too was the water. ... Food was scarce and other consumer goods almost nonexistent. ... Doctors set broken bones without anesthesia. ... Worm dung was the only fertilizer."

He quoted a nurse who told him that Cubans "used to make hamburgers out of grapefruit rinds and banana peels; we cleaned with lime and bitter orange and used the black powder in batteries for hair dye and makeup." "It was a haunting time," Frank wrote, "that still sends shivers down Cubans' collective spines."

The island needed economic reform like a gunshot victim needs an ambulance. Castro had to do something. He wasn't about to tear down his own Berlin Wall and reform himself and his ideology out of existence, but he had to open up at least a small piece of the country to the global economy.

He detested the notion of luring bourgeois tourists to Cuba, but the island needed hard currency and needed it *now*, so the Soviet subsidy was replaced by vacationers, mostly from Europe and Latin America, who brought in hard cash.

Foreigners certainly weren't getting ration cards at the airport, so the island needed some restaurants. Therefore, *paladares*—private restaurants inside private homes—were allowed to open up, though no one from outside the family was permitted to work in them. (That would be "exploitative," even though it paid better than government work.)

Diplomats and other foreign residents didn't get ration cards either, nor would they live there if they had to, so government-run "dollar stores" sold imported and relatively luxurious goods to non-Cubans.

Thus was Cuba's quasi-capitalist bubble born.

And when the ailing Fidel ceded power to his less doctrinaire younger brother Raúl in 2008, that bubble expanded and produced *Elysium*-style stratification that would embarrass the 19th century robber barons.

Cuba was at the end of one era and the beginning of a new one. And the transition produced what was perhaps the most perverse economy in the world.

In the United States, we have a minimum wage. Cuba had a maximum wage—a lousy twenty dollars a month for almost every job in the country. (Professionals like doctors and lawyers made a whopping 10 extra dollars a month.) Sure, Cubans got free health care and education, but as Cuban exile and Yale historian Carlos Eire said,

"All slave owners need to keep their slaves healthy and ensure they have the skills to perform their tasks."

Even employees inside the quasi-capitalist bubble were paid only twenty dollars a month—hence the *quasi*. Hotels, for instance, were owned by the government but managed by Spanish companies such as Meliá International. Before accepting the contract, Meliá said it wanted to pay workers a decent wage. The Cuban government said fine, so the company paid eight to ten dollars an hour. But Meliá didn't pay the employees directly. The company paid the government eight to ten dollars an hour per person, and the government kept almost all of it.

I asked several Cubans in my hotel if that was really true. All confirmed that it was. They don't get eight to ten dollars an hour; they got 67 cents a day. That's not a salary. That's a child's allowance.

Cuban poverty was not like poverty anywhere else, not even in sub-Saharan Africa or in India. In Cuba, poverty was required by law. The maximum wage was just the beginning. Not only were most Cubans not allowed to have any money, but they were hardly allowed to have any *thing* either. The police expended extraordinary manpower and resources to ensure that everyone who was required to live miserably on the bottom actually lived miserably on the bottom. Yoani Sánchez described it sarcastically in her book *Havana Real*: "Buses are stopped in the middle of the street and bags inspected to see if we are carrying some cheese, a lobster, or some dangerous shrimp hidden among our personal belongings."

Perhaps the saddest symptom of Cuba's state-enforced poverty was the prostitution epidemic, a problem the government denied and forbade foreign journalists based in Havana from even mentioning. Some Cuban prostitutes were professionals, but many were average women—wives, girlfriends, sisters, mothers—who solicited johns once or twice a year for a little extra money to make ends meet.

The government defended its maximum wage by arguing that life's necessities were either free or so deeply subsidized that citizens didn't need very much money. (Che and his sophomoric hangers-on hoped to rid Cuba of money entirely, but they couldn't quite pull it off.) The free and subsidized goods and services, though, were as dismal as everything else on the island.

Citizens who took public transportation to work—which included almost everyone, since Cuba had hardly any cars—had to wait in lines for up to two hours each way to get on a bus. Tickets weren't free. Commuters had to pay for their ride out of their twenty dollars a month. At least city buses were cheap. A one-way ticket to the other side of the island cost several months' pay, and a round-trip ticket set a Cuban back almost an annual salary.

Health care was free, but patients had to bring their own medicine, their own sheets, and even their own iodine to the hospital. Most of these items could only be found on the illegal black market and had to be paid for in hard currency. If you had no access to hard currency, you could always try prayer. Even those who had access to hard currency felt anxious about health care. I was warned to bring an entire bag of medical supplies with me—bandages, antibiotics, iodine, gauze—because I'd have a hard time finding these things even with my emergency money.

Cuba sent so many doctors abroad, especially to Venezuela in exchange for oil, that the island was now suffering a personnel shortage as well as a shortage of medicine and supplies. "I don't want to say there are *no* doctors left," said an American man who married a Cuban woman and has returned dozens of times, "but the island is now almost empty. I saw a banner once, hanging from somebody's balcony, that said, 'Do I need to go to Venezuela for my headache?'"

Housing was free too, but it was crumbling. Americans could get houses in abandoned neighborhoods in Detroit for only 500 dollars—which made them practically free—but so what? No one wants to live in a crumbling house in a neighborhood that has been going to the weeds since the '60s. I saw adequate housing in the countryside, but almost everyone in Havana lived in a Detroit-style wreck with caved-in roofs, peeling paint, missing windows, and doors that hung on their hinges at odd angles.

Education was free. And the country was effectively 100 percent literate, thanks to Castro's campaign to teach rural people to read shortly after he took power. But the regime had yet to make a persuasive argument that a totalitarian police state was required to get the literacy rate from 80 percent to 100 percent, especially since almost every other country in the hemisphere managed the same feat at the same time without the repression.

Cuba was short of everything but the air and the sunshine. In her book, Sanchez described an astonishing appearance by Raúl Castro on television, where he boasted that the country was doing so spectacularly well economically that everyone could finally have milk. "To me," Sanchez wrote, "someone who grew up on a gulp of orange-peel tea, the news seemed incredible. I believed we would put a man on the moon, take first place among all nations in the upcoming Olympics, or discover a vaccine for AIDS before we would put the forgotten morning *café con leche*, coffee with milk, within reach of every person on this island." And yet Raúl's promise of milk for all was deleted from the transcription when his speech was published in *Granma*. He went too far. No. Sorry. There was not enough milk for everyone on the island.

There was not enough of *anything* for everyone on the island, not even things as simple as cooking oil and soap. At least the black market filled in some of the gaps. Individuals who, by some illegal means or another, managed to acquire basic goods everyone needs to survive stood on street corners and whispered "cooking oil," "sugar" or whatnot to passersby, then sold it on the sly out of their living room. They were arrested, of course, if they were caught, as were the buyers. Imagine: arrested for buying a bottle of cooking oil! But the authorities couldn't put the entire country in jail. And they'd have to.

"Everyone cheats," said Eire. "One must in order to survive. The verb *to steal* has almost vanished from usage. Breaking the rules is necessary. *'Resolví mi problema,'* which means 'I solved my problem,' is the Cuban way of referring to stealing or cheating or selling on the black market."

But Cuba had two economies—the national communist economy for the majority and a miniature quasi-capitalist bubble for foreigners and the elite. Lest they be mixed, Castro declared that each should have its own currency. The communist economy used the Cuban peso and the capitalist bubble used the convertible peso.

Cuban pesos were worth nothing. They couldn't be converted to dollars or euros. Foreigners couldn't even spend them in Cuba. If I were to step into one of the gruesome shops or restaurants for locals, I'd be asked politely to leave.

I had to use convertible pesos. They were pegged to the U.S. dollar, but banks and hotels only paid 87 Cuban cents for each one. So the government got 13 percent right off the top. That was one reason for having a second currency. The rigged exchange rate was an easy way to shake down foreigners without most even noticing.

It also allowed the state to milk Cuban exiles. A million Cuban Americans lived in south Florida, and another half million lived elsewhere in the United States, and they sent hundreds of millions of dollars a year to family members still on the island. The government got its 13 percent instantaneously, and it got most of the remaining 87 percent later, because almost every place where a person could spend it was owned by the state.

But the real reason for creating the convertible peso was to make damn sure that Cuba's little capitalist bubble was hermetically sealed off from the ragged majority out in the communist economy.

"Foreign journalists report on the creation of ever more luxurious hotels, golf courses and marinas," Eire said, "but fail to highlight the very simple and brutal fact that these facilities will be enjoyed strictly by foreigners and the Castronoid power elite. Apartheid, discrimination and segregation are deliberately built into the entire tourist industry and, in fact, are essential to its maintenance and survival."

Until a few years earlier, Cubans weren't allowed to even set foot inside hotels or restaurants unless they worked there. They were turned back at the door lest they be exposed to the vastly superior lifestyles of the decadent bourgeoisie from capitalist nations like Mexico, Chile and Spain. (I cite these three as examples because the overwhelming majority of the tourists I ran into spoke Spanish to each other.)

The government eventually stopped physically blocking Cubans from hotels and restaurants, partly because Raúl was a little more relaxed about things than Fidel, but also because most Cubans couldn't afford to go to these places anyway.

A single meal out cost an entire month's salary. One night in a hotel cost five months' salary. A middle-class tourist from abroad could easily spend more in one day than most Cubans made in a year.

I had dinner with four Americans I met at one of the *paladares*. Of course the only Cubans in the restaurant were the cooks and the waiters. The bill for the five of us came to around 100 dollars. That was five months' salary.

The Floridita bar in downtown Havana was one of Ernest Hemingway's hangouts when he lived there. He was in the Floridita all the time, and the government placed a statue of him sitting on his favorite barstool grinning at today's patrons. The décor was exactly the same as it was back in his day, but with a staggering difference. Everyone in there was a tourist. Cubans weren't strictly banned anymore, but a single bottle of beer cost an entire week's salary. No one would blow their dismal paycheck on that, not even alcoholics, since Cubans didn't earn enough to become alcoholics. (Score that for the revolution, I guess.) Hemmingway couldn't possibly be happy about what had happened to his old haunt if were he still around.

Cubans weren't happy about it either, but tourists can be the most oblivious people sometimes. I got into an argument with one in that bar when I pointed out how appalling it was that every single patron was foreign. "There are places in the United States that some can't afford," she said defensively. Sure, but *come on*. Nowhere in America does a beer costs a week's pay. If there were such a place, it would be the only place. In Cuba, it cost a week's pay everywhere and for just about everybody. North Korea was the only other country on earth where citizens were forced by the state to be too poor to order a beer.

Cell phones were "allowed," but the monthly fees vastly exceeded the maximum income, so hardly anyone actually had one.

Cubans in the hotel industry saw how foreigners lived. The government couldn't hide it without shutting the hotels down entirely, and the state couldn't do that because it needed the money.

I changed a few hundred American dollars into convertible pesos at the front desk. It was more money than most Cubans made in a year, yet it would last me less than a week at the prices I had to pay. The woman at the counter didn't blink when I handed over my cash—she did this all day and was used to it—but it must have shattered her world when she first got the job.

Imagine working a hotel desk in the United States where foreign tourists change 50,000 euros for a few days' walking-around money. *That's* how much richer Americans were than Cubans. And Cubans were supposed to believe their economic system is better? How could they possibly?

That's why the regime wanted to keep foreigners and locals apart. The amount of money tourists brought into the country exposed the Communist Party narrative as the obvious lie that it was. Everyone who worked in the tourist sector saw it every day of their lives.

Tourists tipped waiters, taxi drivers, tour guides and chamber maids in hard currency, and to stave off a revolt from these people, the government let them keep the additional money, so they were relatively "rich" compared with everyone else. They were an elite class that enjoyed all kinds of privileges—enough income to afford a cell phone, the ability to go out to restaurants and bars and log onto the Internet once in a while—that ordinary Cubans couldn't even dream of.

I asked a few people how much chamber maids earned in tips, partly so I would know how much to leave on my dresser, and also to get an idea of just how whacked Cuban economics were. Supposedly they got around a dollar per day for each room. Some foreigners didn't tip at all, but others tipped more. If the maids cleaned an average of 30 rooms a day and worked five days a week, they'd bring in 600 dollars a month—30 times what everyone else got.

"All animals are equal," George Orwell wrote in *Animal Farm*, his masterful allegory of Stalinism, "but some animals are more equal than others."

Economic inequality is a fact of life. We can't get rid of it any more than we can stop gravity. Not even communist police states, with all the totalitarian might at their disposal, could manage to get rid of it. But only in the funhouse of a communist country was the cleaning lady rich compared with the lawyer.

Yet foreigners and elite Cubans didn't live remotely like rich people did anywhere else. They were impoverished compared with the middle class and even the poor outside Cuba. Spectacular fees for dismal Internet were just the beginning.

Around half the dinners I had were acceptable and one or two were even outstanding, but the breakfast buffets in the hotels were uniformly disgusting. I didn't dare touch the meat or the cheese. Bacon was half raw. Sausage was made from God only knows what. Cheese looked old and discolored. Bread was hard and flavorless. Yet this grim offering was advertised in the lobby as "exquisite."

Maybe if you spent your entire life on a Cuban ration card, that food seemed exquisite, but otherwise—no. The question wasn't what I wanted to eat. The question was what I thought I *could* eat without my stomach rising up in rebellion.

But the real kicker came when I went to a grocery store across the street from the exclusive Meliá Cohiba Hotel, where the lucky few who had access to hard currency shopped to supplement their meager state rations.

The store was located in what passed for a mall in Havana, a shabby and cluttered concrete box that pales in comparison with even the malls I've seen in Iraq, but never mind that. The bodega on the second floor was an extraordinary thing to behold.

I found rice, beans, frozen chicken, milk, bottled water, booze, a small bit of cheese, minuscule amounts of gross meat, some low-end cookies and chips from Brazil, and that's *it*. They have nothing else. No produce, no boxes of cereal, no cans of soup, no pasta, pretty much nothing at all that exists in any grocery store you've ever seen. A 7-Eleven in Omaha, Nebraska, has a better selection. And this place was for rich people. Even Egypt and Iraq had better grocery stores. Potatoes were available at restaurants for foreigners, but not at the store for "rich" Cubans.

Potatoes, I was told, would not be available for another four months.

Cuba's Elysium for the "haves" turned out to be dismal. Homeless people in America had access to more and better food.

Shortly before I left, I met a Cuban-American man and his wife who were visiting from Miami. "Is this your first time here?" he said.

I nodded.

"What do you think?"

I paused before answering. I wasn't worried I would offend him. He lived in Miami, so his opinions of Cuba were probably little different from mine. But we were in a crowded place. Plenty of Cubans could hear us, including police officers. They weren't going to arrest me if I insulted the government, but I didn't want to make a scene either.

"Well," I finally said. "It's ... interesting." He belted out a great belly laugh, and I smiled.

His wife scowled. "I *hate* this place!" she said. She practically shouted it. Fidel Castro himself could have heard, and she wouldn't have cared. She was not going to be quiet about it.

Tourists who visited Cuba and spent all their time inside the bourgeois bubble for the "haves" could easily leave the country oblivious to the savage inequalities and squalor beyond the hotel zone, but this woman was visiting her husband's family in the real Cuba and knew all too well what most of it's really like.

"His family is from here," she said, "but mine's not, and I will *never* come back here. Not while it's like this. I feel like I'm in Iraq or Afghanistan."

I visited Iraq seven times during the war and didn't have the heart to tell her that Baghdad, while ugly and dangerous, was vastly more free and prosperous than Havana. She probably wouldn't have believed it, and anyway Iraq was precisely the kind of country Castro wanted you to compare Cuba with. It was the wrong comparison. So were Third World holes like Guatemala and Haiti. Cuba was not a developing country. It was a developed country that was destroyed by its own government.

Havana was a magnificent European city once. It should be compared not with Baghdad, Kabul, Guatemala City or Port-au-Prince but with prosperous Western cities that were conquered by communists like Budapest, Prague and Berlin. Havana's history mirrors theirs, after all.

An advertisement in my hotel, the Habana Libre, claimed the Sierra Maestra restaurant on the top floor was "probably" the best in Havana. I certainly hoped so, because the restaurants off the lobby made for grim eating.

I saved the Sierra Maestra for my last night and rode the elevator up to the 25th floor. I had my first and only steak on the island and washed it down with Chilean red wine.

The tiny bill set me back no more than having a pizza delivered at home, but the total nevertheless exceeded an entire month's local salary. A comparable steak in America would cost 5,000 dollars. Not surprising, then, I ate alone. Every other table was empty. I felt conspicuous and like a burden to the staff who waited on me as if I were the president of some faraway minor republic.

I stared at the city below out the window as I sipped my red wine. Havana looked like a glittering metropolis in the dark. Night washed away the rot and the grime and revealed nothing but city lights. It occurred to me that the city will look exactly the same, at night anyway, after it is liberated from the tyrannical imbeciles who governed it then.

I tried to pretend I was looking out on a Cuba that was already free and that the tables around me were occupied—and by local people, not foreigners—but the fantasy didn't last. I was all alone at the top of Cuba's drab and eerie Elysium and yearning for home, where capitalism's inequalities were not so jagged and stark.

Four

The Worst Airline in the World

Rome, Italy 2008

If you travel around the world as much as I've traveled around the world, you are going to run into problems. Flights will be canceled. You'll end up sleeping on the floor in the airport. Your luggage will get lost, and you'll have no clean underwear or socks while you wait for your suitcase to show up. You'll get trapped in Minneapolis in December when you're dressed for Africa.

These things happen.

I'm used to it.

But nothing prepared me for the epic hell ride of flying home through Italy from the Middle East for Christmas in the winter of 2008.

I'd just spent several weeks apiece in Lebanon and Iraq and bought a plane ticket from Beirut to Portland on December 22. I should have had plenty of time to get home for Christmas. I had no idea, though, that I'd purchased my ticket from the worst airline company in the world—Italy's national carrier, Alitalia—and that a two-hour layover in Rome would turn into an ordeal that lasted longer than a week.

This was no ordinary travel ordeal. This is no ordinary story about travel delays and aggravated passengers. I wouldn't even believe it if it hadn't happened to me, and by the end of it all, I vowed to *never again* visit Italy for any reason. I won't even fly through it again. I especially won't fly through it again.

I'd placed my most critical and expensive items in my carry-on bag so they wouldn't get damaged or lost. Yet the woman at the Alitalia check-in counter in Beirut's international airport said my bag was too large and would have to be checked. I wasn't happy about that, but I did as I was told and surrendered my luggage. She neglected to tell me that Alitalia's baggage handlers were on strike and that it would be a very long time before I would see my property again—if I ever saw it again.

My flight left Beirut on time, and I had no idea what I was in for in Italy.

After I landed in Rome, the Departures board said my flight to Chicago was delayed two hours. I didn't mind. I had a 24-hour layover there, so I could wait patiently. But an angry stirring of passengers at the flight counter caught my attention.

"What's going on?" I asked an American woman who looked concerned yet approachable.

"I'm not sure," she said. "But somebody told me the baggage handlers on are strike and that we might not be going anywhere."

A few moments passed before I absorbed what that meant. My laptop was in my carry-on bag that Alitalia had forced me to check. My work from Iraq and Lebanon was on that machine. My Nikon camera was in that bag. I didn't want to hand it over, but the airline had forced me to hand it over.

At least I had the presence of mind to make backup copies of my recorded interviews and place them on a flash memory stick that I carried around in my pocket. My photographs, though, were not in my pocket. Alitalia's baggage-handler's union was holding much of my Middle East work hostage.

The man and woman working at our Alitalia flight counter wouldn't tell us what was going on. I assumed they didn't know. They looked slightly stressed, and I felt bad for them. They weren't on strike, but they had to deal with the fallout. And that fallout was about to get nasty.

A 50-year-old Italian man in a fedora started screaming at both of them.

A man standing next to me chuckled.

"Do you understand what he's saying?" I said.

"I'm from Argentina," he said, "but I speak Italian. That man is cursing like you wouldn't believe."

Mr. Enraged was also screaming like you wouldn't believe—wild-eyed, nostril-flared, spittle-flecked screaming.

Listening to him and imagining which curse words he used he was entertaining, but mostly the guy came across like a belligerent jerk. The two Alitalia employees on the receiving end of his tirade weren't responsible for our predicament. The baggage handlers were on strike, but the counter employees were still on the job.

Mr. Enraged was just ahead of everyone else. The rest of us who were booked on the flight to Chicago would learn soon enough that a huge number of Alitalia's employees absolutely deserved to be screamed at.

Our flight was delayed another four hours. Almost every other Alitalia flight in the airport had been canceled. You might think we were lucky that our flight hadn't been canceled. That's what I'd thought at the time, but nope.

"I live in the U.K.," a man said, "but I was born here in Italy. They will not fly us to Chicago. They will do nothing but lie. Trust me. I know how this country works."

They will do nothing but lie. That's how this country works. So said an Italian.

I hate to break it to everyone who yearns to go there on holiday, but he's right.

Our flight was delayed again another three hours, and the man and woman at the flight counter put on their coats and walked away. Several passengers impotently screamed at their backs in Italian. Two hundred of us were left stranded alone.

No one had screamed at them in English. Not yet.

European Union regulations required the airline to book us with another company so we could get home. But they refused to book us with another company. Word slowly trickled into the crowd from passengers who had been stranded in Rome's airport for days. Alitalia hadn't booked any of them on flights with other airlines, nor did the company reserve or pay for hotel rooms as the law required.

Certainly there were worse fates than being stranded in Italy. Daniel, the Italian-speaking man from Argentina, knew that better than most of us. He lived in Indianapolis and worked as a professor of social work.

"Indiana is a big change," he said, "but I like living there." He has fond memories of his hometown of Buenos Aries, but also terrible memories. "There were leftist terrorists and right-hand terrorists killing people all over the country. When the army took over, everyone cheered. But the army was no better, and they went after the intellectuals. Thirty thousand people were killed or disappeared. It was a horrible fascist regime."

Daniel managed to remain calm even after order and civility in the airport later disintegrated. His American friend and traveling companion Greg was about a disgruntled as I was. "No one is coming back here," he said. "They're supposed to rebook us, but they've abandoned us."

"I think we should get some people together and go to the office," I said, "since they refuse to rebook us. Ten people should be enough to put pressure on them."

He agreed, and we asked others standing next to us if they wanted to join us. Everyone seemed to think that was a fantastic idea. I'd only been stranded in Rome for a half day so far, but some had been marooned for days and looked like they wanted to punch somebody.

"Hell yes," a young American man said. "Let's go to the office. I know right where it is. I saw it on my way in here."

He said his name was DJ, and he wore a Palestinian kaffiyeh around his neck.

"You're sure you know where it is?" I said.

"Yeah, man," he said. "Let's go."

"Hey!" I said as loud as I could so everyone in our waiting area heard me. "We're going to the office to demand a new ticket. Who wants to join us?" The crowd roared its approval. I expected just a handful of tagalongs, but it looked like every single person wanted to join us.

So DJ and I led more than 200 people through the terminal toward the Alitalia office.

As soon as I realized I might write about this, I bought a notebook and pen from one of the stores. I wanted to take notes in real time and record more or less accurate dialogue.

"You're sure you know where this place is?" I said to DJ. I had no idea where we were going. We were inside an island terminal that could only be reached by train.

"Yeah," DJ said. "But hang on."

In front of us was a long Alitalia counter staffed by employees who served the entire terminal rather than just our flight to Chicago. DJ stopped and spoke to a man wearing the company's uniform.

"Why are we stopping here?" a woman said.

"I don't know," I said. "This isn't the office."

"This is the blind leading the blind," said a man.

I stepped up to the counter next to DJ. And DJ started screaming at the man standing in front of him.

"I will kick your ass if I see you outside," the Alitalia employee said to DJ.

"Let's go!" DJ said. "Grab your coat and let's go!"

This was not what I'd had in mind when I suggested a trip to the office.

"Hey," a woman said and grabbed my arm. "Look. They've posted the European Union's passenger rights on the wall."

Yep. There they were. Our rights were spelled out in English just behind the foul-mouthed Alitalia employee who, instead of complying with regulations, had just threatened a passenger with violence. The European Union required Alitalia to provide us with food, hotel accommodations and a ticket on another airline since we'd been delayed more than five hours. We were also legally owed up to 600 euros—around 1,000 dollars, —in compensation.

I had already been delayed more than five hours. Some of us had been delayed for days. None of us had received food, hotel accommodations or rebooked flights on a functional airline.

"Hey!" I said to the man who had threatened to kick DJ's ass. "Our rights are printed right there on the wall. You need to book us on another flight or give us a hotel room."

He narrowed his eyes at me and shook his head.

"*Now*," I said.

He ignored me.

When others saw the list of passenger rights on the wall, they became angry, and fast. Italian passengers were no longer the only ones riled up. More than a dozen surged to the counter and yelled in English at the man who refused to do what the law required of him.

"I will call the police!" said the Alitalia man.

The crowd erupted in cheers and applause.

"Yes!" a woman said. "Call the police! Call them now!"

A look of horror and dread washed over his face. He knew his airline was in violation and that the police were not likely to help him.

So what did he do? He put on his coat and walked off the job. Hundreds of furious passengers booed and hissed as he left. I kept an eye on DJ in case he decided to chase the guy down and take him up on his offer to fight.

Instead, DJ found another Alitalia employee to scream at, this time a woman.

"I am a man!" he said. And he was a drunk man. His breath smelled of booze from the airport's café-bars. "Just because my voice is high-pitched doesn't mean I'm in puberty!"

DJ was seriously beginning to lose it. I had no idea what he was talking about anyway. His voice was no more high-pitched than anyone else's.

"Will you please call a manager," I said to the woman. DJ wasn't getting results with his tirade, so I thought I'd play the good cop. "If you can't resolve this by yourself, just call a manager over."

She looked at me, then looked away without even acknowledging that I had said anything. This was becoming a pattern among the staff, and my patience was just about at an end.

"Hey!" I said. "Some of us have been here for days, and your airline is breaking the law."

This time she didn't ignore me. She squinted and jutted her chin.

I gave up. Being polite didn't work, and neither did yelling.

A manager in a tie finally came over. Two dozen people rushed and surrounded him.

"What?" he said. "Is something the matter? What's going on?"

The crowd booed and jeered.

"Oh, come on," Greg said to the manager. "Give me a break."

"You know what's going on," I said. I had been waiting for 10 hours by then, and I was one of the newcomers.

The guy just looked at his feet in embarrassment. Who did he think he was kidding?

"You need to rebook us or put us up in a hotel," I said. "You're in violation of European Union regulations, and you know it."

He looked at me when I spoke to him, but he ignored me and turned away.

"Hey!" I said. "You heard me. Are you going to do your damn job or not?"

He looked at me again, but he still didn't say anything.

An American woman approached the manager in tears and told him her son had just died and that she needed to get to Chicago for his funeral. Would he please just rebook her on another airline?

"No," he said.

And then the crowd lost it.

Five enormous black men stormed up to the manager while punching their hands with their fists.

"Mother*fucker*!" one of them said and flared his eyes and his nostrils. I thought for sure we were about to see blood on the floor.

The black man was hyperventilating and shaking while he tried with all his might to restrain himself from ripping out the man's spinal cord. A few passengers stepped between him and the manager. None of us wanted a riot. But a riot felt imminent.

"Do you know what's going on with these Africans?" a woman said to me. "They've been here for four days, and now the airline is saying there's no record they ever booked a flight at all."

"We want to go home!" the five Africans yelled in unison.

Four days they had been waiting!

"Get it, man?" said the first African man. "We want to go *home*!"

"Where are you guys trying to go?" I asked one of the calmer African men.

"Nigeria," he said. "Now he's saying we never purchased a ticket."

These men had Alitalia boarding passes. They wouldn't have gotten through security without them, so of course they'd bought tickets.

"Unbelievable," said an American man. "The staff is obviously racist against these guys."

"Our luggage is right outside that window," a man said to me. "It's sitting there on the tarmac next to the plane."

One woman told me she checked in her cat in its carrier two days earlier. She was worried her cat might soon die. (In hindsight, I can say that her cat almost certainly died.)

A three-year-old African girl sat on the Alitalia counter and cried hysterically while her father screamed "We want to go *home*!" at the staff.

Three police officers arrived to calm down the crowd. The most enraged of the African men picked up one of the officers, slung the cop over his shoulder and took him away into the restroom. I never found out what happened in there, but it could not have been pleasant.

Here we go, I thought. *This is when it begins.*

I thought about lighting a cigarette. Rules no longer applied. Not if passengers were hauling the cops away with impunity. I doubted anyone would say anything, and I doubted even more that anyone would make me put it out. I was pretty sure that if I lit a cigarette, other people would light up cigarettes too. It actually seemed slightly dangerous, though. The mood in the terminal might shift another notch toward total breakdown.

I kept my cigarettes in my pocket.

Anyone could have pushed the terminal over the edge at any moment. If just one person swung a punch at an employee, the place would explode. I could feel it. The Africans were ready to roll. So were DJ and a bunch of the Italians. Most American passengers seemed a bit more restrained, but even that was beginning to change. The Alitalia staff looked terrified. Their eyes darted sideways as they calculated escape routes.

A young American couple named Sofocles and Tatiana were on their way home from vacation in Greece.

"I thought Athens was screwed up," Sofocles said, "but I've ever seen anything like this."

"We witnessed the riots," Tatiana said, "but this feels much worse."

What? That sounded crazy, but that's what she said. Athens had just erupted in actual violence. Anarchists were throwing Molotov cocktails at the police. Greece was on fire.

Violence in Rome's airport was in the air, but it hadn't actually broken out yet. Tatiana must have felt trapped. We could only leave our terminal by train, whereas the violence in Athens could be avoided by just walking away or taking a taxi to a quieter neighborhood. There would be no walking or running away if a riot broke out in our part of the airport.

The Alitalia manager loosened his tie and wiped sweat off his forehead while dozens of passengers surrounded and screamed at him. I was angry too. *Just rebook us already.* But I also felt a bit sorry for him. Our little mob got its way, though, because he finally did what he was supposed to do and secured accommodations for us at a hotel near the airport.

"There is a shuttle bus outside that will take you to the Airport Palace Hotel," he said to me, Daniel and Greg. "Please tell the others."

"You should make an announcement," Greg said. "There are more than a hundred passengers on the flight."

"Please just let everyone know," the manager said.

He never did make an announcement. He didn't even put up a handwritten sign on the counter. He made Greg, Daniel and me responsible for hundreds of strangers who were, by then, scattered throughout the terminal and mixed in with thousands of others. How were we supposed to find everyone and let all of them know?

Why on earth were Daniel, Greg and I put in charge? The reason, I suppose, is because we took some initiative, but the manager basically told us to do his job for him. So the three of us told 10 people each and told them to tell 10 more people each. Hopefully most of our fellow passengers would eventually find out that hotel rooms finally had been taken care of.

Daniel, Greg and I left the terminal and went looking for the shuttle bus. We couldn't find it.

"I'm going to take a taxi," I said. "I don't want the hotel to fill up while we're just wandering around out here in the rain."

"I'm in," Greg said.

"Let's go," Daniel said.

Sofocles and Tatiana found us and asked if they could share our taxi as well.

"Of course," I said.

So we found a taxi.

"Airport Palace Hotel," I said to the driver.

"The Airport Palace Hotel?" she said. "It doesn't exist."

"I knew it!" Tatiana said. "Oh God, I *knew* it! They lied to us again."

I had no faith whatsoever in Alitalia's staff, but I didn't think even they would go that far.

Our driver called a friend. The Airport Palace Hotel did, in fact, exist.

It was in the ring of crap on Rome's outskirts, a dreary concrete-slabbed wasteland that induced a feeling of physical and spiritual depression in every poor bastard unlucky enough to get stuck there.

No one was at the front desk when we arrived. The hotel seemed entirely empty of guests. Of course it was. Who the fuck would want to stay there? Certainly no one on holiday.

"Hello?" Greg called out toward the back.

A manager emerged from an office while chewing his dinner.

"Hello," I said. "Alitalia booked us for some rooms here."

"Outside," the manager said dismissively with his mouth full of food. He pointed. "Outside. Right. Under the bridge. Right." He then went back into his office and slammed the door.

We stepped outside.

"I guess he's sending us to another hotel," I said.

"Is it just me," Greg said, "or is that man an asshole?"

"He's an asshole," I said.

We followed his directions, but we didn't see another hotel. Every awful nondescript building looked like every other awful nondescript building.

"What are we supposed to be looking for, exactly?" I said.

Nobody had any idea.

"Let's go back," Greg said.

So we went back.

"Excuse me," I said to the manager. "Where are we supposed to go, exactly?"

"Did you follow my directions?" he said.

"Yes," Greg said.

"I don't think so!" the manager said as though we were the stupidest people he'd met in his life.

He then gave us more precise directions, and we found another hotel owned by the same company.

I was startled by the staff at the next hotel. They were perfectly pleasant and helpful.

Daniel, Greg, Tatiana, Sofocles and I sat down to dinner. Christmas was three days away, but I knew we'd never make it.

"Merry Christmas, everybody," I said.

Greg groaned. "Don't say that," he said. "At least don't say that yet."

An Alitalia agent told me to go to the airport again the next morning for rebooking, but I seriously doubted they'd actually book me on a flight that would actually leave. I would have bought another ticket on a different airline so I could be home for Christmas, but the Alitalia staff refused to hand over my luggage. And they refused to let me retrieve my luggage myself. My laptop and camera were being held hostage.

At least a thousand people waited in line for rebooking at the main counter. That's where I'd need to go if I wanted a new ticket on a different airline. It took the staff around 20 minutes to process each passenger. At that rate, it would have taken me more than a week to get a new ticket.

So I went to the check-in counter to get a new worthless Alitalia ticket.

Sofocles and Tatiana were in line already. They let me join them, and we shared contact information. They lived in Chicago, where my luggage might theoretically appear at some later date, and they offered to help me retrieve it if I decided to go home without it.

As we approached the front of the line, I noticed that the man in front of us was checking in luggage.

"Excuse me, sir," I said. "You might not want to check your luggage. The baggage handlers are on strike. The planes aren't flying, and once you check your luggage, they won't give it back."

"*How dare you!*" said the Alitalia woman working the counter.

"You aren't warning this man," I said. "So I'm warning him. Somebody should have warned *me* before I gave you my luggage."

"He's checking in!" she said.

Sofocles and Tatiana laughed out loud.

"He's *checking in*?" I said. "He's not going anywhere. Nobody's going anywhere." I turned around and made an announcement to everybody in line behind us. "They're on strike. You aren't flying today, and if you give them your luggage, they won't give it back."

"That's not true!" the Alitalia woman said. "How can you say that?"

"How can you stand there and *lie* to these people?" Tatiana said.

Passengers in line behind us with luggage shifted and murmured to each other. They had no idea what they were getting themselves into until I told them.

"It's not my job to warn people," I said to the woman behind the counter. "It's yours. Have a little decency, will you?"

She angrily stabbed her keyboard with her fingers as she rebooked me on another Alitalia flight that was supposed to leave on Christmas Eve, the next day. But it did not leave the next day.

When I arrived at the airport the following morning, my flight to Chicago wasn't even on the Departures board. It was canceled before I'd even gotten there.

I stepped up to a counter where a woman sat in front of a computer.

"Excuse me," I said.

She yelled at me. "This counter is closed!"

The relentless rudeness and hostility from company staff would have shocked me if I'd arrived in Italy from the United States, but I'd just arrived from Beirut, one of the most polite cities on earth. I missed the Lebanese so badly it hurt.

I found another Alitalia woman behind a different counter.

"Excuse me," I said.

"Yes?" she said. I was stunned she didn't bitch at me.

"Is the flight to Chicago canceled? It's not on the board."

"I don't know, let me check."

She stepped into a back office and emerged a few moments later.

"Yes," she said, "it is canceled."

"Ugh," I said. "I've been here for days." I was hoping for a little commiseration, but I shouldn't have said anything.

"You've been here for *days*?" she said. "Why? *What happened?*"

"Oh, give me a break," I said. "Don't pretend you don't know what's going on."

She nodded, appeared slightly embarrassed and walked away without saying another word.

The absurdly long line of more than a thousand people from the day before was shortened to a mere hundred or so. This was the line for getting rebooked on a different airline. So I got in line. It "only" took two or so hours to get through it.

Blessedly, the woman at the counter was friendly.

"I can get you on a Delta flight that leaves in an hour," she said.

"Excellent!" I said. "Oh, thank you so much." I wanted to hug her. "I don't suppose my luggage will be on the flight, will it?"

"Unfortunately, no," she said. "But you can look for it in a few days at the lost and found in Chicago. Delta flights leave from terminal 5. Hurry. Go right away. Get to terminal 5 and check in with Delta."

I took the bus to terminal 5 and hurried to the Delta check-in counter. When I got to the front of the line, the man behind the counter said, "What are you doing here?"

"Checking in?" I said.

"This is an Alitalia flight," he said. "And that flight has been canceled."

"It's not even operated by Delta?" I said.

"No," he said. "It's an Alitalia flight."

My ticket said *Alitalia* on the top of it, but I assumed that was because Alitalia booked it, not because it was for an Alitalia *flight*. I might have thought the woman at the counter was incompetent, but I had been lied to so many times by so many Alitalia employees that I knew she'd given me a bullshit ticket and lied about which airline it was for just to get rid of me. She must have done the same to everybody else in that line.

"That is the worst airline in the world," I said. The Delta employee was Italian, not American. I hoped I didn't hurt any feelings of national pride he might have for that airline, but I needed to vent.

"Oh," he said. "I know it. It is a horrible, horrible airline. We hear complaints about them every day. I'm so sorry you have to fly with them."

I went back to the Alitalia terminal. The woman at the desk was either a liar or an idiot, but I wasn't going to give her a hard time. I just needed her to rebook me again, this time for real.

The line was longer than it was earlier, and I'd waited in that line for two hours when it was shorter. I scanned the counter for the woman who had booked me just a few minutes before, but I didn't see her. So I stepped up to the edge of the counter and motioned to the manager.

"Excuse me," I said. Maybe he would know where she went.

"Don't you dare summon me!" he screamed and pointed his finger at me. "You do that with your family, but not with me!"

"*Fuck* you," I said loud enough that everybody in line could hear me. I could hardly believe I'd just cursed at a total stranger, but dozens of people cheered and broke out in applause. *Everybody* wanted to tell this company off. The manager curled his upper lip and glared at us with hatred.

Sofocles and Tatiana were near the front of the line, and they let me join them. I wouldn't have to wait two or three more hours, after all.

"We went downstairs to file a luggage complaint," Tatiana said. "Six guys were just sitting around and laughing and eating at the office. They refused to help anybody. They weren't doing anything and wouldn't even acknowledge our existence. It was unbelievable. Something is wrong with this place."

A manager finally helped her file the complaint. And he told her that 70,000 pieces of luggage were in the basement or out on the tarmac.

An Alitalia man at the counter—friendly for a change!—booked us on what he said was a British Airways flight to London.

"Is this *actually* a British Airways flight?" I said. "Is it operated by British Airways or by Alitalia? I can't be booked on another Alitalia flight."

"I understand," he said. "Yes, it's a British Airways flight, and it's operated by British Airways."

"You're *sure*?" I said. I had a hard time believing anything anyone at Alitalia told me, even if they were convincing and friendly.

"I promise you, it's British Airways."

He lied.

It was an Alitalia flight, as I learned when I got to the check-in counter.

Sofocles, Tatiana and I checked in together. We were basically traveling together at that point. When we got to the front of the line, we handed our tickets to the man at the counter.

"Where did you get *these*?" he said.

"Oh my God," Tatiana said.

"From the rebooking counter," I said. "Is there a problem?"

He didn't say anything. He just tapped a few keys on his keyboard.

A woman worked the window next to him. "How many flights have you canceled today?" I asked her.

"None," she said.

"They're lying again!" Tatiana said.

"You canceled ours to Chicago," I said.

I live in the U.K., a man had said to me two days earlier. *But I was born here in Italy. These people will do nothing but lie. Trust me. I know how this country works.*

We didn't have much time to get to our flight, assuming it would even take off. According to the Departures screen, it was already boarding. I was amazed to see that it was boarding, since it turned out not to be a British Airways flight after all.

I looked at my watch.

"We need our boarding passes," Sofocles said and tapped his foot.

Suddenly the man processing our tickets stood up, put on his coat and walked off the job without handing us boarding passes and without saying a word.

"Where do you think *you're* going?" I said to his back.

He turned around and glowered at me as he walked briskly away.

"We're screwed," Tatiana said.

One Alitalia employee after another had walked off the job right in front of me. In a way, I could hardly blame them. The airport was a zoo full of screaming people. Alitalia had clearly reached a tipping point, as had its passengers.

"Thank God for the United States," an elderly man standing behind me said in an Italian accent.

"You live in the States?" I said.

"I was born in Rome," he said, "but I've lived in Chicago for 35 years."

The woman at the next window gave Sofocles, Tatiana and me our boarding passes.

We ran to the security gate and cut through the line with apologies.

"Excuse me, sorry, our plane is boarding."

Nobody complained.

As it turned out, there was no need to cut through the security line. Our Alitalia flight had been delayed 30 minutes for those of us who'd been rebooked at the last minute. The airline finally did something right.

Tatiana waited at the gate while Sofocles and I went to a café to get sandwiches. Just as we reached the front of the line, the cashier loudly slammed down the Closed sign and walked away without saying a word.

"What the *hell*?" Sofocles said.

"What a strange country," said a Pakistani man standing behind me in line.

Our flight to London actually took off. I didn't have my luggage. I didn't know if I would ever even see my luggage again. But at least I was getting out of Rome's unspeakable airport.

"Thank you for choosing to fly with us," the Alitalia pilot said a few minutes before we landed in London. Several passengers snorted derisively.

Sofocles, Tatiana and I barely made our connection to Chicago. Of course our luggage didn't arrive, but I had a friend in Chicago. I stayed at his house for a few days and waited there so I could retrieve my bags if they showed up at lost and found. My luggage wasn't checked all the way through to my hometown, because I had a separate plane ticket to Portland on a separate airline.

I spent days on the phone asking about my luggage. It didn't show up. Nobody at Chicago's airport even knew if Alitalia's baggage-handling staff had gone back to work yet.

So I gave up and went to the airport to buy a new ticket home on United Airlines. Alitalia would supposedly deliver my luggage to my house if it ever arrived. No point in waiting around. But I thought I'd go to the Alitalia office in Chicago just in case. I braced myself to be screamed at and lied to again.

"Hi," I said to the woman at the Alitalia counter. "I flew here from Rome a few days ago, and I don't have my luggage. Is there any chance it's here somewhere?"

"Actually, yes, there is a chance," she said in an American accent. "We have a whole bunch of bags in the back room."

I handed her my claim tickets, and she went back to look for my stuff. She was in the back office for a quite a while. I hoped she was actually looking.

Finally, she emerged with one of my bags in her hands.

"That's my bag!" I said.

She smiled.

She'd found the bag with my laptop and camera inside, the one that was supposed to be my carry-on bag, the one they'd forced me to check in Beirut. If I could choose only one of my two bags to get back, it would have been that one. The other just had clothes and other easily replaceable items inside.

"Thank you, thank you, thank you," I said.

"You are quite welcome," she said. "And I'm sorry about all this trouble."

"It's okay," I said. "It isn't your fault. I'm just glad to have this bag back. This one has all my valuables in it."

"There is another flight coming in an hour or so," she said. "Check back in two hours and we'll see if your second bag has arrived."

I felt 50 pounds lighter and greatly relieved that Alitalia's staff in Chicago was so much more pleasant to deal with than Alitalia's staff in Rome's airport.

I came back two hours later. The woman who had helped me earlier had been replaced with another.

A handful of people stood in line ahead of me. The young man at the front of the line—who was, I believe, from Mexico—wanted to know if his luggage had arrived.

"We don't have any luggage here," the Alitalia woman said in an Italian accent.

I felt like I had just been whisked back to Rome.

I knew this woman was lying.

The entire back office was full of luggage. I'd seen the pile myself, and one of my own bags had just been retrieved from that pile by her American co-worker.

This Italian woman lived in the United States now, but she'd clearly not yet absorbed her new country's customer-service culture.

"There's a ton of luggage back there," I said. I held up my bag so that everybody could see. "Your *American* co-worker found *this* bag back there just over an hour ago."

The woman was stunned. She hadn't seen me before. She had no idea I'd already been to that counter, no idea that her co-worker had already helped me, no idea that I knew she was lying.

"Well!" she said. "*This* man's luggage isn't back there."

"How would you know if you haven't looked?" the man from Mexico said.

"I just know!" the woman said. "I'm here by myself, and I am very stressed out. Go home! Go home and we'll ship your luggage to you when we can."

"I need my luggage today," the man said. "I have medicine in there that my mother needs."

"Go home!" the woman said. "I know it's easier for you to get it right now, but it's easier for me if we ship it to you."

The man left empty-handed and muttered in Spanish under his breath.

My second checked bag arrived at my house a month later. It had been left outside for days in Rome's winter rains. All my clothing was covered in mold.

Alitalia owes me 600 euros, plus damages. They'll never pay it.

Five

The Battle of Beirut

Beirut, Lebanon 2009

A Syrian-sponsored militia once attacked me and Christopher Hitchens on the streets of Beirut.

Yes, *that* Christopher Hitchens. The famous polemical journalist who went after Henry Kissinger, Mother Teresa, Bill Clinton and even God himself with hammer and tongs. Many considered him the greatest living writer in the English language before esophageal cancer killed him in 2011.

He and I were traveling together in Lebanon with our mutual British friend Jonathan Foreman. The three of us set out from our hotel, the Bristol. Christopher needed a new pair of shoes. Jonathan needed a shirt. I needed a coffee. And I led the way as the three of us strolled down to Hamra Street, where we could buy just about anything.

Christopher hadn't been to Beirut since the civil war ended in 1990 and Jonathan had never visited. I used to live there, though, between the Beirut Spring in 2005 and the 2006 war between Israel and Hezbollah.

My old West Beirut neighborhood of Hamra wasn't the same anymore. It looked the same on the surface, but it had been violated. Hezbollah invaded the previous May, in 2008, with its two sidekick militias, Amal and the Syrian Social Nationalist Party. The city's most cosmopolitan and international district felt much like my house once did after a burglar had broken in. What happened to Hamra, though, was much worse than a mere breaking and entering. Hezbollah and its militant allies shot the place up and killed people.

On our way down to the main shopping street I told Christopher and Jonathan how the Syrian Social Nationalist Party had a serious presence there now. During the invasion in May, its members had placed their spinning swastika flags up on Hamra Street itself. Those flags stayed there for months. No one dared touch them until Prime Minister Fouad Siniora ordered city employees to take them down.

It was a warning of sorts—or at least it would have been heeded as such by most people. I didn't go looking for trouble, Jonathan was as mild-mannered a writer as any I knew, but Christopher was brave and combative, and just hearing about what had happened riled him up.

When we rounded a corner onto Hamra Street, an SSNP sign was the first thing we saw.

"Well, there's that swastika now," Christopher said.

The militia's flags had been taken down, but a commemorative marker was still there. It was made of metal and plastic and had the semipermanence of an official *No Parking* sign. SSNP member Khaled Alwan shot two Israeli soldiers with a pistol in 1982 after they settled their bill at the now-defunct Wimpy cafe on that corner, and that sign marked the spot.

Some SSNP members claimed the emblem on their flag wasn't a swastika, but a hurricane or a cyclone. Many said they couldn't be National Socialists, as were the Nazis, because they identified instead as Social Nationalists, whatever that meant.

Most observers did not find this credible. The SSNP, according to the *Atlantic* in a civil war-era analysis, "is a party whose leaders, men approaching their seventies, send pregnant teenagers on suicide missions in booby-trapped cars. And it is a party whose members, mostly Christians from churchgoing families, dream of resuming the war of the ancient Canaanites against Joshua and the Children of Israel. They greet their leaders with a Hitlerian salute; sing their Arabic anthem, 'Greetings to You, Syria,' to the strains of 'Deutschland, Deutschland über alles'; and throng to the symbol of the red hurricane, a swastika in circular motion."

They wished to resurrect ancient pre-Islamic and pre-Arabic Syria and annex Lebanon, Cyprus, Jordan, Iraq, Kuwait, Israel, and parts of Turkey and Egypt to Damascus. Their vision clashed with Hezbollah's, but the two militias had the exact same list of enemies and they were both Syrian proxies, so they worked together.

Many Lebanese believed members of the SSNP were the ones who carried out many, if not most, of the car-bomb assassinations in Lebanon on behalf of the Syrians since 2005. In December of 2006 some of their members were arrested by the Lebanese army for storing a huge amount of explosives, timers, and detonators amid a large cache of weapons. Then-party leader Ali Qanso responded, saying, "We are a resistance force, and we use different methods of resisting, among which is using explosives."

Christopher wanted to pull down their marker, but couldn't. He stuck to his principles, though, and before I could stop him, he scribbled "No, no, Fuck the SSNP" in the bottom-right corner with a black felt-tipped pen.

I blinked several times. Was he really insulting the Syrian Social Nationalist Party while they might be watching? Neither Christopher nor Jonathan seemed to sense what was coming, but my own danger signals went haywire.

An angry young man shot across Hamra Street as though he'd been fired out of a cannon. "Hey!" he yelled as he pointed with one hand and speed-dialed for backup on his phone with the other.

"We need to get out of here now," I said.

But the young man latched onto Christopher's arm and wouldn't let go. "Come with me!" he said and jabbed a finger toward Christopher's face. These were the only words I heard him say in English.

Christopher tried to shake off his assailant, but couldn't.

"I'm not going anywhere with you," he said.

We needed to get out of there fast. Standing around and trying to reason with him would serve his needs, not ours. His job was to hold us in place until the muscle crew showed up in force.

"Let go of him!" I said and shoved him, but he clamped onto Christopher like a steel trap.

I stepped into the street and flagged down a taxi.

"Get in the car!" I said.

Christopher, sensing rescue, managed to shake the man off and got into the back seat of the taxi. Jonathan and I piled in after him. But the angry young man ran around to the other side of the car and got in the front seat.

I shoved him with both hands. He wasn't particularly heavy, but I didn't have enough leverage from the back to throw him out. The driver could have tried to push the man out, but he didn't. I sensed he was afraid.

So my companions and I got out of the car on the left side. The SSNP man bolted from the front seat on the right side. Then I jumped back in the car and locked the doors on that side.

"He'll just unlock it," Jonathan said.

He was right. I hadn't noticed that the windows were rolled down on the passenger side. The young man reached in, laughed, and calmly unlocked the front passenger door.

I stepped back into the street, and the young man latched once again onto Christopher. No one could have stopped Jonathan and me had we fled, but we couldn't leave Christopher to face an impending attack by himself. The lone SSNP man only needed to hold one of us still while waiting for his squad.

A police officer casually ambled toward us as though he had no idea what was happening.

"Help," Christopher said to the cop. "I'm being attacked!"

Our assailant identified himself to the policeman. The officer gasped and took three steps back as though he did not want any trouble. He could have unholstered his weapon and stopped the attack on the spot, but even Lebanon's armed men of the law feared the Syrian Social Nationalist Party.

A Lebanese man in his thirties ran up to me and offered to help.

"What's happening?!" he said breathlessly as he trembled in shock and alarm.

I don't remember what I told him, and it hardly matters. There wasn't much he could do, and I did not see him again.

"Let go of him!" I said to the SSNP spotter and tried once more to throw him off Christopher.

"Hit him if you have to," I said to Christopher. "We're out of time, and we have to get out of here."

"Back to the hotel," Christopher said.

"No!" I said. "We can't let them know where we're staying."

Christopher would not or could not strike his assailant, so I sized the man up from a distance of six or so feet. I could punch him hard in the face, and he couldn't stop me. I could break his knee with a solid kick to his leg, and he couldn't stop me. He needed all his strength just to hold onto Christopher, while I had total freedom of movement and was hopped up on adrenaline. We hadn't seen a weapon yet, so I was pretty sure he didn't have one. I was a far greater threat to him at that moment than he was to us by himself.

Christopher, Jonathan, and I easily could have joined forces and left him bleeding and harmless in the street. I imagine, looking back now, that he was afraid. But I knew the backup he'd called would arrive any second. And his backup might be armed. We were about to face the wrath of a militia whose members could do whatever they wanted in the streets with impunity. Escalating seemed like the worst possible thing I could do. The time to attack the young man was right at the start, and that moment had passed. This was Beirut, where the law of the jungle can rule with the flip of a switch, and we needed to move.

I saw another taxi parked on the corner waiting for passengers, and I flung open the door.

"Get in, get in," I said, "and lock all the doors!"

Traffic was light. If the driver would step on the gas with us inside, we could get out of there. Christopher managed to fling the man off him again. It looked hopeful there for a second. But seven furious men showed up all at once and faced us in the street. They stepped in front of the taxi and cut off our escape.

None wore masks. That was an encouraging sign. I didn't see any weapons. But they were well built, and their body language signaled imminent violence. We were in serious trouble, and I ran into the Costa Coffee chain across the street and yelled at the waiter to call the police.

"Go away!" he said and lightly pushed me in the shoulder to make his point. "You need to leave now!"

This was no way to treat a visitor, especially not in the Arab world, where guests are accorded protection, but getting in the way of the Syrian Social Nationalist Party could get a man killed, or at least beaten severely. Just a few months before, the SSNP attacked a journalist on that very street and sent him bleeding and broken to the hospital in front of gaping witnesses. A Lebanese colleague told me he was brutally assaulted merely for filming the crew taking down the SSNP flags as the prime minister had ordered. "He didn't do anything to them," she said. "He just filmed their flag."

Christopher was encircled by four or five of them. They were geared up to smash him, and I reached for his hand to pull him away. One of the toughs clawed at my arm and left me with a bleeding scratch and a bruise. I expected a punch in the face, but I wasn't the target.

Christopher was the target. He was the one who had defaced their sign. One of the guys smacked him hard in the face. Another delivered a roundhouse kick to his legs. A third punched him and knocked him into the street between two parked cars. Then they gathered around and kicked him while he was down. They kicked him hard in the head, in the ribs, and in the legs.

Jonathan and I had about two and a half seconds to figure out what we should do when one of the SSNP members punched him in the side of the head and then kicked him.

Christopher was on the ground, and Jonathan and I couldn't fend off seven militiamen by ourselves. I was reasonably sure, at least, that they weren't going to kill us. They didn't have weapons or masks. They just wanted to beat us, and we lost the fight before it even began. I could have called for backup myself, but I didn't think of it—a mistake I will not make again in that country.

Then the universe all of a sudden righted itself.

Christopher managed to pull himself up as a taxi approached in the street. I stepped in front of the car and forced the driver to stop. "Get in!" I yelled. Christopher got in the car. Jonathan got in the car. I got in the car. We slammed down the locks on the doors with our fists. The street was empty of traffic. The way in front of the taxi was clear. The scene for our escape was set.

"Go!" I said to the driver.

"Where?" the driver said.

"Just drive!" I said.

One of the SSNP guys landed a final blow on the side of Christopher's face through the open window, but the driver sped away and we were free.

I don't remember what we said in the car. I was barely scathed in the punch-up, and Jonathan seemed to be fine. Christopher was still in one piece, though he was clearly in pain. Our afternoon had gone sideways, but it could have been a great deal worse than it was.

"Let's not go back to our hotel yet," I said. I covered my face with my hands and rubbed my eyes with my palms. "In case we're being followed."

"Where do you want to go?" our driver said.

"Let's just drive for a while," Jonathan said.

So our driver took us down to the Corniche that follows the curve of the Mediterranean. He never did ask what happened. Or, if he did, I don't remember him asking. I kept turning around and checking behind us to make sure we weren't being followed.

"Maybe we should go to the Phoenicia," Jonathan said.

The Phoenicia InterContinental Hotel was one of the priciest in the city. Management installed a serious security regime at the door. This was the place where diplomats and senators stayed when they were in town. I doubted the guards would allow thugs from any organization into their lobby.

"He deserves a huge tip," Jonathan said as our driver dropped us off.

"Yes," I said. "He certainly does."

The three of us relaxed near the Phoenicia's front door for a few minutes. We would need to change cars but first had to ensure we hadn't been followed.

"You're bleeding," Jonathan said and lightly touched Christopher's elbow.

Christopher seemed unfazed by the sight of blood on his shirt.

"We need to get you cleaned up," Jonathan said.

"I'm fine, I think," Christopher said.

He seemed to be in pretty good spirits, all things considered.

"The SSNP," I said, "is the last party you want to mess with in Lebanon. I'm sorry I didn't warn you properly. This is partly my fault."

"I appreciate that," Christopher said. "But I would have done it anyway. One must take a stand. One simply must."

Even after being forced out during the Beirut Spring of 2005, Bashar al-Assad's government in Damascus still wielded some of its occupation instruments inside Lebanon. The Syrian Social Nationalist Party was one of those instruments, and it counted the regime as its friend and ally. The geographic "nationalism" of the SSNP differed from the racialist pan-Arab Nationalism of the Syrian Baath Party, but it conveniently meshed with al-Assad's imperial foreign policy in the Middle East. It logically followed, then, that the SSNP was also allied with Hezbollah.

The SSNP was first and foremost a Syrian proxy, and Hezbollah was first and foremost an Iranian proxy, but during the previous May when various militias invaded Beirut, the SSNP established itself simultaneously as a de facto Hezbollah proxy.

I still shudder to think what might have happened to Christopher, Jonathan, and me if we were Lebanese instead of British and American.

"If you were Lebanese," said a longtime Beiruti friend, "you might have disappeared."

The next morning I awoke to find more than a dozen e-mails in my inbox from friends, family, and acquaintances, some of whom I hadn't heard from in a long time, asking me if I was okay.

None of us had written about the incident yet, so I wondered what on earth must have happened while I was asleep. Did another war just break out? Did another car bomb go off? I hadn't heard any explosions or gunshots.

As it turned out, the incident on Hamra Street with the SSNP made the news on at least four continents, and possibly six.

Great, I thought. Now *I'm* the story. Christopher was the nearest thing the journalism world had to a celebrity, so pretty much everything he did was news.

Every single reporter without exception got the details wrong. In one version, we got in a bar fight. In another, we were attacked by foppish shoe shoppers. In almost every version, Christopher was drunk or had been drinking. Not one of the reporters who wrote up the story bothered to ask any of us who were actually there what had happened. Some even claimed they had "confirmed" this or that detail, but all they were doing was publishing rumors. It made me think, not for the first time, that first-person narrative journalism, whatever its faults, was far more reliable than the alternative.

Some of my politically connected Lebanese pals were furious when they heard what happened. One friend, whom I'll just call Faisal so he won't get into trouble, said it was time to retaliate.

"They attacked guests in our country," he said as his blood pressure rose, "and they can't get away with it."

I appreciated that my friends were looking out for me, but I felt distinctly uneasy about where he was going with this. A retaliation could easily end badly and might even escalate. Still, I couldn't dissuade him, and he called his bosses and asked for a posse.

Party leaders turned him down, which disappointed him but

relieved me. And it occurred to me later that what Faisal had in mind was likely much more serious than tit-for-tat payback.

"What, exactly, did Faisal mean by *retaliate*?" I asked a mutual Lebanese friend.

"He wanted to shoot them, of course," she said.

He wanted to shoot them!

I later sat down with Christopher over coffee in the hotel lobby and asked him to reflect on the recent unpleasantness.

"When I told you that I should have warned you," I said, "that I take partial responsibility, you said. . ."

"It wouldn't have made any difference," he said. "Thank you, though, for giving me a protective arm. I think a swastika poster is partly fair game and partly an obligation. You don't really have the right to leave one alone. I haven't seen that particular symbol since I saw the Syrianization of Lebanon in the 1970s. And actually, the first time I saw it, I didn't quite believe it."

"You saw it when you were here before?" I said.

"Oh, yes," he said. "But it was more toward the Green Line. I did not expect to see it so flagrantly on Hamra. Anyway, call me old-fashioned if you will, but my line is that swastika posters are to be defaced or torn down. I mean, what other choice do you have? I'd like to think I'd have done that if I had known it was being guarded by people who are swastika fanciers. I have done that in my time. I have had fights with people who think that way. But I was surprised first by how violent and immediate their response was, and second by how passive and supine was the response of the police."

The men of the SSNP had to use force to maintain a hold in West Beirut.

Many of its members were Orthodox Christians, as was its founder Antun Saadeh, while most West Beirutis were Sunni Muslims. They would hardly be any less welcome in Tel Aviv. If its enforcers didn't jump Christopher in the street, their commemorative sign would not have lasted.

"But I was impressed," Christopher said, "with the response of the cafe girls."

"What was their response?" I said. "I missed that."

"Well," he said, "when I was thrown to the ground and bleeding from my fingers and elbow, they came over and asked what on earth was going on. How can this be happening to a guest, to a stranger? I don't remember if I was speaking English or French at that time. I said something like *'merde fasciste,'* which I hope they didn't misinterpret."

I did not see the cafe girls. Or, if I did, I don't remember them. Once the actual violence began, it was over and done with in seconds.

"By then," Christopher said, "I had become convinced that you were right, that we should get the fuck out of there and not, as I had first thought, get the hotel security between them and us. I thought no, no, let's not do that. We don't want them to know where we are. The harassment might not stop. There was a very gaunt look in the eye of the young man, the first one. And there was a very mad, sadistic, deranged look in the eyes of his auxiliaries. I wish I'd had a screwdriver."

"You know these guys are widely suspected of setting off most or all of the car bombs," I said.

"They weren't ready for that then," he said.

"They weren't," I said, "but they're dangerous."

"Once you credit them like that," he said, "you do all their work for them. They should have been worried about us. Let them worry. Let them wonder if we're carrying a tool or if we have a crew. I'd like to go back, do it properly, deface the thing with red paint so there's no swastika visible. You can't have the main street, a shopping and commercial street, in a civilized city patrolled by intimidators who work for a Nazi organization. It is not humanly possible to live like that. One must not do that. There may be more important problems in Lebanon, but if people on Hamra don't dare criticize the SSNP, well fuck. That's occupation."

"It is," I said, "in a way. They have a state behind them. They aren't just a street gang; they're a street gang with a state."

"Yes," Christopher said. "They're the worst. And also a Greek Orthodox repressed homosexual wankers organization, I think."

The Syrian Social Nationalist Party spokesman denied the attack ever took place. He lied.

Six

Darkness in Palestine

Hebron, West Bank 2011

The Palestinian city Hebron is one of the most hate-stricken on earth. Some tourists in the Holy Land cross from Israel into the West Bank to visit the relatively pleasant Palestinian cities of Bethlehem and Ramallah, especially during the Christmas season, when Bethlehem's festivities in Manger Square—where Jesus was supposedly born—are in full swing.

But visiting Hebron on holiday?

Never.

You might as well go to Baghdad on vacation if you're going to Hebron.

But I went to Hebron. I'd been to Iraq seven times, so why not go to Hebron?

Eve Harow drove me. She lived in the nearby Israeli settlement of Efrat, worked as a professional tour guide and knew the Palestinian territories well.

"Hebron's a tough place," she said. "I could never live there."

Eve is a tough lady, but Hebron is tougher. Her "mainstream" Israeli settlement in Gush Etzion looked and felt like a California beach town that had been airlifted off the coast and plunked down somewhere inland.

A tiny Israeli settlement had been set up in the center of Hebron as well, but it had only one thing in common with Efrat: A Jewish population lived there, surrounded by Arabs.

Hebron's settlers were a little more—shall we say—hard-core than the bourgeois Jews of Efrat. And their Palestinian neighbors were much more hostile than those who lived near Efrat.

After the Israelis conquered the Jordanian-occupied West Bank at the end of the Six-Day War in 1967, they established four kinds of "settlements" on the Arab side of the former armistice line: They recolonized the Old City's Jewish Quarter and other parts of Jerusalem where they had been evicted by the Jordanians. They built cheap housing for the working class on mostly empty land. They established middle-class suburbs on the outskirts of Jerusalem.

Everyone knew that Israel would likely absorb these first three types of settlements in a two-state solution to the Israeli-Palestinian conflict. The Islamists of Hamas may wish to shove the Jews into the sea, but the more mainstream and secular Palestinian Authority, founded by Yasser Arafat before his death in 2004, quietly acknowledged for years that most Israeli settlements in the West Bank would one day be annexed by Israel and swapped with additional real estate elsewhere for Palestine.

Not Hebron. That was the fourth kind of settlement, too far away to be annexed. A minuscule Jewish community of just 800 people lived there in a tiny enclave surrounded on all sides by a quarter-million Palestinians. Short of annexing all of Hebron—which even Israel's right-wing parties knew would be madness—the Jews there would eventually have to pack up and go back to Israel or be governed by Palestinians who wanted them gone.

In the meantime, Hebron's Jews refused to leave, and Hebron's Palestinians refused to put up with them. The result? Violence, of course. Middle East–style.

It was the kind of unsolvable problem that made Americans' heads hurt.

I felt a heavy sense of doom hanging over the place before I even got there.

"What do you think of Hebron?" I said to Eve as we headed south out of Jerusalem in her car.

"It's a microcosm of the Middle East," she said. "It really is. There are a few Jews and a lot of Arabs. If Jews are not allowed to live there because they were once driven out, then that validates the ethnic cleansing of Jews from the city in 1948. Ethnic cleansing is wrong, no matter who is the focus. We didn't throw the Arabs out when we came back in 1967, even though they thought we would."

We reached the West Bank in minutes. The hills loomed right over Jerusalem. You will easily see, if you go there, why Israel insisted on retaining defensible borders at least a tad inside the West Bank if a Palestinian state is ever established.

It would be so easy to bombard the city with artillery. The Jordanian army frequently did so when it controlled the area before the 1967 war, and it would be no more difficult for a terrorist organization like Hamas to fire crudely made rockets into the dense population center below. You could almost throw a hand grenade into Jerusalem from up there.

The settlements, though, were even easier targets, since they were *inside* the West Bank.

"So," I said as Eve drove. "Why live in Efrat, or anywhere else out here, for that matter?"

"Because I think Jews should be able to live in Judea," she said, using the Hebrew name for the southern half of the West Bank.

"What about the Palestinians here?" I said. "You say Jews should be able to live in Judea, but most people who live here are Arabs."

"There have a right to live here as well," she said. "I think they can gain a lot more from living in peace with us than they can by waging war against us. I hope that one day they understand that, because we're not going anywhere. I want to live in a world where Arabs don't want to kill me, not because they love Jews but because it doesn't advance their own interests. I want to live in a world where they think about what's good for them rather than what's bad for me."

"Don't you worry that, since you live in Efrat rather than, say, Tel Aviv, you might get forced to move?" I said.

"No more than I fear for the whole state of Israel," she said.

Efrat, though, was more tenuous than Tel Aviv. Jews could only be forced out of Tel Aviv by a conquering army, but there was a chance the Israeli government might one day order residents of both Efrat and Hebron to move back inside Israel's official borders. Efrat would probably be annexed to Israel as part of a deal, but there was no way to be sure. In the meantime, Eve lived on one of the few patches of land on this planet that was technically and legally stateless. It was in limbo, not inside Israel's self-declared borders, nor part of a Palestinian state that didn't exist yet inside any borders.

And people all over the world—including in Israel—argued that even "mainstream" Israeli settlements like Efrat antagonized the Palestinians and made peace all but impossible.

"Lots of people in Israel think you're a major part of the problem just by existing out here," I said.

"Yes," she said. "I know. They don't want to face the truth that they're hated just as much as I am. The PLO was founded in 1964, three years before we came back here. When they talked about liberating territory, they weren't talking about Efrat. We didn't have Efrat then. They were talking about Tel Aviv. Israel is considered a racist genocidal state. Not just the settlers, but all of Israel. Sometimes I feel like I'm living inside a horror film. One of the most insulting things you can say is that I'm against peace because I'm a settler. I live here. I have seven children and three grandchildren, and if there isn't peace, then I'm the big loser. It's the little people who pay the price. It's the little people who go to war, and it's the little people who get buried."

Few places in Israel were quiet during the second Intifada—the terrifying wave of violence between Israelis and Palestinians from 2000 to 2005—and even fewer places were as dangerous as the roads leading from Jerusalem to the settlements.

So many Israeli civilians were shot at that most had to wear the same kind of helmet and flak jacket that I wore while embedded with American combat troops in Iraq.

"I only wore the vest once," Eve said. "I cried the entire time and never put it on again."

Hebron is in the heart of the West Bank, attached to Israel by nothing but a long two-laned highway through Palestinian territory. Violence was not a daily occurrence, but I felt its potential before I even got out of the car.

The road in from next-door Kiryat Arba was under Israeli army control, but it passed through residential and commercial Palestinian neighborhoods.

Everyone on the street could plainly see Eve's Israeli license plates, and the posture from some of the young men walking by was palpably hostile.

Most communication between humans is nonverbal. It's conveyed through body language and is the same across cultures. I wasn't imagining the hatred directed at me from some of the Palestinian men on that road. It was obvious.

And just a few weeks later, several Israeli civilians—including a pregnant woman—in a car much like Eve's were shot to death by Palestinian gunmen on that very road.

Hebron was founded during the Bronze Age, but most of modern Hebron was built during the 20th century. Blocky houses and apartment buildings flowed up and down gently rolling ocher hills like waves of urbanity. Some of the hills were topped with olive-tree orchards. The city center is ancient and should have been beautiful and amazing, but its guts had been ripped out by war. That's where the Jewish settlers lived. Down in the blasted-up city center surrounded on all sides by hostile Palestinians up in the hills.

Eve introduced me to David Wilder, a spokesperson for the community there. He grew up in New Jersey but had lived in the Holy Land for 35 years. He first visited during a one-year program in college and said it changed his life, so he came back after he graduated and had been there ever since.

He appeared hardened rather than softened by middle age.

"Why live *here* instead of in Tel Aviv or Jerusalem?" I said. A muezzin sang out the call to Muslim prayer from a minaret.

"I get to the States more often than I get to Tel Aviv," he said. "And I don't go to the States frequently." He laughed. "I didn't grow up in a religious family. I had a secular Jewish identity. I didn't make contact with religious Judaism until I came to Israel. My wife is Israeli, and her story is similar. After we got married, we decided we wanted to contribute something and to actually *do* it rather than talk about it. And we decided that if Jews should be able to live in a place like Hebron, we should go live in Hebron."

Of course Jews should be able to live in Hebron. Jews should be able to live in Afghanistan too, but that's no reason to pick up and move to Afghanistan.

That's not the real reason he moved there. Jews have little history in far-flung lands like Afghanistan. Hebron, on the other hand, is one of Judaism's oldest cities. It's the home of the Tomb of the Patriarchs, the second holiest site in the Jewish world after the Western Wall in Jerusalem.

"The purpose of the Jewish community here is to maintain access to the tomb, right?" I said.

"That's certainly a primary reason," David said. "This is where Abraham came 3,700 years ago. He lived here. All the patriarchs and matriarchs lived here. King David started the Kingdom of Israel here before he went up to Jerusalem. And with very few exceptions, Jews have always been living here. The last time there were no Jews here before the riots in 1929 was back in 1100, when the Crusaders threw all the Jews out and replaced them with Christians. The Christians have since been replaced with Arabs. But otherwise there were always Jews here. This community is part of a chain that goes all the way back to the beginning of Judaism."

The Tomb of the Patriarchs is roughly 2,000 years old. King Herod built it when the Roman Empire still ruled the city. In 1267, the Egyptian Mamluk occupation authorities declared the building a mosque.

"We share control of the building with Palestinians," David said, "but they tell us straight up that if they can throw us out of here that they won't let us back in the tomb of our patriarchs. They say it's a mosque and that only Muslims should pray there even though it was built by King Herod, who was a Jew. If we don't stay here, none of us will even be able to visit."

Jews and Arabs famously got along well in the Israeli city of Haifa throughout the Arab-Israeli conflict. They lived in the same neighborhoods, on the same streets and in the same apartment buildings. They ate at the same restaurants, attended the same schools, worked for the same companies and drank beer in the same pubs. They *could* get along. Haifa was proof.

Israelis and Palestinians didn't mix much in Jerusalem, but they coexisted reasonably well for the most part in the places where they did overlap, such as Jerusalem's Old City, and their relations were generally civil.

In Hebron, though, they were like antimatter and matter.

Tension between the city's Jews and Arabs was older than the Jewish settlement in the center of town. It was older than the 1967 war. It was even older than the state of Israel.

In the early 20th century, the Grand Mufti of Jerusalem, Mohammad Amin al-Husayni, thrilled to the Nazi cause of exterminating the world's Jews. He and his followers later became Hitler's local proxies. Al-Husayni appears in several photographs with the Führer himself. You can easily find them on the Internet. Even before the war, in late August 1929, al-Husayni ginned up mob violence in Hebron. "Kill the Jews wherever you find them," he said, and his people did. They massacred 67 innocent people in a single day.

Israel didn't even exist at the time. The Holy Land was still part of the British Mandate for Palestine. World War II had not even started yet. Al-Husayni just hated Jews.

Hundreds, though, were saved by Arabs who not only refused to participate but also hid would-be Jewish victims from their murderous neighbors inside their own homes. In the early and mid-20th century, the Middle East, in more ways than one, was like Europe when it came to the Jews. Common human decency existed alongside atrocity. Some thrilled to genocide while others risked their lives for their neighbors. Hebron had a history of lightness as well as of darkness.

The killers committed unspeakable crimes. They castrated men. They raped women and cut off their breasts. An Arab employee at a bakery forced his Jewish boss into an oven and burned him to death.

The terrible events of 1929 still hung over the place when I visited, and the bloody-minded hatred that triggered it still smoldered. The massacre took place back in the days of grainy black-and-white photography, but it was not so long ago—still within living memory. Just a few weeks earlier, al-Aqsa TV, the Hamas channel in Gaza, interviewed a Palestinian woman from Hebron who not only remembered the massacre, but she was proud of the massacre. She said she'd like to see it repeated. "Allah willing," she said to the interviewer, "you will bury (Israel) and massacre the Jews with your own hands. Allah willing, you will massacre them like we massacred them in Hebron. We, the people of Hebron, massacred the Jews. My father massacred them."

"When we came back in 1967," David said, "we had reasonable relations between Jews and Arabs again. There were business relationships, personal relationships. We could walk around the city unarmed, and there were no problems. Things weren't all lovey-dovey, but people got along. Things started to change in a bad way during the first Intifada in the late 1980s. The PLO began rounding up Arabs who were seen talking to Jews and accusing them of being collaborators, so pretty soon the Arabs stopped talking to us."

While it's not true that the first Palestinian Intifada against Israel consisted entirely of civil disobedience and rock throwing, the second Intifada was nevertheless *much* worse than the first. The second consisted almost entirely of suicide bombings and rifle attacks. The road from Jerusalem to Gush Etzion was ferociously dangerous, but Hebron degenerated into a war zone.

Palestinians shot at the Jewish settlers from the surrounding hills with regular rifles and sniper rifles. One sniper shot a baby in the head right on the main street. They fired into David's apartment a number of times. The Israel Defense Forces established a base in the area and launched citywide counterterrorist operations during its years-long Iraqi-style counterinsurgency campaign.

"The Palestinians don't want us here," David said. "They say they don't want us here, and they believe that someday we'll leave, if not because they drive us out then because our own people will force us out. [Palestinian Authority leader] Mahmoud Abbas says that no Jews will be allowed to live in a Palestinian state. Arabs live in Israel, but he insists that no Jews can live in Palestine."

Only an anti-Semite would argue that Jews shouldn't be *allowed* to live in Hebron, one of Judaism's first cities. But it seemed to me that only a fanatic would actually live and raise children in a place where his neighbors routinely tried to murder his family. I wanted to throw my hands in the air and say, "I give up."

Most of the violence came from the Palestinian side, but this isn't a story of angels and demons.

On February 25, 1994, an American Israeli named Baruch Goldstein opened fire on a large group of Muslims praying at the Tomb of the Patriarchs, killing 29 people and wounding another 125.

All by himself, he racked up almost half the body count of the massacre of 1929.

Goldstein shocked and appalled almost every Jew in the world when he murdered those people. One of their own became a full-blown, no-way-to-whitewash-it, mass-murdering terrorist. He didn't stop killing until his intended victims beat him to death.

He belonged to the Kach movement, a far-right political party founded by Rabbi Meir Kahane in the 1970s. Kahane's cultish following may have been the closest thing to the Nazis the modern Jewish world had ever produced, but there was no real symmetry between them and Hamas on the Palestinian side. Hamas ruled the entire Gaza Strip, but the Israeli Knesset banned the Kahanist party for inciting racist violence against Arabs. Hamas won an election once, but the Kahanist party failed to earn even one percent of Israel's vote before it was banned. The Israeli government considers it a terrorist organization—and rightly so, after what Goldstein did.

Goldstein had his admirers, though. Israel never named public squares after him like Hamas had done for Palestinian suicide bombers, but hundreds of Israelis visited his grave to celebrate the attack a week after his death.

David and I walked the streets of the Jewish Quarter. It was at the bottom of a bowl surrounded by densely inhabited hills. I looked up and wondered how clearly we could be seen through a sniper scope. I thought David was nuts for living there, but I was there too, at least for the day. Perhaps both of us weren't entirely right in the head.

"My kids were almost killed out here when somebody shot at them," he said.

"Those are Arab houses up there?" I said.

"Yes," he said and pointed at a house just 20 feet above us. "There's nobody living there now, but that's an Arab house. The last man who lived there was a nice guy. A few years ago a 17-year-old kid jumped down from up there into the playground with a knife.

"Fortunately he was caught. When asked what he was doing, he said he wanted to kill somebody. When asked who he wanted to kill, he did what he was told and said he wanted to kill an Arab. That's why he jumped into a Jewish playground! According to the law here, any conflict between Arabs has to be handled by an Arab court. It can't be handled by us. So we sent him home."

"Do you feel safe here?" I said. Hebron was not scary, but it sure as hell wasn't comfortable. The worst thing about standing at the bottom of the Jewish section of town wasn't the fear of getting shot, which at any given moment was minuscule, but the disturbing awareness that many people who lived in the houses above hated your guts so completely that it took an army to hold them back. The place had a seriously bad vibe.

"If you're afraid, you can't live here," David said, "but Jews in Israel are targeted no matter where they live. I know who lives around us, and I know what they've done. I've seen it. I've seen it many times. Somebody put a teddy bear out here in the market that had wires sticking out of it. It was a bomb. They were hoping one of our kids would pick it up. So the army closed the market."

He took me around the corner and showed me a destroyed home that Jewish settlers had recently occupied before the Israeli army threw them out.

"When we came back in 1967," David said, "there was nothing here. Everything was destroyed. More recently we asked if we could move into empty buildings that were old Jewish property. The government, of course, wouldn't let us."

The Israeli government did not want the Jewish community in Hebron to expand, partly because it would take that much more manpower to keep them alive, but also because the Jewish presence that already existed antagonized the local Palestinians. The government figured that expanding the settlement would only expand the size of the problem, and—fair or not—that was probably right.

"After the baby was killed by a sniper," David said, "we moved in anyway. We put some apartments in here. And after five years, the army evicted us. A year later, two families who didn't have anywhere else to go moved back in, one here and one at the other end. After they were discovered, the government sent hundreds of Israeli soldiers in to pull them out. The soldiers came in with sledgehammers and destroyed everything."

Nobody was allowed to live there. Not Jews, and not Arabs. The building was ruined. Wasted. Snatched away like a toy from squabbling children.

Can't we all just get along?

Not in the Middle East, no.

Hebron would have been a beautiful place if everyone lived together peaceably as they did in Haifa and (for the most part) in Jerusalem, but they couldn't, so it wasn't.

The Israel Defense Forces kept Hebron's Jews and Arabs as far away from each other as possible without kicking the Jews out of the city entirely. The security measures, though, all but ruined the place. An entire swath of the old city was off limits to both sides and in an advanced state of decay. It reminded me of Baghdad a few years earlier, when sectarian Sunni and Shia militias "cleansed" neighborhoods of the other, compelling American soldiers to canton the city with gigantic walls to keep them apart.

"During the second Intifada, a suicide bomber blew himself up down the street and killed a couple from Kiryat Arba," David said. "He came very close to killing a group of 50 kids who were visiting. So the army closed the stores here so nobody could use them as a base for terrorist attacks. It went through the Supreme Court, which okayed it, and they've been closed ever since."

The doors in the Arab neighborhoods immediately adjacent to the Jewish area had all been sealed shut. No one could go in or out, and no one could walk on those streets, not even people who owned property there. The doors were covered in spray paint. The shuttered old city would have overflowed with thousands of tourists and pilgrims from all over the world if it weren't a slum made hideous by hatred and war.

Human life is surely more important than property and the right to move freely, but security in Hebron came at a terrible cost to the city. What the Israeli military called the sterile zone was once a vibrant ancient city. Now it looked like a ghost town, as though everyone had been driven out by a violent catastrophe—which was pretty close to what happened.

I said my thanks and good-byes to David and rejoined Eve Harow.

"So what do you think?" she asked me as we drove past the "sterile zone" on our way back to Jerusalem.

"I think *this*," I said, meaning the streets that had been emptied at gunpoint, "is very disturbing."

"So do I," she said. "Have you talked to anyone else about Hebron?"

"I talked to an Israeli soldier who served here," I said. "He didn't like it. He *hated* it, actually. He hated what he had to do here."

"They usually do," she said.

It's a grim place, but it's more than just that. It's also a warning.

"Hebron," Israeli historian Yaacov Lozowick wrote, "is what happens when Israelis and Palestinians agree to divide a city but can't agree to live together in peace. The blame for lack of peace is irrelevant: Each side will doubtlessly say it's all the fault of the other, but the result won't be any nicer thereby. The myriads of observers, pundits, politicians, dreamers, visionaries and true believers who all know for a certainty that dividing Jerusalem is the key to peace in the Middle East need urgently to visit Hebron."

Seven

Where the West Ends

"The forced collectivization of agriculture decreed by the Soviet master and his party likely cost the lives of more people than perished in all countries as a result of the First World War." – Michael Marrus

"They had gone over the country like a swarm of locusts and taken away everything edible; they had shot or exiled thousands of peasants, sometimes whole villages; they had reduced some of the most fertile land in the world to a melancholy desert." – Malcolm Muggeridge

Ukraine, 2010

I bought a map of Eastern Europe in an old Oregon bookstore that's as big as a couch when unfolded. The most heavily trafficked roads appear as fat red lines on the paper. Almost all of them lead directly to Moscow. Even as late as the year 2012, the nerve center of the former Soviet Empire looks on my map like a world-devouring octopus capturing less important capitals in its tentacles.

On a cold night in late October I pointed at a thin red line on that map leading across the former Soviet frontier into Ukraine from a remote corner of Poland.

"Hardly anyone will be on this road," I said to my old friend Sean LaFreniere. He had just met up with me in Romania so we could hit the road again. "We shouldn't have to wait long at the border."

That logic seemed sound at the time, but I'm here to tell you: never,

ever, choose less-traveled roads in countries that used to be part of Russia. Driving from even the most backward country in the European Union into the remote provinces of Ukraine is like falling off the edge of civilization into a land that was all but destroyed.

Sean and I hadn't learned that yet, though, and we wanted a scenic route. European road trips aren't like road trips in the American West where we live. Outside our major metropolitan areas, huge empty spaces and wide open roads are the norm. Most of Europe is crowded and neither of us wanted to sit in the car for hours in line at the border.

We had no idea what we were in for, but a Polish border guard warned us after stamping our passports.

"It is very *strange* over there," he said. "And nobody speaks English."

Screwing up in the strange parts of the world is never fun and is often miserable, but you learn things by doing it. You see things that governments and ministries of tourism wished you would not. Ukraine is so strange that you can even see these things in the dark. We actually saw more of Ukraine's strangeness *because* we showed up in the dark.

I don't remember what time we crossed the frontier. Eight o'clock in the evening? Anyway, it was dark. When I say it was dark, I mean it was *dark*. The back roads of Western Ukraine are as black at night as the most remote parts of the American West where no humans live in any direction.

Yet Western Ukraine is not empty.

And the roads. Oh God, the roads. I don't care where you've been. You almost certainly have never seen anything like them.

The second worst road I've ever driven on was in Central America in the mid-1990s. It's only ten percent as bad as the road Sean and I took into Ukraine. This one would have been no worse off had it been deliberately shredded to ribbons by air strikes. The damage was so thorough that the surface could not possibly have been repaved or repaired even once since the Stalinist era.

I white-knuckled it behind the wheel while Sean cringed in the passenger seat. I did not dare drive faster than five miles an hour. Even at that speed I had to weave all over the place to avoid the worst of the gaping holes, some of which were as wide as mattresses and deep enough to swallow TV sets.

I saw no cars, no street lights, not even a light from one single house. Ukraine looked depopulated. My maps said there were villages all over the place, but where were they? Did we just drive into an episode of *Life After People*?

"This is exactly like Russia," Sean said. "Exactly."

He had visited Russia two years earlier and will never forget the vast darkness at night on the train between Moscow and St. Petersburg. "We're in Russia!" he said

Then the ghost figures appeared.

They walked on the side of the road in wine-darkness. They did not carry flashlights. They seemed, like us, to be out in the middle of nowhere. It was then that I realized we had entered a town. In the periphery of my headlight beams I could faintly make out a few unlit houses shrouded in shadow away from the road, which was as broken and crumbling as ever. I still hadn't seen any other cars on the road, nor did I see any parked on the side. I don't know if the roads were so bad because nobody drove or if nobody drove because the roads were so bad.

"They should put up a sign on the border," Sean said, "saying *That was Europe. You like that? Now prepare for something completely different.*"

We were on our way to Chernobyl, or at least we thought we were headed there. *City Journal* assigned me to go there and write about the spooky ghost city of Pripyat that, along with the surrounding area in the so-called Exclusion Zone, was struck by a local apocalypse in 1986. The Soviet Union's Chernobyl nuclear reactor number four exploded and showered Pripyat, where 50,000 people lived, and the countryside around it with a storm of deadly radiation. Only 31 people were dead in the immediate aftermath, but the World Health Organization thinks the long-term effects of radiation poisoning will eventually kill another 4,000. More than 350,000 people in Ukraine and nearby Belarus have been permanently displaced. The fire still burns today beneath the crumbling concrete sarcophagus that caps the reactor.

No one should wander around there alone. The Ukrainian military won't let you in anyway if you don't have a guide and a permit. Some of Pripyat's buildings are still lethally radioactive, and there's no way to tell them apart from the relatively "safe" ones without sophisticated instruments. The scrap yard, where fire-fighting equipment was abandoned long ago, is spectacularly dangerous. Even mutant animals are supposedly running around.

Sean and I didn't yet know it, but the Chernobyl administration was about to cancel our permit and refuse to allow anyone entry. They didn't say why, but I assume it was because the zone suddenly became more dangerous than usual. We would not get to go, but going there was our plan and we didn't yet know we would be re-routed. For a while there, we weren't sure we'd get *anywhere* in Ukraine, let alone hundreds of miles away to Chernobyl.

First we had to get to Lviv, the "capital" of Western Ukraine and the heartland of Ukrainian nationalism. That first stop alone was almost a hundred miles away. The road was so shattered I was barely able to drive any faster than I could walk. And we were lost. We couldn't even figure out how to get to Sambir, a small town that was hardly even inside Ukraine at all.

Sambir was spelled Самбір in Ukrainian and only one sign pointed the way. The Cyrillic letters in that particular name resembled the Latin letters well enough that I could figure it out. Then we came to a four-way junction. Road signs pointed to various towns in every direction, but none said Самбір. And none of the towns the signs *did* point toward appeared on my map—or, if they were on my map, I didn't know how to transliterate their names into Cyrillic. Which way we were supposed to be going?

"Let's go back," Sean said, "and ask one of those people on the side of the road."

I drove back the way we came until I saw two ghostly figures shambling along in the headlights. I pulled over and rolled down the window.

"Excuse me," I said. "Do you speak English?" I doubted they did, but this was a way of preparing them for the fact that they weren't going to hear any Ukrainian or Russian from me.

The two stopped walking and stared. A young man, perhaps 20 years old, held his young girlfriend's hand. He stared at me with wide eyes and slowly stepped between me and his girl as if I were a threat.

"We're trying to get to Sambir," I said and paused. "Sambir," I said again in case he understood nothing else but might at least know I needed directions and that he could point. He looked at me and didn't say anything.

"Sean," I said. "Hand me that map."

Sean handed over the map. I pointed at it. "Sambir." I said. "Which way to Sambir?"

The young man took several of cautious steps back. His girlfriend, terrified, moved behind him and peaked over his shoulder. They backed up another five feet or so, then walked away without saying anything.

"Well, that's just great," I said. We were the first foreigners they'd ever seen? Just a few miles from the Polish frontier?

"Go back and take the road that goes to the left," Sean said. "I'm pretty sure it's that one."

"How can you be pretty sure that it's that one?" I said. I had no idea where we were and wanted someone who lived there to tell us.

"It just feels right," he said. "If we see any more people, we can stop and ask."

I was in no mood to argue, and his guess was as good as mine, so we drove back to the four-way intersection and took a left. And we found ourselves in a forest.

"This doesn't look right at all," I said.

"How do you know what it's supposed to look like?" he said.

"I don't," I said. "It just looks like we're going into the middle of nowhere."

"Everywhere we've been is in the middle of nowhere," he said.

Perhaps he was right. Suddenly the road improved slightly. I could increase our speed, so I did, but then BANG. I ran us into a sink-sized hole in the ground at twenty miles an hour. The car shuddered as though a land mine had blown off a wheel.

Sean had rented this car on his credit card. "Oh my God," he said. "Oh my God, oh my God, oh my God."

"It's okay," I said, though I didn't for one second believe it. "There's still air in the tire."

"Not for long," he said and put his face in his hands.

I drove onward again, slower this time. We passed a dark house. Somebody lived out there in the forest.

"There are some people up ahead," Sean said. "Pull over and ask them where the hell we are."

I pulled the car over next to the two figures. Like the others, they looked ghost-like in the headlights. Like the others, they shuffled along as though they were wandering toward no place in particular for lack of anything better to do in a village at night without light.

This time we encountered not two scared teenagers, but an elderly man and his wife.

They looked startled as though they couldn't believe someone was out and about in a car.

"Excuse me," I said. "Do you speak English?" I was certain they didn't.

The woman flinched and the man said, "eh?"

"We're trying to get to Lviv," I said. Then I pointed at the map. "Lviv."

Not knowing better, I pronounced it "Luh-*viv*."

They had no idea what I was talking about.

"Luh-*viv*," I said again, and pointed at the map.

"Eh?" the woman said. "El-*veev?*"

"Da," I said, Russian for *yes*. Many ethnic Russians live in Eastern Ukraine and even ethnic Ukrainians in the west can speak Russian though they'd rather not. The bits of Russian that Sean and I knew were useful wherever we happened to be.

"Da," I said. "El-*veev.*"

She pointed in the direction we were heading. "Poland," she said.

"Unbelievable," I said. We were on our way back to Poland?

"Argh!" Sean said.

"We've been driving around for hours," I said, "and we haven't gone *anywhere.*"

So we turned back. I drove five miles an hour. I weaved around giant holes in the road, but still ran into five or six small ones per second. I had no idea where we were or where we were going. The night was almost half over and we had made zero progress. All we had done so far was damage the car and burn half the gas in the tank.

We eventually came to another small town even though we saw no more signs to even Sambir, let alone Lviv or Kiev. This time a few buildings were lit. One was a gas station. Incredibly, it was open.

I pulled in. Sean and I got out. We both inspected the banged-up wheel. It looked okay and apparently was not leaking air. We were lucky.

A man emerged from the office and asked us—I assume—if we needed gas.

"Do you speak English?" I said and chuckled. I knew he wouldn't.

Of course he didn't. A gas station attendant in rural Ukraine is no more likely to speak English than a gas station attendant in rural Kansas is likely to be fluent in Russian. Unlike the others we'd spoken to, though, he didn't seem surprised or alarmed that the wrong language came out of our mouths.

He filled the tank. I pointed at the map and said "Sambir." He gave us complicated directions that neither Sean nor I could make sense of. All we could really glean from him was which direction to start with.

I heard children giggling behind the gas station office. A young boy and a young girl, each no older than five, peeked their heads around the corner. They pointed at us and laughed as though we wore clown suits and squeaky shoes. Sean and I were the evening's entertainment. We spoke an alien language and that made us freaks.

"Good grief," I said. "Are we going to have to put up with this all week?"

I can only imagine how the locals would have reacted if we were black.

We drove in the dark on hideous roads for another hour. The gas station attendant told us we were supposed to turn left at some point, but we had no idea where.

"I hope it's not like this everywhere," Sean said.

"If it's like this everywhere," I said, "we won't even get to Lviv, let alone Kiev and Chernobyl."

"Turn left here," Sean said when we came to a road that looked promising for no apparent reason.

"Sure," I said. "Why not?"

I turned left. After a few minutes we came to a rusting dinosaur of a factory. It was dark and abandoned and clearly had been for decades. After we passed it, the road somehow managed to get worse. I had to slow down to three miles an hour to prevent the car from breaking apart. We'd need an off-road vehicle to keep going.

"This can't be the way to Lviv," I said. "No one can drive on this road."

So we turned back. And eventually we found the town of Sambir. We found it by sheer chance, but we found it. There were a few cars here and there, and some street lights, too. There wasn't much to it, but it was the closest thing we had yet seen to civilization in Ukraine. And we finally knew where we were on the map.

We had been in Ukraine for four hours and had barely made twenty miles of progress. Lviv was sixty more miles away.

I saw a sign on the side of the road pointing to Львів.

"That must be Lviv," I said. "I guess their в is our *v*. And the letter *i* is the same. I can tell by the way they spelled *Sambir* on the other signs." Over the next couple of days, Sean and I would eventually figure out and memorize the entire Cyrillic alphabet this way.

The road *did* improve after we left Sambir and headed toward Lviv.

"We need food," I said, though I wondered if that would be possible in a countryside that hardly even had light.

"Look for a sign that says pectopah," Sean said.

"A sign that says what?" I said.

"Pectopah," he said. "That's Russian for *restaurant*. That's not how they say it, but that's what it looks like when they spell it."

A few moments later we saw a well-lit building on the side of the road that looked like a restaurant. A sign read "Ресторан."

"There we go," Sean said.

"It even looks open," I said.

And it was.

We stepped inside. The place was half full and a few people were still grimly eating.

"Do we wait to be seated or just grab a table?" I said. I had no idea how to behave in this country. Rural Ukraine doesn't have any handles. We were on the European continent, but we sure weren't in the West any more.

"Let's just sit," Sean said.

So we sat. A waitress stormed over and rudely slapped menus on the table without even looking at us. She couldn't have made it more clear that she was offended by our existence than if she had thrown them.

The menus were incomprehensible. They were thick as pamphlets and had no English translations or Latin letters. I couldn't even differentiate between the main course section and the beer list.

"How are we supposed to order?" I said. I wouldn't mind randomly pointing and just eating whatever she brought, but I might end up pointing at a dessert or even "water" for all I knew.

A large group of people sat at a long table in the back.

"Maybe someone over there speaks English," Sean said. There were about ten of them. The odds weren't too bad.

He walked over.

"Excuse me," he said. "Do any of you speak English?"

"Yes?" a young woman said a bit carefully.

"Thank God," Sean said. "I hate to bother you, but can you help us order some food?"

"I'm from Poland," she said, "and don't speak Ukrainian or Russian. We're all from Poland."

Great.

"But," she added and gestured toward an older man at the head of the table, "he speaks some Ukrainian."

"Yes," the man said. "I can help you."

I stood up and walked to the table.

"Thank you so much," Sean said.

"Hello," I said. "Thank you."

"Of course," the man said. "Should I translate the menu for you?"

I chuckled. That would take at least twenty minutes. The menu was *huge*. "No, no," I said. "Just please tell the waitress we want some chicken or something. We're not picky, we just can't tell her anything."

So he ordered us chicken.

"Do you want vodka?" he said.

"Yes!" Sean said.

"It's after midnight," I said, "and we still have to drive. But damn do I need a drink. So I'll have a shot."

"What brings you to Ukraine?" the Polish woman said.

"We're on our way to Chernobyl," I said.

She gasped and took a step back.

"Are you crazy?" she said. "I'm not sure I want to know you guys."

She must have been half-kidding, but I could tell she wasn't entirely. What was the big deal? Tourists go to Chernobyl now all the time. And I've been to far more dangerous places.

"He's a journalist," Sean said. "And we're both photographers."

I was annoyed that she found our mission repulsive, but tried my best to keep that to myself.

"Thanks for your help," I said. "We really appreciate it."

"Well," she said. "Enjoy your trip to…Chernobyl."

Back on the road to Lviv, Ukraine still looked depopulated. The road was vaguely okay now, but the small towns and villages in the countryside could hardly have been darker had they been hit by an EMP.

The country clearly hadn't recovered from the ravages of the 20th century. Communism was bad in Yugoslavia and even worse in Romania, but the poor souls ruled directly by the Soviet government *really* got hammered, and few so terribly as the Ukrainians.

The Stalinist-imposed Holodomor—Ukrainian for "hunger plague"—lasted from 1932 to 1933 and killed more people than the Nazi Holocaust. It was a deliberately induced famine meant to put down once and for all the weak yet nevertheless extant Ukrainian nationalism.

"In the actions here recorded," Robert Conquest wrote in his gut-wrenching book, *Harvest of Sorrow: Soviet Collectivization and the Terror-Famine*, "about 20 human lives were lost for, not every word, but every letter, in this book." It was, as Wasyl Hryshko wrote, "the first instance of a peacetime genocide in history."

The great Arthur Koestler witnessed it. He describes, in *The God That Failed*, "hordes of families in rags begging at the railway stations, the women lifting up to the compartment windows their starving brats, which, with drumstick limbs, big cadaverous heads and puffed bellies, looked like embryos out of alcohol bottles."

"In one hut there would be something like a war," Ukrainian-born Soviet dissident Vasily Grossman wrote in his novel, *Forever Flowing*. "Everyone would keep close watch over everyone else. People would take crumbs from each other. The wife turned against the husband and the husband against the wife. The mother hated the children. And in some other hut love would be inviolable to the very last. I knew one woman with four children. She would tell them fairy stories and legends so that they would forget their hunger. Her own tongue could hardly move, but she would take them into her arms even though she had hardly any strength to lift her arms when they were empty. Love lived on within her. And people noticed that where there was hate people died off more swiftly. Yet love, for that matter, saved no one. The whole village perished, one and all. No life remained in it."

Ukrainian-born Soviet trade official Victor Kravchenko could finally stand it no more, and so he defected. "Anger lashed my mind as I drove back to the village," he wrote in his memoir, *I Chose Freedom*. "Butter sent abroad in the midst of the famine! In London, Berlin, Paris I could see ... people eating butter stamped with a Soviet trade mark. Driving through the fields, I did not hear the lovely Ukrainian songs so dear to my heart. These people have forgotten how to sing! I could only hear the groans of the dying, and the lip-smacking of the fat foreigners enjoying our butter."

Sean slept in the passenger seat while I drove in a mental fog. I had long been exhausted by the late hour, the stress from being lost on shattered roads, and our near-complete inability to navigate with poor signage in absolute darkness. I drove on autopilot, barely even aware of what was happening, but I snapped back to consciousness when I found myself suddenly bathed in light inside a European-looking city.

I say it was European-looking, but that was really only partially true. The architecture was European, but something was terribly wrong with this place.

The space between each cobblestone on the streets was enormous. Our rental car's tires made a hell of a racket, as though we were driving on washboard or tank treads. The streets had hardly been more maintained than those in the back country. They rolled like roads in Alaska that are forced upward every winter by frost heaves.

"Where are we now?" Sean said as he awoke, motion-sick, from the rolling of the car and the clattering of the tires.

"Somewhere in Lviv, I guess."

Then I realized what else was wrong with the city. It had no economy. We were driving through at three o'clock in the morning, so I didn't expect to see open restaurants or stores, but I hardly saw any that were even closed. Storefronts scarcely existed and I saw no humans at all. There were no cars on the street and hardly any parked. Lviv looked like a European city emptied of people, or like an alternate universe where none of Europe's post-war progress had taken place. It must have looked similar the day World War II ended.

Before crossing into Ukraine, Sean and I drove north and spent a night in the spectacular Polish city of Krakow, which includes the largest still-existing medieval square in the world. Poland seems to have recovered from totalitarianism better than any other post-communist country I had seen. I can't vouch for what Warsaw is like as I have never been there, but much of Krakow looks like it never *had* a communist government or a command economy. Hungary, too, seems to have mostly recovered. At least that's how its capital Budapest looks. So much of Ukraine, though, is still haunted and ruined.

I found a hotel and pulled up in front. Parking was easy. None of the other available spaces were taken.

Sean and I dragged our sorry and exhausted selves up to our room. It wouldn't be too much longer before the sun came up even though the previous day's sun had only just set when we first reached the border. After driving literally all night, we had only covered 100 miles.

"Whoa," Sean said when he pulled open the curtains. "Look at what's outside our window."

Good grief, I thought. *What now?*

We had hardly seen any human beings, automobiles or signs of life or civilization since entering the country. We hadn't seen a damn thing yet that was normal. I had no idea what to expect out that window. A gigantic bomb crater hardly would have surprised me. What I saw instead were statues of angels at eye level atop the roof across the street. In the sunlight they must have been beautiful, but in the dark they looked like imps with sinister wings.

I woke early despite sheer exhaustion. Kiev was hundreds of miles away and Sean and I still thought we were going to Chernobyl first thing the next morning. We had no time to waste in bed even though we needed sleep.

I was also eager to see what Ukraine looked like in the daylight. It's not really fair to judge a country by what it looks like at midnight.

Traffic outside the window was light, but I was relieved to see Ukraine had vehicles after all. There were, however, as many buses as cars on the street. The overwhelming majority of the city's residents used public transportation rather than private automobiles—and I was damned sure the reason was not because they were saving the planet or because there was no place to park. They took buses because they couldn't afford anything else.

Sean and I stepped out for a walk. We had to leave early for Kiev, but you can't get a good read on a foreign city without walking around. So we walked around.

Most people on the sidewalks wore black. Nobody smiled or seemed in remotely good spirits. The entire city seemed to suffer from seasonal affective disorder or outright depression.

I couldn't get past the dearth of cars.

"It's weird, isn't it?" Sean said. "You and I both like the parts of European cities that don't have any cars, but this street *should* have lots of cars. It feels eerie and wrong. Even Russia has plenty of cars."

Even a country as backward and miserable and poor as Iraq has plenty of cars.

I expected Lviv to look and feel like the Polish city of Krakow. They resemble each other in photographs. They're reasonably close together, they date from the same time period, much of both were built when Western Ukraine was governed by Poland, yet they feel utterly different and distant. Krakow is lively. Krakow has a modern economy. Its people suffered terribly during World War II and the communist era, but they have rebounded. Past and present tragedy doesn't hang over them anymore.

Few stores sold much of anything in Lviv. Few restaurants or places to sit and hang out even existed. It's possible that part of the city we didn't see was economically healthier, but we were in the city center, the part of town that's on all the postcards. Lviv's medieval square looks beautiful in the pictures I took of it, but in person it felt like a dead city waiting for burial.

"Hey," Sean said. "There's a McDonald's. We can order by pointing at pictures."

I wanted Ukrainian food. Who wants to visit the other side of the world and eat at McDonald's? But we didn't know how to order Ukrainian food. No one spoke English and menus weren't even transliterated into our alphabet let alone translated into any language I could half understand. I can figure out at least some of what's on a menu in a language that isn't my own if it uses my letters, but not if it doesn't. Sean was right. McDonald's had pictures of food we could point to.

A long line inside moved at an excruciatingly slow pace. We'd have to wait at least 20 minutes before reaching the counter.

An employee replaced the menu showing pictures of egg and sausage sandwiches with pictures of cheeseburgers. Breakfast was over. The crowd in line heaved a collective sigh of disappointment. It was only—what—ten o'clock in the morning? Who wants a cheeseburger at ten o'clock in the morning? No one in line seemed to want one. Neither did I. It was morning and I wanted breakfast. Yet the McDonald's corporate headquarters on the other side of the planet decided Ukrainians want lunch instead of breakfast at ten in the morning. McDonald's was wrong. Sean and I weren't interested in cheeseburgers either. Not for breakfast.

So we left and returned to the main square a few streets away. It looked like dreamy, fantastical Europe when I squinted at it, but only if I squinted hard. The buildings weren't decrepit, but they were in a commercial district with hardly any commercial activity, almost as though Ukraine was still communist. Where were the restaurants? The cell phone stores? The clothing shops? The lawyers' offices? Central Lviv hardly could have been any more lifeless.

I didn't see nearly as many young people around as in Western Europe. The elderly folks looked worn down by a lifetime of poverty, oppression, and brutality. Most of Eastern Europe rebounded after the fall of the Soviet Union, but Ukraine had been left behind. Lviv looked like a Western city that had been shot in the head.

It wasn't at all what I expected. Lviv is in the western part of the country both geographically and politically. It's the capital of Ukrainian nationalism. Most ethnic Ukrainians, at least in this region, feel much closer to the West than they do to Russia. They want to join the E.U. and NATO. They elect politicians who tell Moscow to pound sand. Ukraine might not even exist as an independent country if it weren't for these people. It isn't like Poland or Hungary or the Czech Republic. It didn't just break free from the Warsaw Pact. It broke free from the Soviet Union. It broke free from *Russia*.

At least the city didn't feel sketchy. Russia is famously crime-ridden, but Lviv felt no more dangerous than anywhere else.

"We should go," I said to Sean as he snapped pictures of old buildings for his architectural photography collection. "We have got to get to Kiev. And it's hundreds of miles away."

I hate driving through a place and passing instantaneous judgment, but the shortage of time left me no choice. I may not have correctly understood everything I was looking at, and I'm probably getting some of this wrong, but that doesn't change the fact that driving from the eastern edge of the European Union into Ukraine was a shocking experience. Western Ukraine may be politically oriented toward Europe, but it is an orphan.

The highway out of the city had been recently paved. With the dangerous chassis-busting holes safely behind us, Sean and I could finally drive as if we were in a normal country.

But Ukraine is not a normal country. Well past Lviv on a road that looked more or less like an American Interstate, I saw more pedestrians walking God-only-knows where on the shoulder than I saw cars.

Gentle hills and low mountains gave way to the great steppe of far-eastern Europe that encompasses most of Ukraine, all of Belarus and vast portions of Russia. The landscape was flat as Kansas and almost as empty. Most agricultural fields lay fallow. Horses and tillers plowed working farmland by hand. Sagging single-story peasant houses suffered from dry rot and peeling paint jobs. Ukraine in the daylight appeared to be 200 years in the past.

"I can't believe how these people live," Sean said.

"I've seen a lot worse than this," I said. "You should see what the slums of Guatemala and Cairo look like."

"But these people have no electricity," he said. "And the climate is brutal."

"I've seen rural Guatemalan roofs made of sheets of plastic held down by tires," I said.

"At least they won't freeze to death in the winter," he said.

If you saw my photographs of the Ukrainian countryside, you might think it looks pretty. Many parts of it do, but there's a negative x-factor there, too, something dark about the place that's hard to nail down. Sean felt it more than I did because I had to concentrate on driving.

An oncoming truck driver flashed his headlights at me. Then an oncoming passenger car did the same.

"Something is wrong with the car," I said. "That's the second person who flashed his lights at me."

A third oncoming car appeared over the rise. He flashed his lights at me, too.

"*What now?*" Sean said as I pulled onto the shoulder and stopped.

"We're probably just missing a headlight," I said and hoped it wasn't anything worse.

Sean got out and walked around the car. "The lights are working," he said. Then he kicked all the tires. "The air is fine, too. Even that tire you smashed last night still has air in it."

He got back in and shrugged. I pulled back onto the road.

Just over the slight rise in the road some cops had set up a speed trap.

"Is that why they were flashing us?" Sean said. "To warn us there's cops?"

"Could be," I said. I suddenly found something to like about driving in this country.

And, yes, that is exactly what the flashing lights meant. Whenever somebody flashed his lights at me anywhere in the country, I'd pass a cop in a speed trap within a minute or two. There wasn't a damn thing the authorities could do about it, either. I found this contempt for the government, which everyone knew was corrupt to the core, delightfully post-communist.

The freeway was perfectly smooth now and four lanes wide even though there were hardly any cars on it. Brand new gas stations were *everywhere*. I saw at least six times as many gas stations as you'd find off the exit ramps of American freeways, yet this road carried only one percent as much traffic. Somebody assumed a lot more people would have cars in the future, but there's no way so many gas stations will ever be necessary. The United States was suffering the effects of a burst housing bubble, but Ukraine was in the midst of a gas station bubble.

Small plots of farmland ringed a number of medium-sized cities. Sean saw similar plots outside Copenhagen when he lived in Denmark, but urban Danes tended little farms on the side because it was fun to grow vegetables. Urban Ukrainians farmed on the side so they wouldn't starve.

"I have never been to a country that made me so sad," Sean said. And he's been to Russia.

He and I both snapped out of our gloom and laughed when we saw a tiny Soviet-built car pulling a tiny wooden trailer bursting with turnips. Backwardness and poverty are almost never funny, but there was something undeniably comical about a miniature communist Lada being used in the fields. There was also something admirably resourceful and tenacious about it, like Cubans using shoelaces and spit to keep 1950s era American cars going for so many decades after embargoed spare parts were no longer available.

We found a Ресторан, a restaurant, on the side of the road. A kind old Ukrainian man who spoke English helped us order some food. He insisted that we try the borscht, a beetroot soup from Ukraine that's served throughout the Russian-speaking world. "It's good," he said.

It was not good. No, it was not good at all.

"You're brave to come here," he said.

"We *are*?" I said. "Why?"

I didn't feel brave. I've been to Iraq seven times, to the Lebanese-Israeli border while Hezbollah missiles exploded around me, and to Georgia when Russia invaded. I didn't feel particularly brave even then. I certainly didn't feel brave in Ukraine. Were Sean and I there in the midst of an underreported crime wave?

"Well," the man said. "I guess there are bad people everywhere."

The capital, Kiev, is home to a large population of Russians, around 13 percent of the total. Even many ethnic Ukrainians there speak Russian in their day-to-day lives. The central government has been trying for years to teach the entire country to speak the native language fluently, but most Russians and even many ethnic Ukrainians know it only as a second language—if they know it all. In the more heavily Russian east, and in the Crimea, there is passive and even active resistance. The Ukrainian language, like Ukrainian nationalism, is strongest in the west, especially in the rural parts of the west. Kiev, in central Ukraine, faces toward the east and the west at the same time like the twin-headed dragon on the Russian seal.

The ethnic Russian minority doesn't impose itself or its language on the majority. Rather, until the collapse of the Soviet Union, most of Ukraine was just part of Russia. It was part of Russia before the Soviet

Union even existed. Ukrainians briefly tasted independence after the Russian Revolution in 1917, but in 1921 the western provinces of Galicia and Volhynia were taken by Poland (again) while the rest was conquered by communist Bolsheviks. When Moscow completed its conquest of Poland near the conclusion of World War II, it reabsorbed all of Ukraine and overwhelmed the latter's language, culture, and identity.

Russians still feel a powerful connection to Ukraine, not only because a large Russian minority lives there, but because Ukraine is the place where Russian civilization and culture were born.

The medieval European state Kievan Rus was founded in the 9th century when the northern Viking-descended Rus Khaganate moved its capital south from Novograd to Kiev, which had previously been ruled by semi-nomadic and pre-Islamic Turkic Khazars. By the 11th century, Kievan Rus was a vast state that made up much of the core of the European parts of modern-day Russia and Belarus as well as northern Ukraine. It fragmented in the 12th century and was shattered in the 13th by the Mongol invasion.

So Kiev marks the birthplace not only of Ukrainian culture, but also the birthplace of Russian and Belorussian culture. They are distinct now, but all three are the children of Kievan Rus. They have things in common with each other that they don't have in common with anyone else. Together they form a coherent sort of civilization unto itself even if it's somewhat unhappy, noncohesive, and fractious.

Ukrainian nationalism is hardly the fiercest around. It's strong enough that Ukraine could break free, but the cultural distance between Ukrainians and Russians isn't enormous. It's nothing like that between the Russians and, say, the Chechens even though Chechnya is still part of Russia. Some Russians still refuse to accept that Ukrainians are distinct at all.

No Russian would insist that Poles or Estonians are actually Russians denying their heritage, but many do say that of Ukrainians despite the fact that Ukrainians have their own language, their own folkloric traditions, and a more westward political orientation. Yet these distinct Ukrainian features are weak, especially in the east where many feel a stronger gravitational pull from Moscow than from Europe.

Traffic picked up as Sean and I neared Kiev's outskirts. The four-lane road leading into the city was now as crowded as an American freeway outside a major metropolitan area.

The farther east Sean and I drove, the more Russianized the country became. When we actually arrived in Kiev, though, I was surprised. The capital's outskirts were of course ringed with communist-style apartment towers, but they didn't have the tired, dreary, and relentlessly gray appearance they have almost everywhere else in the post-communist world. Most of the tower blocks had been painted. They looked more like non-descript apartment buildings in Western countries than oppressive communist public housing compounds.

I could hardly believe what I was looking at when Sean and I reached the old part of the city. Kiev today is simply magnificent. Street after street and block after block is densely packed with classical Russian architecture in outstanding condition. Her buildings are beautifully and stylishly lit up at night. The city somehow looks futuristic and classical at the same time. The old part of the city is vast, it is prosperous, and best of all, it was blessedly spared the Soviet urban planning that disfigured so much of Eurasia. If any part of Kiev is truly run-down and decrepit, I didn't see it.

Unlike Lviv, it is thriving. Restaurants, bars, and stores selling anything you might possibly want to buy, including the most expensive and fashionable imported goods, are literally everywhere. The city appears no less prosperous or lively than London or Paris, at least on the surface. Surely many of its residents are struggling, but they don't look like they're struggling, and at the very least they live in a vibrant and beautiful place.

"This city," Sean said, "looks like a cross between Moscow and St. Petersburg, only it's nicer."

Everything we'd seen so far—everything—was the opposite of what I expected.

I knew Ukraine would gradually begin looking more Russianized as Sean and I drove farther east, but I had no idea that meant things would start to look *better*. Russia is painfully backward compared with Europe, so I assumed that as we moved deeper into Russia's orbit and farther from the European Union that the country would keep getting worse. I could not have been more wrong. Driving from the supposedly Westernized part of Ukraine to the Russianized capital was as shocking as crossing the Polish-Ukrainian border, but in the opposite direction.

Ukraine is in some ways the anti-Romania. Most of Bucharest looks grotesquely communist. Hardly anything remains from before Nicolae Ceausescu and his Lady Macbeth of a wife Elena botched the place with their hideous plans. The smaller cities, though, the ones in the north away from the metropole, are beautifully preserved artifacts from the past. Bucharest is a dump of a capital surrounded by a beautiful country.

The problem with Kiev—according to a local joke that is truer than it is funny—is that it's surrounded by Ukraine.

Navigation, though, was an enormous pain in the ass. I bought a map of the city in the United States before we left, but it proved to be almost entirely useless. The map is in English. Cyrillic letters don't appear anywhere on it, not even in a smaller font or in parentheses. Yet all the letters on all the street signs were in Cyrillic. Where my map says "Alexander Street," the street sign says "Александр улице." I could have navigated just fine if my map included the names of things in both alphabets, but it didn't.

"Apparently," Sean said, "just about everyone who visits Ukraine comes from Russia. They have no more use for our language or alphabet than we have for theirs."

Westerners who think Ukraine might one day join the European Union and NATO (and that Russia would let her go quietly) might want to re-evaluate those assumptions. The Western world doesn't seem to even exist when you're in Kiev, but Moscow feels like it's around every corner.

Kiev, though, is not Moscow. It is much more orderly and prosperous. It appears to have been thoroughly de-Sovietized while Russia has been to only a lesser extent and next-door Belarus hardly at all. Crime isn't out of control. Ukraine is at least sometimes capable of holding elections that are not rigged. Kiev strikes me as the kind of place Moscow and St. Petersburg would be by now if Russia had gone the way of Eastern Europe and democratized after the Cold War, if it hadn't expanded so far to the east and half lost its European identity, if it had never been conquered by the Mongols in the 13th century and corrupted with the habits of medieval era oriental despotism.

Russians and Ukrainians are different people today, but they were once the same people. The fact that Kiev is outside Russia, by far the most powerful of the three Kievan Rus nations, leads to both tension and binding. Ukraine doesn't have much serious tension between the ethnic Ukrainian majority and the large Russian minority, at least not the kind that has convulsed former Soviet republics in the Caucasus and former Yugoslav republics in the Balkans. Civil war seems at worst a remote possibility. A Russian invasion, though, might be possible in a perfect storm. And continued Russian pressure and dominance is almost a certainty.

Kiev is a fantastic city, by nearly all accounts better than any in Russia, but it's also, unfortunately, expensive. Luxury cities everywhere are expensive, and Kiev is no exception. Sean and I had little choice but to stay at one of the lesser hotels to keep from hemorrhaging money.

The problem with lesser hotels, of course, is that they are lesser.

I decided to wait for Sean in the bar while he called his wife, Angie. I brought a book to read while I sipped from a glass of red wine. I chose to sit at a table for two by myself rather than at the bar. Within seconds, every woman within a 25-foot radius leered at me luridly. The hotel didn't *look* like a prostitute den from the outside or even the inside, but it was.

A woman in her late thirties at the next table scooted her chair next to mine. She wore a tight black skirt and way too much makeup. Her surgically enhanced breasts burst from her brassiere. I kept reading and pretended not to notice her as long as possible so she would get the idea that I was not in the market.

"Hi," she finally said.

I did not want to be rude, but I waited a few extra seconds before saying "Hello."

"First time in Kiev?" she said. She spoke English better than 99 percent of Ukrainians.

"Yes," I said. "It's a great city."

Getting straight to the point, she said, "Do you want to have sex?"

"No," I said. "I'm meeting someone."

"Girlfriend?"

"I'm married."

"You're meeting your wife?"

"My wife is at home in the U.S."

"So, what's the problem?"

She really did seem to be baffled. If my wife wasn't with me, why *shouldn't* I have sex with a willing woman whose breasts were already half exposed? Was I uptight? Gay? Did I have no libido? Her surprise, genuine or otherwise, actually made me feel slightly ridiculous when I said, "No, I'm sorry, no," but I wouldn't rent a prostitute for myself even if I was single.

"My friend is going to be here any second now," I said and I hoped it was true. Sean could be on the phone with his wife for another hour for all I knew.

I put my nose back into my book and discreetly flicked my eyes around the bar while pretending to read. I didn't dare make eye contact with any other woman lest I have to say no to sex all over again, but the dynamic in the bar was highly unusual and hard to ignore. Half the people in there were women. Every single one of them looked like a prostitute. They propositioned one man after another and were turned down by all of them. So I wasn't the only one acting prudish. I suddenly realized what it might feel like to be an attractive woman in a meet market who desperately wished she wasn't getting so much attention. Yet not even in the sleaziest bars are women approached as aggressively as were the mostly Russian and Ukrainian men in that bar.

I later asked the bartender out of curiosity how much the prostitutes cost.

"It depends on what you want," he said, "but the price starts at 20 dollars."

The rooms in the hotel cost four times as much. The women, then, were a bargain. Yet they still had a hard time finding clients.

I didn't want to eat at the hotel with all the hookers around. Nor did I want to contend with the agonizing difficulty of trying to order food in a place that did not even include my alphabet, let alone my language, on its menus. So I asked the concierge to direct Sean and me to a restaurant that had English menus. There apparently aren't very many, but there are a few here and there for those who know where to go.

The recommended place was decorated with a forest of fake plastic trees. The wait staff wore traditional red and white folk clothing that looked vaguely Bavarian. Our waiter spoke English almost as well as the hookers back at the bar.

"So," I said to him after ordering, "how many people in Kiev speak Ukrainian?"

"Only around 30 percent speak it fluently," he said. Everyone, though, speaks fluent Russian. And, like Americans, they expect everyone they meet, including foreigners, to speak the local language.

A drunk woman wandered over from the next table. She must have heard Sean and me speaking English and must have known that we were foreigners, but she wanted to come over and say hi in Russian.

On and on she went in Russian saying I've-no-idea-what while holding onto the back of an empty chair to keep her drunk self from falling. Her husband and twenty-something son smiled and waved and seemed slightly embarrassed by her behavior.

Then all of a sudden she hugged me. She hugged me and then leaned into me when her drunk feet slipped on the floor. As I held onto her tightly so she wouldn't fall, she looked up into my face like a teenager on a date. God help me I thought she was going to kiss me, and right in front of her family, but her husband jumped up to save everyone from *that* unpleasantness and led her away.

Back at her own table, she took from her bag a box of chocolate covered cherries she had bought earlier. Then she returned to my table and gave them to me.

"*Spacebo*," I said and smiled, slightly embarrassed. I did not want a gift from someone so drunk, but what was I supposed to do? Rudely give it back? Her husband, good sport that he was, nodded that it was okay. Then she returned to her seat.

The waiter gave Sean and me shots of vodka and toothpicked cubes of lard on our way out. "This is our tradition," he said and looked slightly concerned that we might reject what he offered. The vodka was good. I could have done without the lard square, but I tried to pretend it was bacon and that I liked it.

"They do the same thing in Russia," Sean said when we stepped out into the cold late October air. He was relieved we weren't told to drink more often. "In Moscow," he said, "you have to eat *lots* of potatoes for breakfast if you're an American. Russians will pour you so much vodka everywhere you go that you'll otherwise be pickled by noon."

When the Chernobyl administration cancelled our trip to the radioactive wasteland, Sean and I decided to drive south to Odessa on the Black Sea and to Yalta on the Crimean Peninsula. Before leaving for the Black Sea, however, we had to photograph some of Kiev's spectacular monuments.

Without realizing it, I stopped the car in a place where only police cars could park. A cop yelled at me in Russian and waved his arms. I got the point.

"Sorry," I said and rolled down the window. "I'm moving it now."

He then demanded the impossible: "*Speak* to me in *Russian*," he said.

As if I could flip a switch in my head and use a language I never studied. What could I say in Russian off the top of my head? *Vodka, dobre, Gorbachev, da, perestroika, spacebo, dosvidanya*, and *nyet*.

The longer I stayed in Kiev, the more I felt like I was in Russia. I had to try hard sometimes to remember that I was not. I didn't feel that way in Lviv or in the countryside, but Kiev looks and feels so incredibly Russian—and actually *is* partly Russian—that the feeling was inescapable. I was surrounded by Russian architecture, the Russian language, Russian food, businessmen and tourists from Russia, ethnic Russians who lived there, and by policemen who ordered me to speak Russian.

But Kiev seemed to lack Russia's darkness somehow. Aside from the cop, the people Sean and I encountered in the capital were downright chipper compared with those we met in Lviv. They weren't shuffling around, and they did not seem remotely depressed. Kiev is what Moscow and St. Petersburg wish they were. If I had flown into Kiev and didn't see any other part of the country, if Sean and I hadn't made our way there on such awful roads in the remote darkened countryside, I'd think Ukraine was First World and fully developed. But it's not.

The road from Kiev to Odessa is 300 miles of long, flat, and boring. The pavement isn't cratered like the roads near the Polish frontier, so there's that, but I can't think of anything else the journey has going for it except that it ends on the shore of the Black Sea, a relatively warm place with a slightly cooler version of the Mediterranean climate.

On the way down, Sean and I passed one rusted hulk after another, defunct Soviet-era factories abandoned long ago. These things were everywhere. Ukraine experienced a full-blown industrial collapse when Moscow's communist empire burst.

There was no chance Sean and I would find a foreigner-friendly Ресторан between Kiev and Odessa. Three times a day Sean and I had to eat, and most times the very idea filled us with dread. If no one in the restaurant spoke English, and there weren't any recognizable letters, let alone words, on the menu, how could we order? We couldn't even say to the waitress, "just bring us anything."

We were terribly unprepared linguistically for this trip. I felt ridiculous, like we should have studied at least enough Russian that we could order Chicken Kiev and a beer, but we didn't, and I couldn't find a bookstore anywhere that carried an English-Russian or English-Ukrainian dictionary.

You wouldn't be wrong to say that someone who travels as much as I do should have known better. I *should* have known better. In my defense, though, I've been to countries on every continent but Antarctica and Australia and never had trouble ordering food. Hardly anyone in Turkey speaks English, but the Turks use a slightly modified version of the same alphabet we use, so I could figure out enough of the language to get around without any problem. The Arabic alphabet is much stranger than the Cyrillic, but English and French are commonly spoken in much of the Arab world. Far more Westerners visit Arabic-speaking countries than Russian-speaking countries, so translated menus and street signs are common. Ukraine looks and feels far more "Western" than Egypt, but it gets fewer visitors and is harder—and harder than I expected—for the visitors it does get to navigate.

Sean and I selected a random restaurant in a random wasteland of a brutally Sovietized town we had never heard of. That part was easy. All we had to do was look for a sign that said "Ресторан." Only one waitress was working that day. She spoke no English. We were her only customers. No one could help.

After letting us peruse menus we couldn't read for five minutes, she came back to our table and asked what we wanted.

"Um," Sean said.

"We don't speak Russian," I said.

She glowered at us, not quite with hatred, but close. She raised her shoulders and flexed her fingers as if saying, "what the hell am I supposed to do with you two?"

"Chicken?" I said.

She didn't understand what I said. I may as well have said "qwertyplat." She gave her *what-the-fuck* look again. If only they had pictures of food on their menus.

Suddenly I had an idea. It was extreme, but I knew it would work if we dared.

"Sean," I said. "I know a way out of this."

"What?" he said.

I couldn't help smirking. "How badly," I said and giggled, "do you want chicken?"

He thought for a second, trying to figure out what I was thinking.

"No," he said and laughed. "You can't possibly mean…"

He knew exactly what I was thinking.

"Yep," I said.

He looked up into the face of our pissed-off waitress and, with a little boy glint in his eyes, he clucked like a chicken. He put his thumbs in his armpits, flapped his elbows as if they were wings, and let out a "bock *BOCK*."

Our sullen and humorless waitress, so typical in Ukraine, burst out laughing. Sean's clucking was *the* funniest thing she had seen in a week. And she brought us some chicken.

"When we get to Odessa," I said, "we have *got* to get on the Internet and study some Russian. This is absolutely ridiculous. I can't handle being this stupid."

Sean drove when we got back to the car. I rummaged through my backpack for a notebook.

"We are going to learn this alphabet *now*," I said as we merged back onto the freeway.

I ripped out a sheet of paper and wrote down every letter in the Latin alphabet and, next to it, every letter I knew in the Cyrillic alphabet, which was at most a third. I deciphered the rest one at a time by scrutinizing the spelling of place names on road signs. "Kiev," for instance, was spelled "Київ." That gave me a few extra letters right there.

That's how I learned Cyrillic. One letter and place name at a time. By the time we reached Odessa, I had the entire alphabet memorized.

But Odessa wasn't as difficult, at least not at first. We found an Irish pub catering to visitors next to a tourist hotel. And they had menus in English.

Odessa has long been more international and cosmopolitan than the rest of the country. Once an ancient Greek colony with links to the Mediterranean, and more recently a settlement of Muslim Crimean Tatars, the modern city was founded by a decree from Catherine the Great in 1794 and declared a free port. Many of those who built it and lived there in its early days were neither Russian nor Ukrainian, but Albanian, Armenian, Azeri, Bulgarian, Tatar, French, German, Greek, Italian, Jewish, Polish, Romanian, and Turkish. More than a third of the population was Jewish by 1897. It was a world apart even during the worst of the Soviet era. The terror-famine barely grazed Odessa at all.

Today it's a mostly Russian-speaking city, though the old city looks and feels nothing like Russia. It looks and feels remarkably like a gorgeous, atmospheric, and joyous—albeit somewhat generic—city on the Mediterranean. The sprawling suburbs, however, are clotted with ghastly and brutalist communist towers. Outer Kiev must have looked like that before being refurbished.

After the Irish pub, though, Sean and I had a hard time finding a restaurant that could handle our needs in English. Menus weren't as widely translated in Odessa as we had originally thought. I spent hours in the car decoding the alphabet, but that didn't teach me the words for "beer," "chicken," or "steak."

I kicked myself for not asking our English-speaking waiter at the pub when I had the chance. Ordering food was still hard. Sean and I yearned for McDonald's, not because we're fans of fast food, but because we could order by pointing.

We felt like the biggest idiots in the entire country. Being functionally illiterate and incapable of communicating knocked 40 points off our IQs. And no world traveler worth half a damn seeks out a McDonald's on the other side of the world.

"What kind of person," Sean says, "flies ten time zones from home and says, *excuse me, we have just arrived in your country, can you please direct me to the nearest McDonald's?* Am I that guy?"

He was that guy. At least he was that guy in Ukraine. And so was I.

It was arrogant and even a little imperial of me to expect people to speak my language wherever I went. Native English speakers are the only people in the entire world who can get away with it. Hungarians, Vietnamese, Israelis, and Somalis *know* no one else speaks their language. If they want to travel abroad, they have no choice but to learn at least one more language.

The second language most people learn, though, tends to be English. They don't only learn English so they can talk to people from the U.S., Britain, Ireland, Canada, and Australia. They also learn English so they can talk to bilingual Hungarians, Vietnamese, Israelis, Somalis, and so on. A person can get by just fine with English in places as diverse as India, Sweden, Lebanon, Mexico, and Zimbabwe.

It's not much easier for an American to get around in Russia and its sphere of influence speaking English than it would be for a Russian to get around the United States speaking his native tongue. English is not the *lingua franca* in Ukraine, Kazakhstan, or Tajikistan. Russian is.

I knew that long before I left for Ukraine, but I didn't appreciate its significance until after I got there. It was a humbling experience, one that had been a long time coming. It was also instructive. What are the odds, really, that Ukraine will ever join the European Union or NATO when it's still so firmly part of the Russian-speaking world?

We hardly had enough time in Odessa to take a quick look around. Yalta was still a long way to the south at the bottom of the Crimean Peninsula. So we got back in the car, wishing we could have stayed longer in Odessa, but happy to know that Yalta, too, was on the shore of the Black Sea and even farther to the south where it was warmer.

I could understand why Russians wished they had not lost Ukraine. Ukraine is the beach. Ukraine has warm water. Imagine how New Englanders would feel in the winter if South Carolina and Florida seceded.

"If you see a McDonald's," Sean said as we headed south in the car, "you come to a *screeching* halt."

Night fell before we reached the Crimea. Sean and I were both too tired to drive, so we pulled into a gas station to buy cans of Red Bull. CDs were on sale next to the soda and chips. Sean grabbed a couple at random, plus Carl Orff's *Carmina Burana*. The dramatic intro, *O Fortuna*, seemed like the appropriate thing to listen to when arriving in the one part of Ukraine everyone knew might one day, through either war or secession, be reunited with Russia.

Crimea is in Ukraine, but it isn't Ukrainian. This part of the country really is Russian. By this point I had learned the alphabet well enough that I could read, so I knew the gigantic words "Автономной Республики Крым" announced to all visitors at the border that Crimea is an autonomous republic.

Crimea has its own flag. It hosts the Russian navy's Black Sea fleet. It defiantly refuses to place itself within the Ukrainian time zone. Though it's dead south of Kiev, it uses the more easterly Moscow time zone instead. It doesn't have its own national anthem, but I heard the Russian national anthem playing loudly on the boardwalk of Yalta.

This is a town that is long past its prime. It's undoubtedly a nicer place now than it was during the communist era, but, unlike Odessa, it's provincial and tacky. Only a Russian could travel thousands of miles to vacation there without feeling a little let down and that's only because Yalta is Russian and warm. Ukrainians go there because it's nearby and warm.

Only a fourth of its citizens are ethnic Ukrainians. Less than a sixth are Crimean Tatars. Most of the rest are Russians. The government in Kiev has been trying for years to teach everyone in the country the Ukrainian language, but in Crimea it's meeting the stiffest resistance.

One thing the peninsula has going for it, however, aside from an agreeable climate, is its spectacular scenery. While most of Ukraine is flatter than Iowa, the steep craggy Crimean Mountains shoot straight up out of the Black Sea, which shimmers in sun-drenched glory year-round. Even though Yalta is significantly north of the Mediterranean, the climate, at least for a narrow little band near the beach, is startlingly subtropical. It's one of the only places in the world where a native Russian-speaking population can grow palm trees. It's not only the language, but the political autonomy, and the general Russian-ness that set Crimea apart from Ukraine. It's also those mountains and the trees and the moderate sea breeze.

Sean and I hadn't booked a hotel, so we checked out a few places at random. The first was prohibitively expensive. The second, a chopped up former apartment building that must have been beautiful in its heyday, reeked of piss.

A third place was cheap, adequately clean, and had a large room with two beds, so we took it.

A Russian communist-era movie played on the TV. I couldn't understand the dialogue, but it was at least passively propagandistic. The main characters, scientists in white lab coats, worked in a sparkling clean high-tech facility, the kind of place science fiction writers of the 1950s imagined were in our future. The movie portrayed an entirely staged idealized version of an advanced communist utopia without gulags, without long lines for potatoes, and without the NKVD. Ukrainians don't need communist-produced re-runs. They, like the rest of us, need a serious film about Stalinism for a mass audience, a *Schindler's List* of the Soviet Union.

In the morning we strolled the boardwalk. The weather was unseasonably cold, almost freezing even though it was only early November, but the sunshine and the palm trees gave the illusion of warmth. Yalta isn't exactly Miami, but Crimeans really do enjoy a charmed climate, especially compared with the climate Russians suffer in everywhere else.

At the north end of the boardwalk stood an angry-looking statue of Vladimir Lenin. I had the feeling he was still up there not because he was a communist, but because he was Russian. Communism is as dead in Yalta these days as it is in Warsaw. Just a few hundred feet away, and comically in the direct line of sight of Lenin's sculpted furious face, was a McDonald's.

Sean and I had breakfast there and it was disgusting. The sausage McMuffins had two sausage patties instead of just one, and not only were they too salty, they were *off*. But at least I could order one without any serious hassle.

For dinner we found a place with translated menus. Yalta just barely gets enough Western tourists once in a while that it occurred to a few restaurant managers to have a handful of menus laying around in the back in other languages.

Two young college-age women a few tables away heard us speak English. They laughed. They giggled. They tittered. This went on for at least a half-hour. And they couldn't stop staring. Sean and I were like zoo animals. An Arab, a black African, or an East Asian would have a hellish time visiting this place.

Yalta was nice in a basic sort of way, but it lacked the polish and vibrancy of Kiev and the relative cosmopolitanism of Odessa. No one should ever fly from the other side of the world just to go there. It reminded me of what Samuel Johnson once said about a bizarre volcanic basalt formation in Northern Ireland called the Giant's Causeway. "Worth seeing? Yes; but not worth going to see."

Crimea is a de-facto independent Russian-speaking republic, but if it weren't for Soviet premier Nikita Khrushchev it would still be part of Russia. In 1954 he moved an internal Russian border around and placed Crimea in Ukraine. It didn't seem like a fateful decision at the time, one no more significant than giving Idaho a slice of Montana. He had no idea any part of Ukraine, let alone all of it, would ever break loose from Moscow. He should have known it was possible since it had happened before, but he did not see it coming, or at any rate didn't care, so this Russian-majority region is marooned outside of Russia.

Perhaps the only reason Russian leader Vladimir Putin hasn't moved to "correct" Khrushchev's mistake is because there isn't much point. Ukraine's current government headed up by Viktor Yanukovych was friendlier than the previous government of Viktor Yushchenko, which Putin did everything in his power (short of invasion) to smash.

Ukraine's 2004 election was rigged. Yanukovych was declared the winner when the majority wanted the pro-Western Yushchenko instead, whom somebody almost fatally poisoned with dioxin. His face was hideously disfigured by the toxin for a while, but slowly recovered. The results of that rigged election were reversed by the Orange Revolution, when general strikes broke out and thousands took to the streets and said *no*.

In 2009, Russia turned off its supply of natural gas and let Ukrainians freeze in the winter, purportedly because of a financial dispute over prices and debt. The punishment was preferable, of course, to Stalin confiscating Ukrainian *food* in 1921 and 1922, but the message was a familiar one: if you don't follow dictates from Moscow, you will be punished.

The crisis likely wouldn't have been triggered at all if Ukrainians had elected a pro-Russian government. Moscow was already cheesed off by Yushchenko's noises about Ukrainian ascension to the European Union and NATO. The Russian media portrayed Ukraine as a traitor state over it. There wasn't much Moscow could do to stop the likes of Lithuania and Poland from joining NATO, but it won't likely ever let its Kievan Rus cousins leave without resistance.

These kinds of problems don't exist between Russia and Crimea. It might mean war if they did, or if a stridently pro-Western government in Kiev expanded its writ a little too enthusiastically, but that hasn't happened.

Moscow doesn't actually care very much about Yalta. The city made history when Stalin, Franklin Delano Roosevelt, and Winston Churchill met there at the end of World War II to agree about which parts of post-fascist Europe would be in the Western camp and which would be in the communist bloc, but it has been a backwater ever since even if it's a slightly pleasant one nowadays.

What Moscow cares about in Crimea very much is Sevastopol. That's where Russia's Black Sea fleet makes its home. Neither Sean nor I dared take any photographs of it, not even discreetly from the car as we drove past. It's not a good idea to take pictures of military installations anywhere in the world, especially not Russian military installations.

In Sevastopol, once again, I found myself forgetting I wasn't in Russia. The overwhelming majority of people who live there are Russians. The language they speak is Russian. Actual Russian soldiers and sailors were all over the place.

When the Soviet Union cracked up and Ukraine declared independence, Russia initially refused to cede Sevastopol and Crimea at all and only later relented when it signed the Peace and Friendship treaty with Kiev. Moscow need not worry overly much. Its fleet's lease won't run out until 2042. And if Ukraine tries to revoke it, Russia will almost certainly seize it by force, most likely to cheers and applause by locals who would feel liberated. Ukraine barely holds onto the Crimea oblast as it is, and on even numbered days I can't help but wonder how long even that is going to last.

Before heading back toward Kiev, Sean and I first had to see the remote and far-flung Sea of Azov. The western side is Ukrainian, and half of that is Crimean. The eastern shore is all part of southwestern Russia. It is so far east from any place in Europe normal travelers would want to go that it seemed, at least in my mind, more Central Asian than European.

"It almost has to be strange," Sean said, and I agreed. "I want to say that I've been there. Who goes to the Sea of Azov?"

I felt slightly silly, however, for thinking it must be exotic in anything other than name. It's just a large body of water. Right? Water is water. How strange could it be? It wasn't purple or made of Dr. Pepper. Just because hardly any Americans ever see it doesn't mean there has to be anything odd or even interesting about it. I *felt* that it must be unusual, but my head told me it can't be. It's not on another planet. It's just a remote and obscure Russian sea. Visiting would almost certainly be anti-climactic. We still wanted to go, though, on the off chance that our gut feelings were right.

So far, most of what we'd seen had defied expectations, but this time our gut feelings were right.

We drove a few hours from Sevastopol and out onto a long narrow spit, certain it would be easy to find the beach since the water was less than a mile from the road. Yet all I could see was a hideous post-industrial wasteland with no way to reach the water on the other side. The sea was just off to our left according to my map, but every street heading that direction was gated and shuttered. Was it possible we drove all the way to the Sea of Azov and would not get to see it? I drove along the desolate road that took us through unspeakable squalor for another half-hour. A sad billboard advertised cheap holidays on that blasted up shore for those who could not afford Yalta.

I was just about to give up when I saw an ungated dirt road branching off to the left. I took the turn and we found ourselves in the creepiest place I had yet seen in the country. Broken glass, barbed wire, crumbling walls, junked automobiles, and garden variety refuse were everywhere. If there were people around, I couldn't see them or hear them. The entire area was derelict and forlorn.

Some dogs detected our presence and barked. I felt a powerful sense that we shouldn't be there. The dearth of other humans added to my sense of uneasiness, but at the same time I didn't want anybody to see us. I'm not sure why, exactly, but a tingling feeling told me we'd be in trouble if anyone did.

A narrow path led to the beach through a thicket of weeds. A wooden sign pounded into the sand showed a camera with a red slash through it. *No pictures.* Why shouldn't anybody take pictures? There was nothing even remotely interesting or apparently sensitive that I could have photographed.

A strong wind came off the sea, whipping the water into a furious lather. Dark rain clouds on the watery horizon headed inland. The beach in both directions was cluttered with the hulking industrial wreckage of a ghost port.

Sean took out his camera.

"Don't," I said.

"But there's nobody here," he said.

All I heard was the wind and the surf.

There seemed to be no one in any direction for miles, so I unzipped my Nikon from its case and took a few pictures.

We stood there in silence and took in the desolate scene for a while.

"You were right," I said, "about the Sea of Azov."

"This is why nobody comes here," Sean said.

We were technically in Europe, but it looked like the nastiest parts of Iraq. The sound of machine-gun fire would not have seemed out of place.

I have never been anywhere that looks and feels more like the rotted dead center of the Soviet Empire. This place was so utterly godforsaken and misery-stricken I had a momentary feeling that the Union of Soviet Socialist Republics had never fallen apart, that, Mordor-like, its malice truly is sleepless, that it's still crushing parts of the world in its totalitarian fist.

The West won the Cold War, but this place experienced none of the springtime of Budapest, Prague, or even of Yalta. This part of Ukraine suffered nothing but ruin. It looked like the end of the world. The only things missing were corpses and rats.

Eight

The Slow Rot of Hosni Mubarak

Cairo, Egypt 2005

There's no way around it: your first impression of a new city and country will be powerfully influenced by whatever you see in your first 15 minutes of walking around. It's important, then, that you choose the location of your hotel very carefully.

My starting place in Egypt was the Hotel President on the island of Zamalek in the Nile River, supposedly Cairo's Beverly Hills. The place looks nothing like Beverly Hills. It's packed from one end to the other with medium-rise apartment towers, most of them knockoffs of the concrete monstrosities that ring cities in the old Soviet bloc. I found shops, cafés and restaurants on the ground floor, but most were quiet, simple places, dimly lit on the inside, and they were spaced far apart as though Zamalek, despite its packed urban density and higher concentration of wealth per capita, could only support a thin spread of modest establishments.

The streets were remarkably quiet for the center of a metropolitan area of nearly 20 million people, though I heard blaring horns faintly in the distance across the river on the busier mainland. The sidewalks were wide and shaded by dusty green trees. A vaguely vegetable smell, presumably from the Nile, coated the air like a thin slime. A dense foglike haze enveloped the city, partly from automobile pollution but also from farmers out in the delta burning crop waste. It gave my sleepy Zamalek neighborhood a surreal, ghostly pallor that added to the dislocation I always feel when arriving in a new country.

Foreign embassies were all over the island, most of them right next to each other. They were the former mansions of rich Cairenes built in various European styles at the turn of the last century. But after Gamal Abdel Nasser and his so-called Free Officer's Movement overthrew King Farouk in 1952, these magnificent homes were nationalized by the state. Nasser wrenched Egypt into the orbit of Soviet Russia with predictably disastrous results. Most of the island's residents have been living in those drab apartment buildings ever since.

Nasser was long gone, though, by the time I arrived, as was his replacement Anwar Sadat, whom Islamist army officers assassinated in 1981 for signing a peace treaty with Israel. Egypt's current president, Hosni Mubarak, had no interest in Nasser-style radicalism, nor was he brave enough to risk anything if he had to pay a price as Sadat had. He'd been ruling Egypt as a standard-issue status quo authoritarian for the previous quarter-century. The entire country was drowning in torpor. His regime calcified long before I got there.

At midnight I walked along the bank of the Nile. Two commercial pleasure boats—one lit up in neon and both playing Arabic music too loud—passed each other on the otherwise dark and quiet waters. International hotels skycrapered behind them. Women were allowed out of the house during the day, nearly all with their heads wrapped in scarves, but every person I passed on the street that night was a man. Cairo is 10 times larger than Beirut, Lebanon—where I lived in at the time—but it's two or even three orders of magnitude more conservative.

I was surprised that Zamalek was considered upper-class. The sidewalks were crumbling. Almost every apartment building, whether ugly and modern or lovely and Victorian, was coated in soot and grime. Many parked cars had been idle so long, they looked like they were covered in volcanic ash. Only the embassies were clean and well maintained.

Some of these people had money, though. Zamalek was dour on the outside, but when I saw through the front windows into the living rooms of some apartments in the older buildings, I had to revise my opinions.

It's hard to feel sorry for someone who has high ceilings, color-washed walls, wedding-cake moldings and chandeliers in their living room. My house in the States is not as nice as many of these. Zamalek's problem was that the neighborhood wasn't kept up, as if civic pride didn't exist.

In the 1980s, when travel writer Douglas Kennedy visited Alexandria, the largest city on the Egyptian Mediterranean, renowned painter Sarwat el-Bahr explained a key Egyptian concept to him. "Do you know why America does not understand Egypt? Because they do not understand the meaning of the word *Maaleesh*. In English, *Maaleesh* means 'doesn't matter,' and it is the one word you need to understand Egypt. In America everything is *now, now, now*—make the money now, make the career now. But in Egypt, everybody believes in life after death, so everything in life is *Maaleesh*."

That's how much of Zamalek looked and felt. It simply didn't matter if the public spaces were dreary. Not to the locals anyway. But it mattered to me. Zamalek disappointed—considering what it was supposed to be like—and I went back to my hotel and picked up my copy of *Travels with a Tangerine* by Tim Mackintosh-Smith, a British Arabist expat who lives in Yemen.

"Few visitors have liked Cairo on first sight," he wrote. "'Uff!' exclaimed an eighth-century caliph, 'She is the mother of stenches!' Later, a geographer wondered why anyone should have wanted to build a city 'between a putrid and mephitic river, the corrupt effluvia of which cause disease and rot food, and a dry and barren mountain range devoid of greenery.' The ground teemed with rats, scorpions, fleas, and bugs, the air with miasmas. In Cairo Symon Semeon buried his companion Brother Hugo, who had succumbed to an attack of dysentery and fever 'caused by a north wind.' My guidebook, compiled a century after I.B.'s visit, was disturbingly frank about the dangers of living in a polluted high-rise city where light and air rarely penetrate the dark alleyways. Its author, al-Maqrizi, warned that 'the traveler approaching Cairo sees before him a depressing black wall beneath a dust-laden sky, from which sight his soul shrinks and flees away.'"

What I saw wasn't nearly as bad as all *that*, at least. And the next day, when I found 26 July Street and the streets adjacent to it, I changed my mind about Zamalek. (I later changed my mind again and again about not only Zamalek but also all of Cairo.)

26 July had an elevated freeway that ran right over the top of it, giving the street a dark, *Blade Runner* feel. That may sound like a complaint, but somehow it worked. It reminded me a bit of Chicago, a city I love and wish I could visit more often. You can barely see the sky from the sidewalk, but the street is brilliantly lit up at night. All the usual neighborhood goods are for sale: shoes, watches, clothing, glasses, pharmaceuticals, snacks and so on.

I found a terrific Italian restaurant called Maison Thomas. The sign in the window said *"Le Caire Fondee en 1922,"* decades before Nasser drove all the non-Arabs out of Egypt in his Arab Nationalist "revolution" from above. Maison Thomas, unlike so much of Cairo and even the quieter back streets of Zamalek, felt truly modern. Its patrons were well dressed, most of them more so than me. The waiters and waitresses dressed sharply in black and white. Women and men—and I couldn't tell if they were single or married—went there on dates. None of the women wore the hijab, the veil or the abaya. Almost everyone seemed to be in a good mood, and almost everyone smoked imported cigarettes rather than Egypt's crap Cleopatra brand. My charming and disarming waiter seemed like the happiest man alive, as if nothing in the known universe pleased him more than bringing me food and a beverage.

I had to look hard, but I did find tiny pockets of sophistication. A first-class bookstore across the street called Diwa carried some of the best titles from the West as well as from the Middle East. A whole shelf was devoted to Arabic literature translated into English and published in beautiful eye-catching trade-paperback editions. Many of the original English titles were among the finest works of literature the West has ever produced. In the History and Current Events sections, I found books by Edward Said, David Frum, Thomas Friedman and Bernard Lewis. (No Salman Rushdie, alas.)

Cairo was ahead of bookstore-free Tripoli, then, at least in some ways, and miles behind Beirut. But Cairo is so large that you could fold Beirut and Tripoli into it five times each and have room left over.

For good or for ill, whatever happened there would have an enormous impact on the rest of the region.

Egyptian blogger Big Pharaoh gave me an insider's tour of Cairo and the ghastly political situation facing his country.

He took me down 26 July Street on foot to the bridge over the Nile connecting Zamalek to the mainland. As we walked up the entrance ramp—built for cars, not for people—he asked if I ever walked like this in Beirut. "In Egypt you can walk wherever you want," he said. "There are no rules or laws here."

Well, I thought. There were laws against involvement in politics. But I knew what he meant. The Egyptian government didn't micromanage its citizens. Good on Hosni Mubarak for that one, at least. Egypt was a police state, but at any given moment it didn't feel like one.

"There are no laws in Lebanon, either," I said. "You can do pretty much whatever you want there."

As soon as we crossed the river, the amount of traffic—both pedestrian and automobile—multiplied exponentially while the economic conditions plunged. Zamalek was hardly the most charming place in the world, but it was exquisite compared with the rest of the city. Mainland Cairo was loud, crowded and crumbling. I could see that it must have been beautiful once, and some of its architecture was strikingly European, but it looked a bit like Prague must have during the 1970s, decades before its postcommunist restoration.

Hideous concrete tower blocks stretched to the horizon in every direction from the relatively compact downtown.

I thought to myself that it looked more than a little Soviet, but it wasn't until I visited 13 postcommunist countries in Eastern Europe and the former Soviet Union and then returned to Cairo during the so-called Arab Spring that I realized just how accurate that observation actually was.

I was surprised, but I shouldn't have been. Nasser's Egypt was a Soviet client state, though officially "socialist" rather than communist. In the 1950s he purged Egypt of its tolerance, its riches, its openness and its variety. He brought in Russian advisers, ramped up the secret police and ruthlessly smashed everyone who opposed him. He expelled nearly all the Greeks, Jews and other minorities in his attempt to make Egypt monolithically Arab. (Egypt before Nasser was not considered an Arab country. Before him, Egypt was just Egypt.) His nationalization of industry and private property turned the economy into an incompetently micromanaged catastrophe.

"Can we talk about politics out in the open?" I said to Big Pharaoh.

"Yes," he said. "We can say whatever we want."

"Is it because we're speaking in English?"

"No," he said. "We could do it in Arabic too."

"You're not worried about the secret police?"

"Not anymore," he said. "It is a real change from last year. Last year there was no way. But it's better now, more open. Do you know why?"

"Tell me," I said.

"Because of pressure from George W. Bush."

That was the only piece of good news I had to report from Egypt during the time of Hosni Mubarak.

We walked underneath an overhead freeway. I had to shout so he could hear me. The entire world looked as though it were made out of poured concrete, and I could taste the black tang of exhaust in the air.

Big Pharaoh pointed out a set of campaign posters on a wall. It felt good seeing campaign posters in Egypt. It was a long way from Libya, where menacing portraits of Muammar Qaddafi and no one else were plastered up everywhere. The main opposition to Hosni Mubarak, however, was not a liberal coalition but the Islamist Muslim Brotherhood.

"Do you know what that says?" he said as he pointed at the Arabic script above the portrait of a candidate's face. "It says 'Islam Is the Solution.'"

We made our way to the nearest subway station and descended the steps. It was clean down there—much cleaner than the subway stations in New York City—and I said so.

"It is almost brand-new," he said.

"How old is it, exactly?" I said.

"About 10 years," he said.

I was amazed that such a miserably poor country could build a brand-new subway while American taxpayers said they couldn't afford to build any new trains. How was that even possible?

"It must have been hugely expensive," I said.

"France and Japan helped us pay for it," he said.

"Japan?" I said. "Really. Why Japan?"

"To earn some goodwill, I guess," he said.

As our train pulled into the station, I made my way toward the first car.

"Not that car," he said. "The first car is only for women."

The genders weren't segregated as in Saudi Arabia. Women could ride any car on the train. But sexual harassment and sexual assault in Egypt were so off the scale compared with almost everywhere else in the world that the government gave women their own train car so they wouldn't have their asses grabbed by aggressive, lecherous men.

"I got in that car on accident once," he said. "By the time I figured it out, the doors closed. I got out at the next stop and was fined seven pounds." Seven pounds is less than $2, but half of Egyptians earned less than $2 a day.

We got off the train in the center of downtown and emerged next to a huge, well-lit roundabout. Perhaps it was because he and I arrived after dark when the night washed the grime away, but Cairo suddenly looked like a European masterpiece. It was not at all what I was expecting after seeing the squalid condition of so much of the rest of the city. I changed my opinion of Cairo—again.

"This is amazing," I said. "What a terrific downtown. Look at these buildings!"

"They are from another era," he said. "They are just relics. They have nothing to do with what Egypt is now."

"But they're real," I said, "and you still have them. No country builds streets like this anymore anyway."

It felt like an Arab New York or, rather, an Arab Rome. Later, though, when I went downtown again by myself during the day, I understood what he meant. Downtown Cairo is all sparkle and no substance at night. Cities can't lie during the day. Even this neighborhood, which surely once was exquisite, seemed to have all the prosperity sucked out of it. Only an empty husk remained. Egypt had clearly had a rough couple of decades. In the harsh afternoon sunlight, the neighborhood looked like it had been lifted hundreds of feet into the air and dropped back on the street.

I've seen photographs of this part of town that make it look sort of okay. Their smaller-than-life size conceals the backwardness, the gloom and the depressed condition of the place since Nasser took out his blunt instruments and went to work on it.

"I am going to take you to an Egyptian bar," he said. "Is that okay?"

"You mean an Egyptian bar where no tourists would ever go?"

"Exactly," he said.

"Perfect," I said. "That is exactly what I want to see."

We walked past a women's underwear store. "When the Muslim Brotherhood comes to power," he said as he swept his arm in front of female-shaped mannequins modeling panties and bras, "they will ban this."

He led me into an establishment called Cap'dor. Instead of glass windows it had wooden shutters painted red and green. The floor was laid with gray tile, the walls lined with wood paneling. There was not a single woman inside. Apparently that's how it always is in that bar. They didn't even bother to install a women's restroom. Beer was the only beverage available.

"There are some prostitute bars around too," he said.

"Is it legal here?" I said. "Prostitution is rampant in Lebanon."

"No," he said, "but the law is lax. The bar owner just pays off the police and no one cares."

We ordered two stout bottles of Stella beer.

"Best beer in Egypt," he said. "The company was started by a Greek guy in 1897."

The bartender brought us carrots, sliced tomatoes and *ful* beans. We dug in.

I wanted to know what he thought of the Muslim Brotherhood. Many in the Western press described the organization as moderate, but compared with what? Al-Qaeda? Sure. But it was hardly moderate compared with anything in the West.

"They are moderate because they don't have guns," he said. "They don't kill people. But most of the armed terrorist groups we see now were born out of the ideology of the Muslim Brotherhood. My biggest fear is that if the Muslim Brotherhood rules Egypt, we will get Islamism-lite, that they won't be quite bad enough that people will revolt against them.

Take bars, for example. Most Egyptians don't drink, so they won't mind if alcohol is illegal. The same goes for banning books. Most Egyptians don't read. So why should they care if books are banned? Most women wear a veil or a headscarf already, so if it becomes the law, hardly anyone will resist."

"How many people here think like you do?" I asked him.

"Few," he said. "Very few. Less than 10 percent probably."

We ordered more Stella beers. He practically inhaled all the *ful* beans. I didn't think they were that great. They had little taste, actually.

"There probably aren't many Muslim Brotherhood guys in this bar," I said.

He laughed. "Ha! No way. This is a secular working-class bar. Just the fact that they're here makes them liberals."

The patrons didn't look liberal. He used that word in the most elastic way possible. These men were secular, sure, since they drank beer, but there were no women around. This was a man's establishment. How many of these guys, I wondered, were responsible for the government giving women their own car on the subway?

It was odd, I suppose, to see my pale face, blue eyes and black leather jacket in Cap'dor. No one stared, but almost all the other men's eyes lingered on me a bit longer than usual. They seemed curious and slightly pleased that someone from somewhere else decided to hang out in their place.

I asked Big Pharaoh what he thought would happen if Egypt held a legitimate free and fair election instead of a rigged one staged by the government.

"The Muslim Brotherhood would win," he said. "They would beat Mubarak and the liberals."

It was obvious just from walking around that liberalism in the genuine sense of the word found little purchase in Cairo. Women wore headscarves. A large percentage of men wore robes. It was a traditional place despite its size. The vibrant culture that must have existed when the European Quarter was built had passed into history.

"I've had a theory for a while now," I said. "That some Middle East countries are going to have to live under an Islamic state for a while and get it out of their system."

Big Pharaoh laughed grimly.

"Sorry," I said. "That's just how it looks."

He buried his head on his arms.

"Take Iranians," I said. "They used to think Islamism was a fantastic idea. Now they hate it. Same goes in Afghanistan. Algerians don't think too much of Islamism either after 150,000 people were killed in the civil war. I hate to say this, but it looks like Egypt might have to learn this the hard way."

"You are right," he said. "You are right. I went to an Egyptian chat room on the Internet and asked 15 people if they fasted during Ramadan. All of them said they fasted during at least most of it. I went to an Iranian chat room and asked the same question. Fourteen out of 15 said they did not fast for even one single day."

"Egypt didn't used to be like this," I said.

"Nasser's biggest crime was not establishing democracy when he took over," he said. "Back then, Egyptian people were liberal. It would have worked then. But not now."

Progress is a funny thing. Westerners like to think it moves in a straight line. In America that's pretty much how it is. No serious person would argue that American culture was more liberal and tolerant in the 1950s than it is now or that it was more liberal and tolerant in the 19th century than it was in the 1950s. But Egypt moved in the other direction. Why?

"When Nasser took over," he said, "people were angry at Britain and Israel. He nationalized all the industry. He banned political parties. He stifled everything. Banned the Muslim Brotherhood. Banned the Communists. Banned all. When Sadat took over in 1970, he had two enemies: the communists and the Nasser remnants. So to counter these threats, he did what the United States did in Afghanistan during the Cold War: he made an alliance with the Islamists. He brought back the Muslim Brotherhood, which had fled to Saudi Arabia when Nasser was around. He used them to destroy the left.

"That was part of it," he continued. "During the oil boom of 1973, a lot of Egyptians went to Saudi Arabia to work. Then in the 1990s, two important things happened. After the first Gulf War, Saudi Arabia began to Saudi-ize its economy and said they no longer needed Egyptian workers. Egyptians came home contaminated with Wahhabism. Egypt's economy kept getting worse. Unemployed members of the middle class either sat around and smoked or got more religious. That was when Islamism moved from the lower class to the middle class. Now it is moving even to the upper class."

"Egypt will get over it after a while," I said, "just like Iran is getting over it now."

"That will take 25 years! I don't have 25 years!"

The Iranian ayatollahs had so far been in power for 26 years.

I felt bad for Big Pharaoh. Even the Egyptian capital, despite its immensity, hardly had a place for a person like him.

The bartender came around and gave everyone a glass with a green liquid in it. Hey, I thought. Free drinks. I guessed beer wasn't the only thing they had in the bar after all.

"What is this?" I said.

"It's the water the beans were cooked in."

I stared at him.

"This is bean juice? Are you serious?"

"Yes," he said. "You will love it."

"I don't know about that," I said.

"There is a first time for everything," he said.

"Okay," I said. "Here goes."

I took a small sip.

It was horrendous.

"No," I said. "This isn't working for me."

I wanted a glass of red wine. And I wanted some women around. Hanging out at a wiener roast is no fun. It reminded me of something Carsten Niebuhr wrote in 1774: "Young men who like their comforts, and a dainty table, or who wish to pass their time pleasantly in the company of women must not go to Arabia."

"A friend of mine recently went to Algeria," Big Pharaoh said. "When he came back he told me that there are far fewer veiled women there than there are here. It is much more liberal in Algeria because there they have tasted Islamism. Egypt does need to experience what happened in Iran and Algeria … as long as I am in the U.S. or Canada when it happens."

Even though he would rather live in the United States, he was seriously looking into immigrating to Canada. It might be easier for him to qualify for an immigrant visa. "If I live in Canada, I will be in the apartment above the party."

"The apartment above the party?" I said.

"America is the party," he said. "And I will be living right above it. So I'll be in the apartment above the party. And I'll go downstairs a lot."

"I sincerely hope you can make it out of here," I said, although I partly felt bad because his leaving would only contribute to Egypt's brain drain.

"Mubarak is a horrible, horrible man," he said. "He is the reason we are in this thing. He has oppressed all the liberals."

Optimism came naturally to me at the time. Beirut, where I lived, was looking up. The Lebanese had cast off Syrian occupation without firing a shot. The city felt like I imagined Berlin did shortly after the fall of the Berlin Wall. Hezbollah had not yet ignited the war with Israel in 2006. That would happen seven months after I left Cairo. Nor had Hezbollah invaded Beirut. That wouldn't happen for another two years. Nor had the Syrian civil war erupted, which would—rather predictably—spill into Lebanon.

Beirut seemed to have a bright future ahead of it. I was wrong about that, but Cairo's bleak future was obvious.

"You want to feel good?" he said. "You want to be optimistic? Go back to Beirut."

I had to check myself. Perhaps I was wrong about the Muslim Brotherhood. Maybe they really were moderates, and Big Pharaoh, as one of the few Egyptian liberals, was being paranoid and excessively partisan. It happens.

So I called senior Muslim Brotherhood leader Essam el-Erian and asked for an interview. He was the Brotherhood's smooth media man, the go-to guy journalists liked to talk to when they need a fresh quote or wanted to know what the Brotherhood stood for and thought. He spent time in Egypt's dungeons, not because he was a terrorist (he wasn't) but because, like Egypt's liberals, he was an enemy of Hosni Mubarak.

I felt some sympathy for him even though his politics were radically different from mine. Though I couldn't say I wanted to see him in power, that didn't mean I wanted to see him repressed or in prison.

"Your campaign slogan is 'Islam is the solution,'" I said. "If Islam is the solution, why did millions of Iranians move to the United States after the 1979 revolution? Why do so many people in Afghanistan hate the Taliban?"

He laughed. Not a belly laugh, but a knowing laugh, as though he fielded a version of that question every day.

"Listen, Mr. Michael," he said. "Iran is not Egypt. Egypt is not Afghanistan. Afghanistan is not Sudan. Sudan is not Algeria. There are different models of Islamic life. We have a very long civilization here. It is ancient. We have common values here between Muslims and Christians and even Jews."

I liked his answer but could not take his word for it. I needed specifics. It's not enough to say that Egypt isn't Afghanistan. That was obvious anyway. *How* was his ideology different from that of the Taliban?

"Okay," I said. "What kind of model for Islamic life does the Muslim Brotherhood have in mind for Egypt?"

"I cannot answer specifically now," Erian said. "We are not in power. We are struggling for democracy. All people must be respected in a democratic system. It is very important to be tolerant."

Nice-sounding boilerplate, but it was a dodge. I decided to get back to this later rather than beat him over the head right at the start.

"If the Muslim Brotherhood were in power in Egypt," I said, "would you cooperate with the West against al-Qaeda?"

"From the first moment we are against al-Qaeda," he said. "We condemn all violent activities. We condemned it then. But we have doubts about the way the West fights terrorism. This way of fighting is the wrong way. We need a concrete definition of terrorism before we can cooperate."

"What's your definition of terrorism?" I said.

"We need an international meeting and conference to decide on a definition."

"Good idea," I said. "So if you attended an international conference, what definition of terrorism would you suggest?"

"I am not going to give you a definition," he said. "We need dialogue and consensus. It is not only for the Muslim Brotherhood to decide."

"But what would you say to Western governments if they agreed to a dialogue with you? What is *your* definition of terrorism? Never mind what anyone else thinks."

"I cannot give you an answer now," he said.

This guy was more useless than government ministers I've interviewed. But I had to give him credit. He was extremely well practiced in the art of saying nothing.

I decided to try another angle on the first question he'd dodged.

"Would the Muslim Brotherhood ban alcohol in Egypt?" I said. "Would you ban books?"

"We are not going to do anything without discussion. We are not in power."

"Should women be forced to wear a veil or a hijab?" I said.

"You must understand," he said. "We are outlawed. We can clarify these points after we are free."

"Why don't you clarify now?" I said.

"We need fresh air. We need fresh air before we can clarify this."

"People want to know what you stand for," I said. "My job is to help you explain yourselves to them."

"The government likes to confuse people about what we really believe," he said.

"Tell you what," I said. "You clarify your vision of an Egyptian Islamic state now and I promise to get the word out."

"We need fresh air before we can clarify anything," he said.

He went round and round like this, refusing to even hint at what their Islamist program might look like. It seemed plain enough to me that his deliberate obfuscation was a ploy to feign moderation and conceal a hidden extremism.

"Mr. Michael," he said. "It is late and I am tired. Just two more questions please."

We had only been talking for a few minutes. And he hadn't yet answered even one question.

"Okay," I said. I had plenty more questions I wanted to ask, but if I was only allowed two, I needed to ask something he couldn't dodge quite as easily. "If you could change three things about American foreign policy, what would they be?"

"Respect human rights and international law," he said.

We could have dug into that one for hours, except of course he wouldn't let me. Instead of dwelling on it, I moved straight to the last question, one that tends to be a lightning rod for Islamists.

"What do you think about the fatwa against Salman Rushdie?" I said. Since he wouldn't answer my question about whether or not he wanted to ban books in Egypt, perhaps he would give it away when discussing the world-famous "blasphemer" whom Iran's Ayatollah Khomeini sentenced to death for his novel *The Satanic Verses*.

"It was the wrong way to treat," he said. "Ignoring would have been better."

What could I say? It was a good answer, the best answer there is. He did know how to put on a moderate face when he wasn't blatantly dodging my questions.

I can only assume he had a definition of terrorism that Westerners would think is extreme. Otherwise he would have told me what it was.

I can also only assume he would like to ban booze and veil women. Otherwise he would have said that he didn't.

If I was wrong about the Brotherhood—and if Big Pharaoh was wrong—it was the Brotherhood's fault for dissembling.

I couldn't go to Egypt without seeing the pyramids, especially since they're less than an hour from the center of Cairo. So I hired a grizzled 60-year-old driver named Nabil to pick me up at my hotel in late morning.

He and I cruised from the center to the outskirts through miles of shabby apartment towers. I saw precious little economic activity—

unsurprising since half the country earned less than $2 a day—and couldn't escape the sense that most of Cairo, despite being the Arab world's cultural capital, was actually a cultural void packed with people who spent nearly all their energy struggling just to get by. The culture produced by Egypt and consumed by the rest of the region was created by a minuscule minority.

The quality of the apartment towers was inversely proportional to their distance from downtown. The farther Nabil drove from the center, the worse everything looked. Soon the tenements were nothing more than red brick warehouses for humans, many of them without windows and no doubt without air-conditioning.

Nothing was worse than the slums on the outskirts. Streets weren't paved. Each neighborhood had its own garbage dump where children played barefoot. Lush agricultural land—tended by farmers with oxen and adorned with what presumably were date palms—was checkerboarded throughout the slum blocks. The housing was horrid, but the landscape was verdant and subtropical, and it helped take the edge off the ugliness.

I wanted to raise my camera to the window and take pictures, but I was worried it would embarrass Nabil. I imagined he wished every tourist who came through Egypt did not have to see what I was seeing. So I pretended I didn't.

"So, Nabil," I said. "What do you think of Hosni Mubarak?"

"He does many good things for people outside of Egypt," he said. "For Americans, Europeans and Israelis, he is a man of peace. I like that. But he does nothing for us. Look at these poor people."

At least Mubarak didn't plaster his picture up everywhere like Qaddafi did, at least not in Cairo. Unlike Nasser, he didn't even attempt to gin up a cult of personality. He was not a mass murderer like Saddam Hussein, not a totalitarian like Bashar al-Assad. He was just a standard-issue strongman who'd leave you alone if you stayed out of his way, though he ran Egypt like it was his private plantation.

One Egyptian, however, told me that outside Cairo, Mubarak's portraits were more common and sinister. He looked like everyone's dad in the pictures I saw. In Upper (southern) Egypt—the stronghold of the Salafists and the Muslim Brotherhood—he was supposedly decked out in sunglasses and an officer's uniform.

"Do you have any children?" Nabil said.

"No," I said. "I'm married, but I don't have any children."

"Good," he said.

Good? Middle Easterners tended to be slightly horrified and confused by Westerners who don't have children.

"Why is it good?" I said.

"Raising children is a huge responsibility," he said. "I have three, and it is so hard. I have an electrician's degree, but the government doesn't pay enough money for us to live on." Apparently, finding electrician's work in the private sector isn't much of an option. "So I drive car," he said.

I had agreed to pay him $12—his asking price—to drive me out to Giza and wait for me for two hours while I looked at the pyramids and the Sphinx. Twelve dollars for a half-day's work may be a lot in Egypt (I don't know), but it seemed like nothing to me. So I quietly decided I would pay him $20 instead if he didn't try to extract any more from me.

"What do you do for a living?" he said.

"I'm a writer," I said.

"Oh!" he said, delighted. "What do you write about Egypt? You write about pyramids?"

"Sure," I said. "I'm also interested in politics. Mubarak and the Muslim Brotherhood."

He twisted up his face.

"I not like them," he said. "I like women. And I like beer."

"Beer and women are good," I said. He grinned and gave me a high-five.

We pulled off the freeway and turned onto a dirt road between the tenements. A cart drawn by a donkey got in our way. Nabil sighed. "Cairo traffic," he said.

He stopped the car at the edge of the city of Giza. The silhouette of a pyramid towered above us in the haze, easily as high as a skyscraper but *much* wider and more imposing. Two horses were tied to a post on the sidewalk next to us.

"Do you want to ride camel or horse?" he said.

Actually, I wanted to walk. I especially didn't feel like being a dorky tourist riding a camel. I'd ridden an ass-busting camel once already, in Tunisia, and that was enough.

"A horse," I said, not wanting to be a pain by insisting on walking.

Horses are more trustworthy. Camels have been known to chase down their owners (while bellowing like Chewbacca) when they get disgruntled and are finished taking orders. I admire that about them, but I didn't need any drama from an animal that weighed hundreds of pounds more than me.

Nabil summoned a horse man who introduced himself to me as Mohammad.

Mohammad offered to help me mount the horse, but I didn't need it. He mounted his own and we set out into the street alongside automobile traffic.

This was a stupid way to travel in Cairo.

"Watch your legs!" he shouted as a filthy bus roared past.

A driver rounded a corner too quickly and clipped my foot with his mirror.

"Watch your legs!" Mohammad said again.

After riding a few blocks, we reached the gateway to the pyramids. I saw then why we needed horses. The area around the pyramids was *huge*, much larger than I had expected. And it was all sand. There was no road to drive on. It would not have been possible to walk around and see everything in under four hours, let alone two.

I paid my admission, and as we passed the gate, a policeman carrying a horse whip and a gun walked up to us.

The officer screamed something at Mohammad in Arabic. Mohammad screamed something back at him. The policeman then cracked his horse whip on the sand and narrowed his eyes at us.

Having no idea what the problem was, I pretended to be a perfectly happy and oblivious idiot, hoping it might tone down the temperature by a degree or so.

Mohammad said something nasty to the policeman in Arabic and then led our horses away as the officer's face flushed with hatred and rage.

"Asshole," Mohammad said. I acted as though I hadn't heard that.

Mohammad led his horse and mine away from the abusive policeman and toward the base of the pyramids of Giza.

"Welcome to the beginning of the great Sahara Desert," Mohammad said.

I have climbed to the top of the Maya pyramids in the Petén Jungle of the Guatemalan Yucatán. Spectacular as they are, their life size is smaller than I had expected before I arrived. The pyramids at Giza are much bigger. They're impossibly large monuments that seemed the size of small moons. No doubt they'll still be standing thousands of years after we all are gone. Egypt one day may no longer be Egypt, but the pyramids will remain as though they belong to eternity. They will weather as slowly as great mountains.

Some of the more deranged Islamists have threatened to destroy them, as the Taliban destroyed ancient Buddha statues at Bamiyan with ack-ack guns, but now that I was looking at them in person, I had to laugh. The pharaoh's tombs at Giza aren't going anywhere unless someone detonates a nuclear weapon on top of them. Even then I wouldn't count on their being destroyed. They would probably have to be nuked a second or third time.

"Are you a Yankee?" Mohammad said. "Or are you Southern?"

"I'm a Yank," I said. From Oregon.

"Can you believe you are here?" he said.

I didn't know what he meant, and he read that on my face.

"Every day people tell me they can't believe they are here after flying thousands of miles."

"I came here from Beirut," I said.

"Ah," he said. "Okay. You live in the Middle East. You know where you are then."

He and I rode our horses at a full gallop until we reached the first pyramid, then we slowed to a trot. A man dressed in Bedouin garb ambled by selling warm bottles of Coke. I bought one for 50 cents and offered Mohammad a sip.

"Can we climb to the top?" I asked, not really sure I actually wanted to.

"No," Mohammad said. "A tourist recently tried it. He fell and lost himself. It is no longer allowed."

He led me to a lookout point where all three pyramids were visible in a line, the perfect place for a photo. I suddenly wished I had come in late afternoon, when the light was better for pictures. Glare from the afternoon sun washed out all color and left no shadows for contrast.

Mohammad had been right earlier. The pyramids really are the beginning of the great Sahara Desert. The suburb of Giza was barely visible in the haze on one side while sand stretched to the horizon in the other direction. Metropolitan Cairo had reached its absolute physical limit and could sprawl no more. I wondered where on earth jobs and food would come from as the city grew ever larger. The place would turn into a Malthusian death trap if it didn't get its economic house in order.

Two uniformed police officers rode on horseback to where we were standing. They exchanged pleasantries with Mohammad as he handed them several Egyptian pounds. Then they left. The entire meeting took less than 10 seconds.

"Why did you just do that?" I said, feeling defensive on his behalf as I narrowed my eyes at the officers' backs.

"They are poor, and good people," he said. "The state does not pay them. Look after the poor, and God will look after you."

They did seem like nice enough gents in the nine seconds I saw them in action, as long as I didn't think about the fact that Mohammad, rather than the government that ostensibly employed them, paid their salary. Since they were armed men of the law, I couldn't help but wonder what would have happened if Mohammad *hadn't* given them any money, and I remembered the shouting match he had earlier with the enraged policeman with the gun and the whip.

We got back on our horses and rode leisurely toward the Sphinx. Mohammad rode silently, but he seemed to be in a pleasant enough mood.

"What do you think of the Muslim Brotherhood?" I said.

"Those are bad words, my friend," he said.

"Bad words?" I said. "Why, exactly?"

"They are bad people who know nothing," he said. "I have no school. But I know war is terrible and that we should take care of our country." I hadn't said anything about war, but it was the first thing he thought of when I mentioned Islamists. He wore a somber look on his face now.

He was a simple man and probably charged too much money to lead me around on a horse, but he seemed a decent enough fellow, and I did not get the sense he was jerking me around and telling me only what I wanted to hear. Some Middle Easterners in the tourism business say "I love America!" in the most unconvincing voice possible. It's obvious fakery. I can tell when they do it just for form's sake. Mohammad didn't seem the type to pull that with me.

"What do you think about Hosni Mubarak then?" I said.

"He is a good man," he said.

"Hmm," I said.

"What?" he said, aware that I didn't agree. "What do you want to say? Tell me what is in your heart."

"He's a dictator," I said. *And an asshole*, I wanted to add. Mubarak had been in charge of Egypt for decades, and the place was in terrible shape. It wasn't his fault that the country was not liberal, but he was certainly to blame for persecuting the liberal minority that did exist. It guaranteed his rule, sure, but it also guaranteed that the main opposition to his rule was the Muslim Brotherhood, since they could organize in mosques no matter what the state did. The liberals had no such sanctuary and couldn't compete, couldn't even attempt to convince their neighbors and fellow Egyptians that neither Mubarak nor the Brotherhood had the answers. He did it on purpose so he could tell his supposed friends in America that he was all that stood between the Islamists and an Iranian-style regime. He may have been right, but it was partly his fault.

"I understand what you mean," Mohammad said and nodded. "In America you change presidents without fighting. Here if we change presidents we could have a war."

"Maybe," I said. "And maybe not. It's awfully convenient for him that you think that."

"Listen, my friend," he said. "If we have a president who is not from the army, we will have another war. Only the officers know how to keep us at peace." I presumed he meant only the officers know better than to humiliate Egypt by picking another losing battle with Israel. Perhaps that was true, but even Syria's Bashar al-Assad knew better than to go full tilt against Israel. He fought Israel indirectly through Hezbollah in Lebanon.

The pyramids were much bigger than I had imagined, but the Sphinx was a great deal smaller. It looked especially tiny with the gargantuan pyramids as a backdrop. Only in close-up photos does it take on much size.

As we got near the Sphinx, the angry policeman from earlier returned on foot. He cracked his whip on the sand again and stared holes through Mohammad and me with his black eyes. He didn't look like a starving policeman to me. He was fat, actually, and his rosy cheeks made him look like a boozer.

"This man will guide you to the Sphinx," Mohammad said.

Oh, for God's sake, I thought. The Sphinx was right there. Only a blind man would need a guide. Mohammad didn't want to pay this jerk off, so now I had to do it? I suddenly liked him less, but it was hard to say how much pressure he was actually under. I had witnessed some of that pressure earlier, and it was a lot. There is no legal recourse at all when you're abused by policemen in Egypt.

The menacing officer stared at me, whip in hand, with undisguised hatred as I dismounted my horse. I smiled at him as though I were the perfect American idiot utterly clueless about what was happening and incapable of reading body language or hostile intent. What I really wanted to do was break his face with my fist. I'd be in deep shit if I didn't pay him. That came across. He was mugging me, basically, and hardly even bothered to pretend otherwise.

"Do you speak English?" I said in the most genial voice I could muster as we walked together toward the Sphinx.

He actually smiled at me and shrugged his shoulders. Playing nice was paying off. What else could I do? I seethed inside even after he decided to cool it. He didn't care at all about making a civilized impression on foreigners. I despised him for that on Egypt's behalf as well as my own. The code of Arab hospitality was completely lost on this man.

It only took two minutes or so to reach the Sphinx. Other tourists were there snapping the shutters on their digital cameras. I took several pictures and ignored the policeman completely, refusing to look at him or acknowledge that he even existed.

I walked around to look at the Sphinx from several different vantage points and stayed much longer than I would have if the bastard weren't on my case. You want baksheesh? I thought. Then you're gonna wait for it, pal.

I kept the policeman waiting for as long as I could stand, then started walking back toward Mohammad and our horses without looking back at him. Clandestinely I pulled one Egyptian pound (less than 20 cents) out of my pocket for the baksheesh he "earned" in no way whatsoever. I didn't want him to ask for money and see me pull a big wad of cash out of my pocket and demand I give him one of my larger bills.

"Hello again, Mohammad," I said as I approached.

"Hello, Mr. Michael," he said. "How was the Sphinx?"

"Grand," I said.

The policeman walked just behind me and to my right as I fantasized about cracking him in the nose with the back of my elbow. I mounted my horse and let the man wonder if I was actually going to give him baksheesh or not. Then, not wanting to start yet another furious incident, I handed him the Egyptian equivalent of 17 cents.

"*Shukran*," I said—thank you—in the iciest tone I could manage.

No, fuck *you*, you son of a bitch, is what I was thinking. Would you treat my mother this way if she were here instead of me? Even tourists at the pyramids, of all places, get a taste of the petty humiliations people have to put up with every day in Third World police states. Imagine living in a country so messed up that it could be your job to roam around all day with a whip and a gun angrily extorting money from everybody you come across. No wonder Mohammad was fed up with this man and had the nerve to scream at him earlier.

This is what you have to put up with thanks to your pal Mubarak, I wanted to say to Mohammad as we rode away, but I didn't. He was a nice enough man, and he knew that already. He was shaken down by the cops every day when he went to work.

I went to a cozy restaurant and pub back in Zamalek and ordered a bowl of pasta. A 20-something Western woman sat alone at the next table reading an English-language newspaper. We smiled hello to each other.

"Are you a student here?" she asked in an Australian accent.

"No," I said. "I'm a writer. You?"

"Just traveling," she said.

"By yourself?" I said.

"I've been traveling alone for four months. I started in India and I'm working my way to Spain."

"Did you go through Iran?" I said. I wanted to go to Iran but doubted they'd give me a visa. The regime didn't like my job or my passport.

"I can't go there," she said.

"They're blocking Australians, too, eh?"

"Well, not exactly. What I mean is *I* can't go there." I figured she must have been to Israel and that the Iranians wouldn't let her in if she had the Zionist Entity stamp in her passport.

She whispered, "I work for the Department of Defense."

It's a good idea to whisper that sort of thing in the Middle East. Conspiracy theories are out of control, especially in Egypt.

If she and I had some privacy, I would have asked about her job. But I couldn't expect her to tell me anything interesting where others could hear. Australia didn't have sinister designs on Egypt, but neither did the United States. That didn't stop Egyptians from hatching dark, elaborate fantasies.

The waiter brought my pasta. It was so undercooked I could barely eat it. I should have sent it back, but I didn't want to be difficult. He, like many Egyptian waiters, was so embarrassingly friendly and charming, I didn't have the heart to complain.

"What's it like traveling by yourself in Egypt?" I asked her.

"Difficult," she said. "I'm leaving tomorrow."

"Is it difficult because you're a woman?"

"This is the absolute worst place for a woman to travel alone," she said. "Men harass me constantly. They hiss, stare and make kissy noises."

"A Syrian friend told my wife if she ever goes there to carry a spare shoe in her purse. If any man gives her trouble and she whacks him with the bottom of the shoe, a mob will chase him down."

She laughed. "Syria is wonderful. I mean, it's much more oppressive than Egypt. But it's also more modern. No man ever bothered me there. No men bothered me in Lebanon, either. I was surprised. Lebanese and Syrian men are more respectful even than European men. The worst part is that Egyptian men won't back down when I tell them to leave me alone."

I remembered Cairo's subway, how the first car in the train was only for women.

"I'm having the time of my life, though," she said. "Tomorrow I'll be in Spain. It will be fun to be a single woman in Spain." She winked at me, gathered her things, and got ready to leave. "Happy travels," she said. And then she was gone.

I met Blake Hounshell in the lobby of the Hotel President in Zamalek. He was an American student studying Arabic at the American University of Cairo and the founder of the group blog *American Footprints*, formerly known as *Liberals Against Terrorism*. He would later become the editor of *Foreign Policy* magazine.

"Let's go somewhere off Zamalek, shall we?" I said. "This city is huge and I need to see as much of it as I can."

"What would you like to do? Have lunch? Coffee? Smoke *shisha*?" A *shisha*, or hookah, is an Arabic water pipe, like a bong for flavored tobacco.

"How about all of the above?" I said.

"I know just the place then," he said, "in a cool neighborhood where lots of young people like to hang out."

He hailed us a cab and we hopped in the back. I had no idea where we were going, but a cool neighborhood where lots of young people like to hang out sounded perfect.

But the neighborhood he took me to looked grim and depressing, much more so than Zamalek, and was not at all what I expected from a place where hip young people had colonized. But I kept my gripes to myself.

"You have to revise your expectations downward in Cairo," he said, as though he knew what I was thinking. "This probably looks Stalinist to you."

"It isn't *that* bad," I said. But it was, actually, almost that bad. Much of Cairo looked Stalinist.

"No, it's not pretty," he said. "But you get used to it."

He led me into what counts in Cairo as a nice restaurant. The floors were orange tile. The chairs were made of wicker. A mild feeling of gloom hung over the place like a cloudy day just before rain.

"Do you like living in Cairo?" I said as we sat down. A beaming waiter brought us two menus and bowed.

"Well, it's a big sprawling mess," he said. That was certainly true. "You either hate it or love it. I think I'm in the latter category. I was bored back home in the States, and I'm not bored here at all."

He and I have different personalities. I worried that I'd be bored and alienated into depression if I lived in Cairo after I saw all the sights, though I loved living in Beirut, a vastly more sophisticated and prosperous city that was also thrilling and edgy. It's impossible to be bored there for even five minutes.

Going from Lebanon to Egypt was like descending into a poorly lit basement.

How far the mighty do fall. Fifty years earlier, Cairo was a relatively wealthy, liberal, cosmopolitan jewel of North Africa and the Middle East. Nasser's cultural and economic wrecking ball smashed the place as totally as the communist regimes he aligned himself with. Mubarak was no communist—that's for damn sure—but he was spectacularly uninterested in cleaning up Nasser's mess. *Wall Street Journal* reporter Stephen Glain once aptly described Egypt as a "towering dwarf." I don't think the description can be improved upon.

Hounshell and I ordered sandwiches, soft drinks and a *shisha* to share as we talked politics.

"There are 21 political parties," he said. "But 16 don't really exist. They are newspapers, not parties. Their reporters aren't really reporters. They have no handle on policy or ideas whatsoever. Some of them even sell access. If someone wants to smear a businessman, for instance, space can be bought for that in their pages."

The only real opposition to Mubarak's National Democratic Party, the Muslim Brotherhood, had been active in Egypt for 77 years at that point and had painstakingly built a formidable political machine through the mosques even while banned.

The two main liberal opposition parties, al-Wafd and al-Ghad, were tiny, disorganized and woefully unprofessional. They were fringe parties, not broad-based popular movements. It's not that the Muslim Brotherhood truly represented everyone else—they didn't. But the liberal parties had not been around for as long and hadn't been free to operate normally or build themselves up. Their ideas found little traction in Egypt anyway. The country was, for all intents and purposes, a two-party state, with Mubarak's military regime on one side and the semiunderground Islamists on the other.

Hounshell and I passed the *shisha* pipe between us. The tobacco flavor was apple, widely considered the best.

"The MB is going to win around 100 seats in parliament," he said. (As it turned out, they won 88.) "That's 100 out of 444 seats, plus another 10 appointed by Mubarak directly. That's a lot of seats considering that they only ran 120 out of fear of being smacked down by the state if they posed too much of a threat."

It *is* a big deal that the Muslim Brotherhood won more than half the seats they contested, especially since Mubarak's NDP still cheated and even opened fire with live ammunition on voters.

"All the ministers are members of parliament," he said. "So the minister of energy," for example, "has to face an election. In all the races where these big guys are running, we are seeing vote rigging, vote buying, intimidation and cheating."

During one of the early rounds of elections in Alexandria a street battle erupted between NDP guys wielding swords and Muslim Brotherhood members who came at them with chairs. The army fired tear gas at groups of voters in Brotherhood strongholds to keep them from reaching the polls.

How extreme was the Muslim Brotherhood, really? That's the argument that never ended in Egypt, in large part because the Brotherhood refused to admit where it stood. People saw what they wanted to see. Anti-Islamists feared the worst while optimists hoped the Brotherhood's self-identification as moderate was sincere.

Would they actually ban alcohol if they came to power? Who knew? They wouldn't say. Would they force women, even foreign women and Christian Egyptians, to wear the veil? No one had any idea.

"Islam is the solution" was their rallying cry, but they said they wanted to build an Islamist state democratically.

They also claimed, at least sometimes, that they were not sectarian—a difficult thing to believe considering that they wanted an Islamist state. "I went to a Muslim Brotherhood rally," Hounshell said. They chanted 'Muslims and Christians, we are all Egyptians.'"

The problem for Egyptian Christians (who make up between 10 percent and 15 percent of the population) wasn't that the Muslim Brotherhood wouldn't recognize their right to live in Egypt and be Egyptians. The problem was that they stood a real chance of losing some of their already diminished rights and being forced to live by the code of another religion.

Mubarak's regime was secular, yet even under *him*, Christians were blatantly discriminated against when it came to government jobs. In a country where huge swaths of the economy are controlled by the government, that's a serious problem. They also had trouble building churches. Muslims could build mosques, no sweat, but Christians faced years of bureaucracy, and regime apparatchiks routinely said no. So Christians feared that if the Brotherhood ever ascended to power, the already existing discrimination from the secular state would only increase under an Islamist state. Why wouldn't it?

"The Muslim Brotherhood is run mostly by old people," Hounshell said. "The old guard is definitely less moderate and less democratic. But they are also more willing to make concessions to the regime. They really don't believe in democracy. The younger members, though, are more democratic. At least they seem to be. They talk a good game, but the way this will all play out if they ever come into power ultimately is unknowable."

To those who were easily and perhaps willingly fooled, Mubarak appeared to cry uncle after sustained U.S. pressure to open up his one-party state and hold real elections. But the reforms were a farce—and hailing his just-kidding charade as a sign of progress in the Middle East was naive and reckless.

Human-rights activists and independent politicians—most famously Saad Eddin Ibrahim and, more recently, Ayman Nour—continued to be harassed, arrested and booked on trumped-up charges. And since kicking around his opponents during "campaign season" wasn't enough to guarantee victory, Mubarak worked over the voters as well.

In early 2005 he announced that he would allow candidates other than himself to run for president. Millions of Egyptians were ecstatic. Finally they would have an actual choice in an election—a first-time experience for everybody. Yet no one who wasn't already registered to vote under the old system, where Mubarak was the only candidate, would be allowed to vote in the supposedly real election at the end of the year.

The Egyptian government knew better than to imitate the Syrian and Iraqi Baath Parties by claiming to get 99 percent or even 100 percent of the vote. That didn't mean Mubarak actually won a normal election. It only meant he was a tad less obvious about it.

He was still pretty obvious, though. The democratic opposition parties only won 3 percent of the seats. It all went according to government plan, then. Kicked-around parties like al-Wafd and al-Ghad had no better chance of beating Mubarak at his game than the Green Party had of winning the White House in the United States.

"Rigging elections is a sport here," American political scientist and long-time Cairo resident Josh Stacher told me in his office. "There are 2,000 different ways to do it, and the methods vary by constituency and region. When all else fails, they just physically block people from voting."

All else failed in the Nile Delta during the third round of elections, including the physical blocking. Military police fired not only rubber bullets but also live ammunition at voters, killing at least eight and wounding more than 100.

Mubarak's regime didn't fail merely in politics. It spectacularly failed in every way a state can possibly fail. The economy was moribund. The habitable regions of Egypt were so overpopulated that cemeteries and garbage dumps had been transformed into slums packed with millions of people. Barely half the population could read or write. The state was a mafia with an army; its grubby paws stifled and profited from practically everything. Just walking around, I felt hopeless depression and dread like a dead weight.

Democratic and Republican administrations in Washington both described Mubarak as a moderate and an ally. They gave him $2 billion a year. To a certain extent he was "our son of a bitch." And that was precisely the problem.

Stacher explained how it looked to Egyptian eyes. "Mubarak's NDP fires tear gas at people who line up to vote. 'Made in the USA' is stamped on those canisters. When this sort of thing happens, lots of people here compare themselves to Palestinians living under foreign occupation."

The popular Egyptian notion that Mubarak was an American "puppet" is understandable to a point. The U.S. government was far too cozy with the man. At the same time, it was a bit of a stretch. His state-run media organs propagandized relentlessly and hysterically against the United States, arguably more so than any other newspapers and TV stations in the Middle East.

The U.S. was frequently compared to Nazi Germany. (At the same time, Egypt's media wallowed in Holocaust denial.) Al-Qaeda's man in Iraq, Abu Musab al-Zarqawi, was described as an American agent. Colin Powell, according to government weekly *al-Ahram al-Arabi*, accused the Sudanese government of genocide in Darfur as part of an American plot to steal oil. Just a few months earlier al-Mihwar TV had the audacity to air an interview with an Egyptian general who claimed that Vice President Dick Cheney admitted that the September 11 attacks were hatched by rogue elements in the White House. These are mere samples of what Mubarak's government-controlled media cranked out on a regular basis. No one who airs and publishes this kind of nonsense can honestly be counted as a friend or an ally, let alone a "puppet."

The Bush administration, to its credit, pushed for democratic reforms in Egypt, but it wasn't enough. Gently prodding a dictator who is otherwise treated politely and as a friend doesn't work if he's not a reformer. The Nasser-Sadat-Mubarak regime created Egypt's 21st century problems in the first place, and Mubarak turned out to be a little like Assad in Damascus. He created problems only he could solve, and he refused to deliver.

The very idea of a good autocrat is for the most part an oxymoron, but they do pop up here and there. Robert D. Kaplan defined such a rare creature as "one who makes his own removal less fraught with risk by preparing his people for representative government." Mubarak missed that mark by a couple of time zones.

Still, his government could only do so much damage to a thousand-year-old city like Cairo without physically tearing it down. I wanted to see the oldest parts of the city, places where dreary human storage units didn't make up the skyline. I also wanted to see the blogger Big Pharaoh again. I liked the guy, and his pessimistic view of the place more or less lined up with mine. So we met at my hotel and took the subway as near as we could to Khan el-Khalili, the ancient souk near the Fatimid walls of the old city.

We got off the subway a half-mile or so from our destination and walked through a concrete catastrophe of a neighborhood on the way. Most storefronts were either closed permanently or shut behind grimy metal gates that pulled down in front of the entrances like garage doors.

"Don't eat anything from these guys," Big Pharaoh said as he gestured to a man selling food that was spread out on a rickety outdoor table. "If you eat that, you'll *die*."

"I'll *die*?" I said. "From what?"

"From a horrible disease."

I'm sure he exaggerated, but I duly noted his warning.

"We're coming up to the place where a bomb went off earlier this year," he said. "Are you okay with that?"

"I live in Beirut," I reminded him.

"Are you sure?" he said.

"Yeah, I'm sure," I said and laughed. "It's not going to explode again. Who planted it, anyway? Al-Qaeda?"

"Some guy in an extremist organization. Don't worry, everyone hates them."

He complained about how some parts of Cairo that used to be beautiful became squalid, in particular one area where derelict European-style architectural wonders were blanked out by an octopus of freeway on- and off-ramps.

"May God damn Nasser in hell all over again!" Big Pharaoh said.

"Plenty of countries built ugly crap like that after World War II," I said. "It wasn't just Nasser. I know what you mean, though. Even most Westerners have no idea how badly he ruined this place."

"Some of them love charismatic dictators," he said. "Like Castro and Qaddafi."

"Qaddafi is only charismatic if you're outside Libya," I said. "Inside he has all the charisma and charm of a serial killer."

Nasser wasn't as bad as the mad scientist ruling Tripoli. No doubt about it: Egypt was in far better shape than Libya. Egypt had people who could say what they wanted without being yanked from their beds in the night, as long as they didn't act on their opinions in public. Egypt had intellectuals. Egypt had art. Egypt had opera. Egypt had restaurants with menus. Most Egyptians didn't partake of Cairo's high culture, but at least it *existed*. In Libya it did not. Not under Qaddafi. He wouldn't allow it.

We walked past an old mosque set 15 feet below street level, built by Sharf el-Din and his brother in 1317–37 A.D. Just in front of the entrance was a de facto courtyard of sorts created by the walls of the two buildings next to it on either side. The entrance was shut, and the lights set up to illuminate it were turned off. This mosque, unlike most, had no minarets.

I walked down the stairs and tried to open the slender wooden doors in case they were open. They weren't. Just to the right of the entrance was a plaque identifying the mosque as Monument Number 176.

You can spend a lot of time gawking at extraordinarily well-preserved monuments if that's what you're looking for in Egypt on holiday. Cairo suddenly seemed a better tourist attraction that I had so far given it credit for. The city as a whole is pretty shabby, but Beirut—which is in much better shape—is effectively only 150 years old. It lacks the sense of history and wonder that Cairo, dumpy as it is, can rightfully boast.

Big Pharaoh and I continued walking toward the old market on a busted-up sidewalk walled off from four lanes of traffic by a metal fence that looked like a 5-foot-tall mile-long bicycle rack. Shuttered and boarded-up storefronts eventually fell away and were replaced by brilliantly illuminated shops selling all manner of oriental art, jewelry, housewares and textiles.

On our left was an 800-year-old Shia mosque built by al-Saleh Talai in 1160 A.D. (This one was Monument Number 116.) Marble Roman-style columns flanked the entrance below a classical Islamic arch. The doors of this mosque were made of tarnished hammered metal and looked original. It appeared to be in pristine condition, at least on the outside, for such an old building. I thought of an old saying about Europe and the United States, where Egypt can stand in for Europe. In Europe (and Egypt), 100 miles is a long way. In America, 100 years is a long time.

"You see those men in white robes and white hats?" Big Pharaoh said and pointed with his eyes toward two traditionally dressed men crossing the street. "They are Shias from India who moved here with Sadat's permission to live next to the Fatimid mosques and take care of them."

The Fatimids founded Cairo and built the oldest remnants in the historic center. Some parts of the ancient city walls still remain, along with an enormous metal door—impenetrable by medieval armies—at one of the gates.

"Khan el-Khalili is just up ahead," Big Pharaoh said. "You will love it. It is very exotic."

"Is it exotic to you?" I said.

"No," he said. "But it will be exotic to you."

I'd spent enough time in Arab countries by then that the exoticism had worn off, but I could still appreciate it. Khan el-Khalili is exactly, precisely, what I always imagined the Middle East would look like before I went there. Shopping—or buying things, I should say—never interested me much, but getting lost in the twisting narrow streets while gawking at gold, silver, hookahs, spices, jewelry, antiques and dramatically colored bolts of cloth reminds me that I was far from home and that I should savor my time while I could.

Some of the hustling shopkeepers could be endearing and entertaining when they weren't annoying.

"Welcome to my country!"

"How can I take your money from you?"

"I don't cheat as much as the others!"

Neither of us wanted to buy anything, though, so we set off for food.

I saw small birds the size of my fist being roasted by an ancient man at a food cart.

"Do you know what those are?" Big Pharaoh said. They looked like tiny chickens.

"Nope," I said.

"They're pigeons," he said. "They are stuffed. The cooks stuff rice—" he broke off laughing. "They stuff rice up its ass."

"Do you want a kebab?" the cart owner asked. "A pigeon kebab?"

"No, thank you," I said and walked on.

"We don't waste food in Egypt," Big Pharaoh said. "We eat every part of the cow here." That seems to be the case almost everywhere in the world except in the U.S. and Canada. "We eat the brains, the testicles and even the eyeballs. But I have *never* eaten an eyeball." Every man has his limits. "And I never will." He didn't mention testicles one way or the other.

"The brains are delicious," he said. "You would love it!"

Perhaps. But neither of us particularly wanted bovine noodle for dinner that night. So he took me instead to a restaurant called Egyptian Pancake near the entrance to Khan el-Khalili.

"This is the best pancake place in all of Egypt," he said.

Egyptian pancakes are more like slabs of thick pita bread than the breakfast fare in the United States. I ordered mine stuffed with white cheese and tomatoes. Big Pharaoh ordered his stuffed with beef. We ate at an outdoor table and talked about travel.

"I went to the Greek side of Cyprus when I was 5," he said.

"I didn't like the Greek side of Cyprus," I said. "The Turkish side is more interesting. The Greek side has no identity. It's like a gigantic outdoor frat house for British louts on a budget. It could be anywhere. If I flew all the way across the world just to go there, I would be pissed."

"I got lost on the beach," he said. "I was 5 years old. I remember screaming for my mother, and of course I was screaming in Arabic. I went up to all these Greeks asking if they had seen my mother, tears streaming down my face, and none of them understood me. I remember thinking, Well, I am going to spend the rest of my life here in Cyprus."

"Obviously your parents found you," I said.

"My father found me, and I ran up to him and hugged him like crazy."

"Where else have you been?" I said.

"Bulgaria," he said.

"I would love to visit Bulgaria," I said.

"I went there when it was communist," he said and laughed. "Communist Bulgaria! It was bad. My father didn't make as much money then as he does now. So when we wanted to go on vacation, all we could afford was a communist country."

We both thought that was funny. But, hey, I was willing to visit a communist country. I went to Libya, for God's sake, when I could have gone to Prague.

"Bulgaria is beautiful, though," he said. "The mountains, the forests, amazing. We went to a place called Butterfly Island. It is the most beautiful place I have ever seen. In the spring, the entire island is covered in butterflies." He made sweeping gestures with both his arms. "I had not even heard of it until my family went there."

I had not heard of it until he told me about it.

"What's the best trip abroad you ever took?" I said.

"My best trip ever was to Los Angeles. I was in heaven! When my family came home and the plane touched down in Egypt, my sister wept." He drew lines down his cheeks with his fingers. "She wept."

Nine

The Road Up IED Alley

Mushadah, Iraq 2008

"Al-Qaeda terrifies the locals," said Major Mike Garcia before he put me in a convoy of Humvees with 18 American military police (MP) on their way to the small town of Mushadah, just north of Baghdad. "The only people Iraqis may be more afraid of is their mothers. When we arrest or detain people and threaten to call up their mom, they completely freak out. 'Please, no, don't tell my mother,' they say. Women are quiet outside the house, but they severely smack down their bad kids inside the house. When your Iraqi mother tells you to knock something off, you knock it off."

The American military has slowly figured out how to leverage Iraq's culture to its advantage, but only to an extent. Locating, killing, capturing and interrogating terrorists and insurgents is the easy part. The hard part is training Iraqis to do it themselves.

Our destination in Mushadah was the local police station, where American military police officers train and equip Iraqi police officers and where it's still too dangerous for either Iraqis or Americans to walk on the streets.

"I am not trying to scare you," said Captain Maryanne Naro. "But don't get out of your vehicle unless something catastrophic has happened to it."

I walked the streets of Baghdad every day with soldiers from the 82nd Airborne Division, but that clearly wasn't going to happen in Mushadah.

"It's pretty bad up there," she added. "AQI [al-Qaeda in Iraq] is all over the area because they've been pushed out of Baghdad, Ramadi and Fallujah."

Just driving to Mushadah from the base at Camp Taji was dangerous in a weird sort of way.

"Our convoys are hit with IEDs every day on the road," she said.

I swallowed hard. "Should I really be going up there?" I said.

"Oh, don't worry," she said. "It's fine."

I laughed. *It's fine*? How is that fine? Nothing, except perhaps the kidnappers, is scarier in Iraq than IEDs, especially now that Iranian-manufactured armor-piercing EFPs—explosively formed penetrators—are deployed by Shia militias.

"None of us have been hurt," she said. "They're just small harassment attacks. Most of the IEDs are mortar rounds, and the Humvees are armored. They usually just pop tires and blow off our mirrors. They do it to piss us off."

"The route-clearance team is out there right now," mission leader Sergeant James Babcock said as he showed me which of the five Humvees I was to ride in.

Mine was in the middle of the convoy. The Humvee behind mine was recently hit with an IED.

"That shrapnel can't go through the armor," Sergeant Babcock said when he saw me taking a photograph of the damage. "The doors are armored and the windows are bulletproof. All that shrapnel did was tear holes in the trunk and rip through cases of Gatorade. It was kind of annoying."

"No one fires off EFPs in the area?" I said, referring to the unstoppable molten copper penetrators.

"Nah," he said. "It's just al-Qaeda here."

We saddled up, left the base and drove north. Everyone locked and loaded their weapons on the way out of the gate.

"Hopefully we won't have any fireworks for you today," my driver said.

Well, I thought, it certainly would be *interesting* if there are some fireworks for me today. Not every Humvee in Iraq is up-armored, and not every IED-laced road in Iraq is free of those terrifying EFPs. And so, I figured, if I'm ever going to be hit with an IED, this would be the best day.

It was a strange feeling, a bit like being in a shark cage—inches away from mortal peril, but kinda sorta okay ... as long as an IED didn't explode *under* the vehicle.

"AQI always puts the IEDs in the same places on this road, in culverts and holes they already dug," Captain Naro said. "We just swerve around them."

"Are they stupid?" I said.

She gave me a look, as if the question was a little too cocky, that it was dangerous to dismiss al-Qaeda as stupid. I agree in general, of course, but I can't help but think that putting IEDs in the same places over and over again isn't too bright.

Getting into a Humvee with the Army in a war zone can be a little bit stressful all by itself. The ranking officer inside often reminds everyone else of the safety procedures—which are not at all like the safety procedures you'll hear from a stewardess on United Airlines just before takeoff.

"Combat lock!" he might yell, which means everyone must lock their door so no one can open it from the outside and shoot people inside.

"Everybody remember what to do if someone throws a grenade in the truck?"

No, I did not remember. It is not something anyone ever taught me.

"Yell 'Grenade grenade grenade!' and get the hell out as quickly as possible. If you don't have time to get out, turn your back to the blast and hope for the best."

Fast-moving targets are harder to hit. And because the IEDs don't explode on their own, the odds of any Humvee in particular being hit were no greater or less than the odds of any other Humvee being hit. Riding in the front of the convoy was no more dangerous than riding anywhere else. And riding in the middle or in the rear wasn't safer. Of course that didn't stop me from trying to convince myself that I rode in the lucky Humvee that wouldn't be hit for some reason.

There weren't any fireworks that day, at least not against my convoy. But we still weren't safe once we reached the police station.

"Get inside," Sergeant Anthony Doucet said to me when we stepped out of the Humvees. "This place is a mortar magnet."

Every place in Iraq is hot during the summer, but the Mushadah police station was merciless. Only two rooms had air conditioning. The rest were miserable sweatboxes.

Captain Maryanne Naro was supposed to join us, but she had to remain at Camp Taji. That was too bad. I was hoping to see how Iraqi police officers interacted in person with an American woman who outranked almost all of them.

"The police won't leave the station," Major Garcia had told me, "unless Americans are there to protect them. They wouldn't leave under any circumstances until Captain Naro showed up and was willing to go out on patrol. They were ashamed that a woman had more guts than they did."

"They will go out alone now for something real basic," she said. "Otherwise, if Americans aren't with them, they'll hide in the station. They're hard to work with at times, like they're kids."

Incompetence, though, is the least of their problems.

"About half of them are corrupted," she said, "and it's hard to get the bad ones out. Some of the higher-ups are corrupted too, but it's hard to prove. They help al-Qaeda, they set up illegal checkpoints, and they raid civilian houses so they can steal stuff."

Not surprising then, local civilians are just as afraid of the police as the uncorrupted police are afraid of the neighborhood.

"Locals come in here all the time and talk to Americans," she told me. "They're afraid to give intel to the Iraqi police."

Mushadah is a bad area with bad police and a bad police station. The building itself is filthy and ramshackle. The stairs to the second floor are murderously uneven, not because they've been damaged but because they were built by incompetents. I've seen dodgy construction in Iraq—even at Saddam's palaces, believe it or not—but this station was the worst. I'll spare you a description of the bathroom, but I was warned in no uncertain terms not to touch anything.

A high wall surrounded and protected the station, but one side had recently been destroyed by a mortar round. A spring windstorm had blown down the wall on the south side.

The whole place was almost destroyed not long ago. An al-Qaeda suicide bomber filled a dump truck with explosives and tried to ram it into the building, but the whole thing tipped over when he drove too fast around a corner. He would have killed everyone inside had he succeeded.

Sergeant Doucet led me to the front door from the inside so I could photograph some of the Iraqi police standing at attention.

"How many of these guys do you suppose are al-Qaeda infiltrators?" I said. I just couldn't look at them without wondering.

"I don't know," he said. "We speculate about it. We don't investigate them or anything like that."

"You *don't*?" I said. "Why not?"

"We aren't passive about it," he said. "If we suspect someone has gone over the edge, he'll raise a red flag and we'll deal with it."

"How much support do you get from local civilians?" I said.

"Locals bring in tips against bad guys all the time," he said. "Several times a week. What they tell us is not very tangible, though. Sometimes it's useless. Someone will come in here and scream, 'There's bad guys out there!' We'll ask where. 'To the west!' they'll say. Well, no crap."

"Residents are still afraid to give intel on bad guys," he continued. "Insurgents will kill them if they do. The area is totally unsecured. Even if we question people who live right in front of an IED trigger point, they won't say anything. But, look, forget what you see on the news.

People in this community are just like people in any other community. This guy is pissed off at that guy, and you have to deal with it."

I've been in parts of Iraq where local civilians cooperate with the Army and police and where they do not. Civilians cooperate as much as security on the streets will permit them. The dynamic here isn't all that hard to understand, or even that foreign. If you want to see how this has played out in America, watch Elia Kazan's *On the Waterfront*, the classic film from 1954 starring Marlon Brando about the mafia's infiltration of a longshoreman's union. No one in that story wanted to cooperate with the police in their murder investigations against the mob because they were terrified that they would be "next" if they did.

"We have a medical facility here," Sergeant Doucet said. "Local civilians can come here and use it, and they do."

They did while I was there. A three-year-old boy was badly burned at his house—how, I don't know—and he was brought in to be treated by a medic.

I let the medic tend to the boy and stepped into the tactical operations center, one of only two rooms in the station that had air conditioning.

"Hello again, sir," Sergeant Babcock said and pulled up a chair for me. He then gave me more background and asked me not to take pictures of anything in that room.

"Lots of Iraqi police here had orders to work in Baghdad," he said, "but they refused. They are Sunnis. This is a Sunni area. Baghdad, as you know, is mostly Shia. Their names and license plates mark them for death. They work here but are counted as AWOL and are not being paid."

Some of the Iraqi police are honorable men. (And they are all men.) I don't want to leave you with the impression that all of them are terrorist infiltrators. They aren't.

"Because of logistics problems, we have to go to Baghdad for fuel," Sergeant Babcock said, "and we have to go to a Shia area. It's very dangerous for them and they ask us to go with them. They have problems getting ammo as well. There are always problems with ammo."

And there are severe problems with other stations.

"The Taramiyah station was hit by insurgents earlier this spring," he said. "It was completely destroyed. Only six officers from that station are brave enough to come to work here."

A poster on the wall caught my eye. It showed a grainy photograph of an AK-47 and a masked man who looked like a terrorist. "Citizens of Iraq," the poster read. "Effective immediately: Any weapons carried or displayed in public will be confiscated by Security Forces. This weapons confiscation plan has been endorsed by the Prime Minister. This is for the safety of you, your family and the citizens of Iraq."

Sergeant Babcock introduced me to the man in charge of the station, Captain J. Dow Covey from New York City.

"Do you know the *Weekly Standard* magazine?" Captain Covey asked me.

"Of course," I said.

"My buddy Tom Cotton was just written up there," he said. "It was pretty cool seeing him in that magazine."

"What did he do to get in the magazine?" I said.

"He's like me," he said. "He's a Harvard Law grad who joined the Army after 9/11. I'm an attorney."

"You're an *attorney*?" I said. "What are you doing out here in Iraq?"

"I practiced law for three years," he said, "then got into investment banking. When 9/11 happened, I just had to sign up with the Army. Investment banking is a lot more stressful than this."

"You're kidding, right?" I said.

"No," he said and laughed. "I am totally serious."

If he was deployed in, say, Kurdistan, I could see it. But Mushadah was stressful. Less stressful than investment banking? Investment banking in New York must really be something.

Not much happened the first half of my day at the station, so I lounged with the MPs in their broiling quarters. None had anything positive to say about the Iraqi police they were training.

"What can you really ask for in a lazy society? You go in their houses and the floors are covered in pillows."

"You can tell who is corrupt because their convoys *never* get hit."

"This place wouldn't be so bad if it wasn't so fucking hot. I can deal with being shot at and blown up, but 150 degrees is a bit much."

"Some Iraqi police recently left the station, we got hit with a bunch of mortars, then they came right back inside. This sort of thing happens a lot. It makes us suspicious."

"We're giving them 50,000 Chevy trucks, and it's like a junkyard out back. It's like *Sanford and Son* out there. They drive stuff better than we can afford, and they don't even take care of it."

"I miss Baghdad. One day we'd be walking out on the street buying sandwiches and playing soccer with kids. The next day we'd get in a firefight with burning tires and RPGs and shit. The next day we'd be hanging out and chilling like normal again. It's a weird place and really keeps you on your toes."

"It's not like Germany or Japan, where people wanted a change. The Kurds up north wanted a change, so they got one. The Arabs don't, so they aren't. They hardly change even with *us* here."

The Iraqi army in the area isn't faring much better.

"They are severely infiltrated by al-Qaeda and the Mahdi Army," Colonel John Steele told me back at Camp Taji.

The Iraqi army soldiers who aren't double agents are still nowhere near ready to defend their own country.

"We assess, train and help provide logistical support to prevent catastrophic failure," he said. "Their logistics are very immature. They are always short on ammo. And we have to hold their hands and make sure they don't kill themselves and others. We still do some unilateral U.S. actions even though we want to become partnered with the Iraqi army in all our operations. But we first want to make sure they have all the skills they need to survive in combat."

Most American soldiers I spoke to about the Iraqi army and Iraqi police—not just in Mushadah but also in Baghdad—have a dim view of their local counterparts. I wanted to know what the colonel thought.

"Do you trust them?" I said.

He paused for a long time and answered very carefully.

"We won't tell them about sensitive operations until the last second," he said. "I trust some individuals, though, because I know them. I'd share a foxhole with them as far as ideology goes, but I'm not sure how good their skills are when they are shot."

Pride is much more important in Arab culture than it is in the West. Humiliation is therefore more painful. I wondered if this created problems when Americans train Iraqi soldiers and police officers. What must it feel like for local men to be yelled at by foreigners who showed up uninvited and knew their job better than they did?

Colonel Steele insists it isn't a problem.

"They don't want to be babied," he said. "They want to be treated as equals and adults. Their shame culture actually helps. Our new recruits recently complained about having sore feet during a march. When they noticed our female soldiers are in better shape than they are, they never complained again. Also, when we first had them try on our body armor, it nearly broke their spines. They want to be physically capable of wearing it too."

It's at least possible that some of the infiltrators may be turned over time. Some former insurgents elsewhere in Iraq are now openly siding with the Americans.

There's also this: "We give them rudimentary skills and a work ethic," he told me. "They attend the same classes on character and honor and professional conduct becoming a soldier that our own people attend."

Is he optimistic? "I am optimistic," he said. "But only for one single reason. Because I talk to the average Joe in Iraq. I meet the children and parents. Iraqi parents love their children as much as I love mine."

Sergeant Babcock invited me to a meeting with Iraqi police Colonel Hameed, the man who was responsible for the station on the Iraqi side.

Sergeant Babcock, Sergeant Doucet, an interpreter, the colonel and I sat together in the only other room at the station that had air conditioning.

"You are most welcome," the colonel said to me in an obviously insincere tone of voice. Some of the MPs think he's corrupt. I don't know if that means they think he works with al-Qaeda.

"Thank you," I said. "May I take your picture?"

"No," he said, "please don't." It didn't sound like he actually cared, though, as if he was only pretending to need protection from terrorists.

He and the American MPs discussed fuel logistics.

"The only reason the Iraqi police got fuel on the last mission," he said, "is because you were with us. Otherwise they wouldn't have given us anything."

Suddenly Captain Covey, the New York City attorney, nearly broke down the door as he barged into the room.

"Hey!" he screamed at the colonel. "I'm tired of you motherfuckers stealing our fuel cans. I'm going to kick *all* you motherfuckers out of here. I'm sorry for interrupting your little meeting, but at noon I want every single one of you people *off* this post." He stared at the interpreter. "Translate that!" he said.

He slammed the door behind him. Everyone looked at each other. A quietly horrified expression washed over the face of the colonel when he saw me taking notes.

The meeting was over, obviously. I stepped into the hallway and asked the nearest MP what was going on.

"Sixty-one fuel cans have been stolen over the last week by Iraqi police officers here," he said. "Three more were stolen today. These are fuel cans that Iraqis and Americans risk their lives to go get."

The tension in the hallway was palpable. None of the Iraqis could look me in the eye.

"Can the captain really kick the Iraqis out of here?" I asked Sergeant Babcock.

"Actually, he can," he said. He sounded mortified at the idea.

Colonel Hameed walked up to Sergeant Babcock. He was furious.

"Your captain offended us by coming in here and yelling like that," he said. "I need you to find a solution."

"I'm a staff sergeant," Sergeant Babcock said. "He's a captain. I'm also an MP and he's infantry. I have to obey him, whether I like it or not."

"This station does not belong to his family," the colonel said curtly. "This is unacceptable. The building is ours, and he is our guest. A guest cannot fire the owner of the house."

"We'll go talk to him and come back," Sergeant Babcock said.

As it turned out, the whole thing was a screwup. Somebody forgot to update the board and account for three fuel cans that were taken legitimately.

Captain Covey was embarrassed.

"Would you really have kicked them all out of here?" I said.

"In the state of mind I was in then, yes," he said. "I was ready to do it. But I calmed down and would have gotten in trouble anyway. So no, I wouldn't have actually done it."

Sixty-one fuel cans really had been stolen earlier in the week, however. The Iraqi police were in serious trouble.

Another Iraqi police colonel, whose name I did not catch and who no one thinks is corrupt, arrived on the scene and yelled himself hoarse at his deputies.

"Coalition Forces are screaming at us!" he hollered. "Screaming at us because *you* keep stealing fuel!"

He kicked an empty metal garbage can and knocked it clanging to the floor. The Iraqi police officers glowered at him as if they wanted to scream back and were trying mightily to restrain themselves.

An American MP walked past me. "That's the first time I've seen those guys yelled at," he said and grinned with satisfaction.

Shortly after noon, an international police adviser from Michigan named Paul taught an hour-long class to the Iraqis about how to take weapons from potentially dangerous people who are under arrest. The officers seemed to learn as much sitting through that course as I did. Apparently they had never gone over the procedures before.

I couldn't help wondering as I watched the Iraqis: Which of you work for al-Qaeda?

Maybe none of them did. I don't have a sense of how many infiltrators there actually are, although Captain Naro thinks the number could be as high as 50 percent.

"Please don't publish my picture," Paul said to me after the class. "And use only my first name. Only my wife knows I'm in Iraq."

I wanted to know what he thought of the trainees. He has trained police officers in not only Iraq and the United States but all over the world. He could, perhaps, see them through more worldly eyes than the American MPs, who had a narrower range of experience.

"They've made leaps and bounds in the past two months," he said. "Every day they make progress. Today they made progress."

"Are you optimistic about them?" I said.

"Oh, absolutely," he said. "The Iraqi police are like sponges. It's all new to them."

"Lots of American soldiers I've talked to about the Iraqi army and Iraqi police don't think very highly of them," I said.

"Look," he said. "The other contractors I know who train the police are also optimistic. Many file extensions to stay longer because they feel like they're making a difference. I never hear anything negative from any of them. We watch the Iraqis progress over time because we work with them daily. Most American soldiers don't see the progress, because they observe the Iraqis from more of a distance. You yourself are only seeing a snapshot in time. If you think it looks bad now, you should have been here two months ago."

It was time to head back to Camp Taji. The MPs and I saddled up in our Humvees while, in front of us, Iraqi police officers piled into their trucks. We would escort them out of the station, then they would be on their own. They were going out alone, apparently for something "real basic," as Captain Naro had told me.

The Iraqi police truck in front of my Humvee had an office swivel chair crazily bolted into the flatbed. A policeman strapped himself into that and manned a mounted machine gun.

"Is he really going out all exposed like that?" I said.

"He is," Sergeant Babcock said. "I can't quite decide if that's pathetic or if it's a testament to the human spirit. Maybe it's a little of both."

We drove back down IED Alley to Camp Taji. It was four in the afternoon and so unbearably hot. The air conditioner in the Humvee hardly did anything. I desperately wanted a shower so I could wash Iraq off my skin.

Nothing exploded on our way back.

Major Garcia wanted to know what I thought. I didn't know what to say.

"Whether we like it or not," he said, "and whether we like them or not, they are the future of this country."

Ten

Ho Chi Minh's Nightmare

Hanoi, Vietnam 2014

During the 1970s, Vietnam's capital, Hanoi, was a bombed-out disasterscape overseen by grim ideologues who seized power after forcing out the ruling French imperialists. They imposed an egalitarian reign of terror, imprisoned dissidents, executed tens of thousands of "rich" people and landlords and waged a brutal war against their American-backed countrymen in the south. The once lovely French buildings were falling apart. Older Vietnamese homes looked even shabbier. People queued up in long lines past government stores with bare shelves to exchange ration coupons for meager handfuls of rice. Citizens were not allowed to socialize with or even speak to foreign visitors—not that many showed up. The only traffic on the street was the occasional bicycle.

In the summer of 2014, Hanoi was an explosive capitalist volcano. Though it is still developing—Vietnam was a Second World nation, if you will—on just my ride in from the airport, before I even reached my hotel, I saw factories, malls, high-rises, energy-production facilities and infrastructure projects, including the construction of an enormous new terminal at the airport that will almost double the capacity to 10 million annual passengers. I could tell within minutes that Hanoi has transformed itself more dramatically than almost any other city in the world during my lifetime. Once a closed and paranoid backwater, it looked and felt like a free country even though it was not, and it was rapidly on its way to becoming a formidable economic and military power.

"Many revolutions are begun by conservatives," Christopher Hitchens said, paraphrasing John Maynard Keynes, in an interview with *Reason* magazine, "because those are people who tried to make the existing system work and they know why it does not. Which is quite a profound insight. It used to be known in Marx's terms as revolution from above."

That's exactly what happened in Vietnam, although this time the revolutionaries weren't conservatives. They were communists.

Hanoi had a rough 20th century. The French invaded and made it the capital of colonial French Indochina in 1887. The Empire of Japan seized the city in 1940 and annexed Vietnam to its brutally fascistic Greater East Asia Co-Prosperity Sphere. Ho Chi Minh declared Vietnam an independent state after the end of World War II, and his Viet Minh forces controlled a few scraps of territory, but the French returned in force in 1946 and didn't leave until Ho's communist army forced them out in 1954. Hanoi then became the capital of the misnamed Democratic Republic of North Vietnam.

Decades passed in squalor and brutality. Ho's centrally planned Marxist-Leninist system ravaged the economy, and war with the United States and the American-backed government of South Vietnam—which included aerial bombardment of Hanoi itself—made the devastation all but complete. More than a million Vietnamese died.

The North Vietnamese won their civil war in 1975 and imposed the same draconian economic and political system on the south, but by that time it had already proved itself disastrous. "Nothing had been repaired in years," reporter David Lamb wrote of the city in the 1970s. "The old French colonial buildings appeared in danger of collapse. Everything was in a state of poverty and decay."

The south's former capital Saigon suffered at once when the north took over. "All the schools were shut down," said southerner Tuong Vi Lam, who vividly remembered when her side lost the war. "My aunts and uncles were in college, and they had to quit. They just couldn't get there. Property was confiscated and given to northerners. Communist propaganda was even put in our math books. We had questions like this: 'Yesterday a soldier killed three Americans and today he killed five. How many Americans did he kill total?' The books don't have those kinds of questions anymore, but they did for five or 10 years."

Vietnam was finally independent and unified, but it fared no better than the Soviet Union, North Korea or Cuba, and almost everyone knew it, including plenty in the communist leadership itself.

In the mid-1980s, a fight broke out in the party between those who wanted to continue with the old system and those who had already benefited from quiet microcapitalist reforms in 1979. Southerners made noise about returning to the precommunist system that they knew from personal experience worked so much better. The relative economic success of other Southeast Asian nations, especially Thailand, was obvious even to the ideologues.

So the reformers won the argument, and in 1986 the government officially abandoned Marxist-Leninist economics and announced the Doi Moi reforms, defined as its attempt to create a "socialist-oriented market economy." Presumably, party leaders left the word *socialist* in there because they were embarrassed by the failures of Marxism. Or perhaps they feared that their supporters—however many they still actually had—were allergic to the word *capitalism*. Maybe they just had to save face and couldn't admit to the subjects they lorded over that they'd been wrong about everything. No matter. Vietnam officially junked communism a mere 11 years after winning the civil war and imposing it on South Vietnam.

State subsidies were abolished. Private businesses were allowed to operate again. Farmers could sell their produce on the open market and keep the proceeds instead of giving them up to the state. The results were spectacular: Before Doi Moi, the command economy contracted and inflation topped out at over 700 percent, but it later dropped to single digits. After years of chronic rice shortages, Vietnam became the world's second largest exporter of rice, after Thailand. In 2013 the economy grew by 8.25 percent, compared with less than two percent in the United States.

"The number of malls, shopping districts and restaurants is amazing compared with when I was a kid," said motivational speaker Hoan Do. "Eighteen years ago the entire country was broken down. There was hardly any technology, but now even poor people can go to an Internet café and log onto Facebook and YouTube."

The United States didn't normalize diplomatic relations until 1995, so American companies were late foreign investors, but their presence was obvious by the time I got there. It was impossible to miss the Starbucks, KFC, Pizza Hut and Burger King franchises. General Motors, Dell, Visa, General Electric and countless others, including clothing and footwear manufacturers, invested there too. The Vietnamese wanted and expected even more and hoped to soon get it with the Trans-Pacific Partnership (TPP) with 11 Pacific Rim nations that would pry loose outdated bureaucratic trade obstacles on all sides while at the same time enforcing labor standards, environmental protections and intellectual-property rights.

Vietnam even had its own high-tech start-ups. "The incubation and funding of tech start-ups is still a fragmented segment of our economy," said Nguyen Pham, founder of the start-up incubator 5desire, "but we're working on streamlining the process and modeling it rigorously after those in Silicon Valley. We organize technology events that attract world-class foreign speakers and investors. One of our notable events was Hackathon Vietnam 2014 in August, where we partnered with Formation 8, a well-known venture-capitalist firm from Silicon Valley, and the Ministry of Science and Technology in Vietnam. More than 1,000 people attended, more than 60 percent of them developers. Joe Lonsdale, co-founder of Palantir Technologies and managing partner of Formation 8, has spoken at our events, as have Ngo Bao Chau, mathematics professor from the University of Chicago, and Jonah Levey, the CEO and co-founder of Vietnamworks."

Vietnam's transformation was entirely the result of the government's surrendering to reality, scrapping the ration system and letting people buy and sell what they want. It took some time for a middle class to emerge, but in just 11 short years, from 1993 to 2004, the percentage of Vietnamese living in poverty dropped from 60 percent to 20 percent. Businessmen, investors and employees could keep their profits and wages and prosper on their own, not despite the fact that they weren't being micromanaged but *because* they weren't being micromanaged. The only thing stopping a similar economic explosion in Havana was the Castro regime's control freakery. Cuba's president Raúl Castro was easing up a *little* bit from his brother Fidel's brutal rigidity, but it would be a long time indeed before Havana looks like Hanoi, even if Raúl were to convert to libertarianism at once.

Hanoi appeared to take naturally to capitalism and business, but this was all a recent development. Saigon (which the government renamed Ho Chi Minh City in 1975) was considerably wealthier. "When the communist leadership decided in the mid-1980s to put Karl Marx and Adam Smith into an economic blender and see what came out," Lamb wrote, "Southerners, exposed to capitalism for decades, were far more comfortable than their northern brethren in adapting to the demands of free markets."

Saigon remained capitalist through 1975, whereas Ho Chi Minh and his cadre imposed communism on Hanoi more than a generation earlier. Soviet-style economic imbecility didn't last long enough in the south for business and economics to fall out of living memory as they did in the Soviet Union, North Korea and Cuba.

Hanoi took longer to open up and prosper after Doi Moi for two reasons—and it still lagged behind Saigon despite the breathtaking progress. Initially, the communists-turned-capitalists wanted Saigon to be the business capital, and they would simply sit around while the money flowed from the south to the north. Let the southerners do all the work; the north could benefit almost as much, albeit indirectly through taxes. Though Hanoi eventually and more slowly liberalized too, the economic opening followed a much longer period of command economics. Visit Hanoi for yourself, though, and you'll see no evidence that this was the case. Both citizens and state figured out how to thrive in the meantime, as if they'd been doing it all along. Some nations and peoples are just faster learners than others.

Hanoi assaulted all five senses. The streets smelled of fried food, incense, barbecue, mold and exhaust, sometimes all at once. The sounds of growling motorbike engines and banging construction were endless, and they were punctuated by vehicle-mounted loudspeakers announcing God-knows-what all day.

And the climate: God, it is horrendous during the summer.

The sky was white the day I arrived, the city almost foggy like Seattle in January, but the ambient air temperature outside was 99 degrees Fahrenheit with 108 percent humidity. Air-conditioning units dripped so much moisture onto the sidewalks that it appeared as though rain had recently fallen. After just five minutes outside, I felt like I'd been hosed down with hot water. Wearing any clothing at all was unbearable. I wanted to crawl into a freezer. Yet the locals zoomed by on motorbikes, many wearing jackets and gloves, oblivious to or at least remarkably tolerant of the sauna-like weather.

Hanoi was exhausting in the heat, but it was the opposite of boring. The city burst with frenetic activity, especially economic activity.

Luxury boutiques, technology stores selling Apple products, high-fashion clothing outlets and international food chains were easy enough to find, but Hanoi was overwhelmingly dominated by individual street-front proprietorships. Half the population seemed to have gone into business for themselves. Some of the largest companies were still owned or controlled by the state, but the vast majority were too small to be centrally managed. The economy looked and felt entirely unregulated.

On a single block alone I saw the following for sale: Vietnamese flags, Ho Chi Minh T-shirts for tourists, candles, incense, bolts of cloth, used clothing from the U.S., fake money to burn in offerings to ancestors, *Angry Birds* toys, exotic fruit I don't even know the names of, meat skewers, pho, iPhones, tea, jewelry, Italian shoes, French pastries, spices, herbs, motorcycle helmets, bootleg CDs, bootleg cigarettes, Japanese barbecue, carpets, funeral boxes, silk, paintings and bootleg paperbacks with misspelled blurbs on the back.

Women wearing conical hats roamed the city selling fruit, fried pastries and other items to passersby. They congregated around pagodas and tourist sites. I stopped an elderly vendor and asked for a small portion of what looked like Vietnam's version of doughnuts. The woman smiled and placed a handful in a plastic bag and said, "200,000 dong."

That was ten dollars. For a fistful of fried bread.

I laughed.

"Come on," I said.

Vietnam was not an expensive country. I didn't know what she would have charged a local person, but surely much less than ten dollars. She thought I was rich and therefore wouldn't mind paying so much, but I was nowhere near rich, at least not by Western standards. (Only a lucky few writers ever get rich.)

"200,000 dong," she said again.

"I'll give you 20,000," I said. That was about one dollar and probably more than the locals would have paid.

"200,000," she said again.

Seriously? She wasn't even going to come down to 180,000?

"Forget it," I said and walked away.

That night I paid six dollars for an entire meal plus a bottle of beer, so I knew the lady on the street had tried to drastically overcharge me. I swore not to buy anything that didn't have a price tag on it somewhere.

My waitress that evening correctly sensed that I had just arrived (newcomers are obvious everywhere) and gave me some advice.

"The street sellers," she said, gesturing outside the window with her eyes, "are not good. If you're a foreigner, they'll charge you 10 times what everyone else pays."

Indeed. It had taken me no time at all to figure that out. I appreciated, though, that she was looking out for me. She didn't know me, but she was looking out for me. And she helped me out with the language—which is a pain and a half. The Vietnamese language uses six different vocal tones, and if you're not used to tonal languages, you can easily screw up saying even "hello" and "thank you." A single syllable sound like *Ha* can be made into six different words, depending on which tone you use and which markings you put above or below the letters in writing.

The Vietnamese use a modified version of the Latin alphabet, but it's harder to casually learn a few words and read than that it first appears. You must pay attention to the tone markings, not just the letters, if you want to even begin making sense of it. *Má* and *Mã*, for instance, are not the same word. They look similar, and to my tone-deaf ears they sound exactly the same, but they're different words.

I thanked the waitress for helping me out as best she could with the language, and especially for warning me about scammers prowling the streets, but no one else ever tried to egregiously overcharge me, at least not to my knowledge. Even the taxi drivers used the meter without my having to ask, which was unheard of almost everywhere else I had been in the world. Even European taxi drivers have tried and sometimes succeeded in ripping me off.

Before I left home, I had read all kinds of horror stories on the Internet about scam artists and hasslers of every conceivable variety in Vietnam, but I hardly ran into any of them. I don't know if it's because I got lucky, because I've learned how to not look like a sucker or because the problem was much less severe than it used to be. I didn't know, but I suspected it was the latter. Everything else was changing at rocket-ship speed, so why not the hassling?

After dinner I returned to my room in the busting Old Quarter, flicked off the lights and heard the honking and growling of motorbikes as a bat flew past my window.

I awoke early and jet-lagged the next morning and set out at six to find some relief from the hideous climate. The air outside was 82 degrees Fahrenheit and humid. Hardly ideal, but it certainly beat the 99 degrees of the previous day. At least I could walk around for a *few* minutes before my shirt was soaked through with sweat.

How miserable it must have been fighting a war in that country. They say war is interminable boredom punctuated by moments of sheer terror. I've been to war zones myself and can attest to the truth of that statement, but war in the sticky and sweltering jungles must have been interminable *misery* punctuated by terror.

I was advised to check out Le Mat on the outskirts of the city. There you will find the Snake Village, where you can pull up a barstool and order some snake wine. The bartender will kill a cobra, pour its blood into rice wine and drop the snake's still-beating heart into the shot glass.

If you don't want to drink blood, you can have it with bile instead.

I refused. Why make my stomach churn and possibly heave just so I can write about it? The description of the drink itself was enough. I went to Iraq seven times during the war, but drinking snake wine was over the line. I didn't care whether or not that made sense.

What I wanted was coffee. I was jet-lagged in a bad way, and if I didn't have caffeine I'd need a nap. And if I succumbed to that nap I'd sleep for eight hours, miss most of the day and be up all night when everything was closed. So I headed back toward Hoan Kiem Lake during early business hours, and when a young woman on the sidewalk beckoned me over and told me about a café upstairs, I eagerly agreed to let her show me the way.

She led me inside a building that looked like a parking garage, though nobody parked there. Empty boxes, a discarded broom and other detritus were strewn about. There was a café upstairs? Really? I felt a twinge of uncertainty. What kind of café would be above this? The building looked derelict.

I resisted the twinge of uncertainty. The young woman seemed friendly enough, and she wore a shirt with a café logo on it. I followed her into the elevator. We rode up to the fourth floor, then she pointed toward a rickety-looking stairway leading up to a gloomy fifth floor. The way was unlit, the walls filthy, the air hot and still. I saw no other people and heard no sounds but the traffic outside. I had a hard time believing the kind of café I wanted to hang out in was up there.

If I were anywhere in the West, I would have turned around and gone back to the street, but my instincts were different abroad. I ascended the stairs, feeling curious about what I'd find but doubtful that I would like it.

I reached the top of the sweltering stairway, pushed open a glass door and found myself in a café worthy of South Beach in Miami tucked into an air-conditioned aerie. The place was packed with comfortable sofas and chairs and stylishly dressed Vietnamese with laptops and iPads drinking from cups of Italian-style espresso. The entire south wall was made of glass from floor to ceiling and revealed a 180-degree view of the lake and the skyline below.

Almost everyone in the café was staring at a personal electronic device.

Who during the Vietnam War on either side of the conflict could have imagined that such a bourgeois place would ever appear in Hanoi while the Communist Party still ruled? Ho Chi Minh sure as hell didn't expect this. Nor would he have wanted it. Fidel Castro would have hated it. Of that I assure you. Pol Pot would have wanted to murder everyone in there.

The world was becoming more and more alike everywhere. Outside of basket-case countries like North Korea, Syria and Iraq, we all seemed to be heading in the same direction toward the same destination. And with everyone looking at the little screens in their hands all the time, even while sitting with friends, I had to wonder: Where exactly, as a species, were we going?

Whatever the answer to that question, Hanoi was no longer an impoverished totalitarian backwater. It was a global city now. And despite the name of its government, communism was finished.

The city was friendlier to businesses than many in the United States. I asked a local man who worked for an American company how hard it was for foreigners to invest and go into business there. "The Vietnamese government makes it easy," he said. "Just present them with a business plan, tell them what you want to do, and you're good to go." The same went for small businesses. All you have to do, he says, "is rent the space, pay the taxes, and that's it."

The food was startlingly good for even a nominally communist country. Vietnam was the only place I'd ever visited that has or had a communist government and still had good cuisine, and I'd been to 15 formerly communist countries plus Cuba, which is still communist. I'd rather travel to Eastern Europe than Western Europe for my own reasons, but I couldn't recall a single quality meal I'd ever had in Europe's former communist bloc. Marxism bulldozed restaurants along with everything else, and all industries take time to recover. Chefs in post-communist Europe just hadn't had as much time to master their craft. Cuba's food was still mostly terrible, even though a handful of restaurants were privately owned. The biggest problem there is a chronic shortage of quality ingredients. Yet Vietnam—which is still nominally communist and was actually communist through the mid-'80s—somehow had outstanding food everywhere, even on the street. I don't know if it's more a testament to the ingredients, the cooks or the cuisine itself. Surely it's partly all three.

Although you could eat rat for dinner if you really wanted to. (I didn't want to.)

Prosperity never guarantees an aesthetically pleasing urban environment. To this day, most of Bucharest, Romania, looks like a totalitarian anthill despite belonging to the European Union. Hanoi, though, was nice on the eyes.

The city center is dominated by the charming but chaotic Old Quarter and the more stately and orderly French Quarter just minutes away on foot. Both neighborhoods are anchored by Hoan Kiem Lake, the cultural center of the city. Its name means "Returned Sword," after the weapon the gods supposedly gave Emperor Le Loi in the 15th century, which he used to drive out the invading Chinese.

Hoan Kiem Lake, however, is just the most famous. The entire city sparkles with lakes, and it's studded with an even larger number of ancient Buddhist pagodas with vertical Chinese characters on the walls.

The most exquisite buildings are French and Chinese, but the simpler Vietnamese homes are also delightful. Many look as though the architects mashed Victorian, French, brownstone and Thai architecture together, then squeezed the final product into a vise to make it taller and narrower. (Homes and businesses are taxed by how much width they take up on the street, so narrower is cheaper than fatter.)

The communists were wrong about everything, but at least they elided some of the mistakes made by their comrades elsewhere, in their wars against everything old. Hanoi is blessedly free of an asteroid belt of Soviet-style garbage architecture on the outskirts that blights so many formerly communist cities in Europe. I did see a few soul-crushing structures made of poured concrete here and there, but for the most part this stuff was either never built, has been torn down or has been overwhelmed by an explosion of new and better construction in the meantime. The city *has* grown exponentially in size since the bad days, so perhaps the ugly stuff has just been drowned out. In 1979 the population was less than a million, but today it exceeds 7 million, making Hanoi larger than all but America's three largest cities.

But while much of it looks like a First World city, it sure doesn't feel like one.

"Not in my wildest dreams," said an Australian man I bumped into on holiday, "could I have imagined what an absolute madhouse Hanoi is."

I was a little less shocked after living in Beirut, but I was still shocked. He's right. Hanoi is an absolute madhouse. It is the diametric opposite of dead cities like Havana and—especially—Pyongyang.

The city thunders with a never-ending cacophony of honking, zooming, blaring, shouting, pounding and jackhammering, even late into the evenings. Mostly it thunders with motorbikes.

Only the richest people own cars. Everyone else careens through the streets on mopeds and scooters with little or no regard to traffic signals, speed limits or road courtesy. Crossing the street in the Old Quarter is a terrifying experience. No one will stop for you. They'll go around, sure, but they'll never stop to let you cross—*ever*. Your only option is to pick a direction, pick a speed and step into traffic. Trust that they don't want to hit you any more than you want them to hit you. But if you hesitate or try to dodge them, you'll make yourself an unpredictable hazard. They won't be able to figure out your vector and they'll hit you. You're better off closing your eyes, holding your breath and crossing blind than trying to dodge them. You have to let them go around you. If you lack confidence, just follow a little old lady. I'll admit that I did that myself a couple of times.

Just as shocking as the madness of traffic is the amount of traffic, with mere inches between motorbikes as they pour down the streets like a river of metal and rubber and helmets. The entire surface area of the roads is often covered with them. Late one evening, I overheard an exasperated elderly Englishman wonder aloud to his wife, "Where are all these people going? They can't all be going to work at this hour. They're just riding around."

From the rooftop of a Lebanese restaurant, I watched a group of pedestrians cross a six-lane intersection. Motorbikes furiously swarmed around them at top speed like a whirlpool as they crossed. I anxiously figured the odds that I'd get hit before I left the country approached 50 percent, but it never happened. Nor did I see anyone else get hit.

But the emergency rooms in the hospitals *have* to be busy. I saw a young man ride his motorbike an entire city block while texting on his phone, dodging other traffic using only his peripheral vision. Young women ride "sidesaddle" on the seat behind their boyfriends without holding onto anything. One sudden stop or turn and they'll fly at top speed into traffic. One woman rode past me with a 50-pound dog on the seat behind her trying with all its might not to fall off as she zoomed around town. I even saw a family of five piled onto a scooter. None wore helmets or other protective gear. Who even knows how many laws would be broken simultaneously if a family did that in the U.S.?

Sidewalks in the Old Quarter are obstacle courses of street hawkers, food stalls, elderly ladies selling fried dough and vegetables and people squatting on tiny stools eating dinner. Sometimes there are so many parked bikes in the way that pedestrians have no choice but to wade out into dangerous traffic to get around them.

But in the French Quarter—which in some places looks like an immaculately restored, near perfect copy of France—the sidewalks are clearer, the streets easier to cross. They're wider, so motorbike riders have no choice but to respect the red lights. Not even the Vietnamese can blow lights through huge intersections without getting smashed. (Note to self: Next time you visit Hanoi, stay in the French Quarter.)

I hired a 60-year-old man to show me around and asked if he had a car. "The middle class doesn't have cars yet," he said, adding that he didn't even *know* how to drive. At once I felt ridiculous even for asking. Of course he did not have a car. I had noticed the obvious. Motorbikes make up 99 percent of Vietnam's traffic. It's strange, in a way, since nice houses larger than mine make up a large percentage of the city. Perhaps the middle class would rather spend its money on housing than transportation. But Hanoi is a bit like Manhattan, though it's not remotely as vertical. There's no room on the streets for everyone to have a car. They wouldn't be able to park. They wouldn't be able to *move*. No matter how rich these people become in the future, they can't defeat physics. Urban planners would have to pull down the city and start over before everyone could have a car. The government knows it too and punishes would-be drivers with an almost 200 percent car tax.

Most of these people will be stuck riding motorbikes of one kind or another for the foreseeable future. But it wasn't long ago that most of them rode bicycles. And before that, they walked.

"You should go to the Royal City Mall," a local man told me, "and learn about Vietnam."

A peculiar suggestion. I'd learn about Vietnam by going to a mall? *Really*? I've been to malls all over the world. Most are the same as malls everywhere else. I find them antiseptic and dull and hardly ever visit them when I'm at home.

But I understood why Hanoi's Royal City Mall was considered an educational experience as soon as I got there. It shattered every idea I had about Vietnam when I was growing up after the war, and it still stunned me even after spending a week in the city.

The entrance looked like a Roman emperor's palace surrounded by luxurious high-rises. The inside was vast and burrowed deep underground. You could walk around in there for miles without retracing your steps, past sparkling fountains, gourmet restaurants, local boutiques as well as international chain stores, snack shops, playgrounds, an ice-skating rink and—best and strangest of all—a huge area designed to look like a somewhat cartoonish version of Hanoi's Old Quarter without all the hazardous traffic, the noise, the banging construction, the obstacles on the sidewalks and most blessedly of all without the heat or humidity. The place is as opulent as Las Vegas.

In fact, the indoor replica of the Old Quarter was exactly what a Las Vegas mogul would build if he decided to create a Vietnam-themed hotel and casino like the Disneyish knockoffs of Venice, New York City and Paris. I could not help but laugh. The Vegas version of Hanoi existed in … Hanoi!

I could only imagine how a Cuban would feel if he were whisked there from Havana with a ration card in his pocket and his state-imposed maximum wage of twenty dollars a month in his wallet.

The Royal City Mall was unique too because it was by far the most impressive I'd seen. The Vietnamese man who told me to go there knew I'd react this way, which is surely the reason he told me to go there.

It *couldn't* be a mall for just the elite. Thousands of Vietnamese were in there at the same time I was, and all day long thousands more kept coming in. And Royal City was just one huge mall of many in Hanoi, all visited by thousands each day. Most of these people had to be middle class. There weren't that many rich people in the city.

How strange, I thought, that such a place existed in a country run by a government that calls itself the Communist Party. Ho Chi Minh would have mortared it out of existence, but he's as dead as his ideology. Go ahead and dismiss malls if you want, but they beat the pants off long lines in the heat for handfuls of rice.

Even the best malls can be a little garish, but you can't live in a country where every street looks like the Latin Quarter of Paris. No such country exists. Not even France can live up to that standard. The city center of Paris is the most magnificent urban environment in the world, but the outskirts beyond the Boulevard Périphérique are far more dreary and drab and communist-looking than anywhere in Hanoi.

Those in the United States—and I sheepishly include myself in this category—who have scoffed at the Mall of America should instead be glad we live in a nation where building and hanging out in such places is possible. Because until recently, the Vietnamese didn't.

People yearn to be bourgeois all over the world. When they have the ways and the means, they like to visit climate-controlled shopping centers. They buy things. They have dinner. They see movies in the Cineplex. They go there on dates. They take the kids. They hang out with friends. Say you hate malls all you want, that the Vietnamese caught the disease of consumerism, that they're losing their souls to consumption just like Americans, and you may have a point.

But if you want to stop people from living this way, you will need to put them in camps.

Totalitarian regimes are categorically different—and drastically more repressive and destructive—than standard-issue authoritarian states. Think of the gulf separating Josef Stalin's Soviet Union from Vladimir Putin's Russia. They were both repressive, sure, but there's no question about where the vast majority of us would rather live.

Jeane Kirkpatrick nailed the salient differences between the two types of regimes in 1979.

"Traditional autocrats," she wrote, "leave in place existing allocations of wealth, power, status, and other resources which in most traditional societies favor an affluent few and maintain masses in poverty. But they worship traditional gods and observe traditional taboos. They do not disturb the habitual rhythms of work and leisure, habitual places of residence, habitual patterns of family and personal relations. Because the miseries of traditional life are familiar, they are bearable to ordinary people who, growing up in the society, learn to cope, as children born to untouchables in India acquire the skills and attitudes necessary for survival in the miserable roles they are destined to fill. Such societies create no refugees.

"Precisely the opposite is true of revolutionary Communist regimes. They create refugees by the million because they claim jurisdiction over the whole life of the society and make demands for change that so violate internalized values and habits that inhabitants flee by the tens of thousands in the remarkable expectation that their attitudes, values, and goals will 'fit' better in a foreign country than in their native land."

Hitler's Nazi regime produced similar results, as did the Taliban regime in Afghanistan. ISIS did the same in Syria and Iraq: Millions of Sunni Muslims fled fanatical psychopaths with whom they clearly didn't share values and habits despite having a religion in common. Millions of Cubans fled to South Florida from Havana, thanks to Fidel Castro. And millions of Vietnamese fled the south after the communist north conquered it in 1975 and sent thousands to "re-education" camps. Most came to America.

Vietnam in 1975 was precisely the sort of revolutionary communist state that Kirkpatrick had described in her 1979 essay, yet the government regime-changed itself with a Marxist-style revolution from above into the kind of standard-issue authoritarian government it once went to war against in U.S.-backed South Vietnam.

Despite having terrible relations with China, Hanoi explicitly followed Beijing's economic and political model. The tradeoff was simple: The state would yield on economic freedom as long as citizens didn't demand political freedom. Princeton professor and China expert Perry Link summed it up as "Shut up and I'll let you get rich."

Perhaps none of this should be surprising. "Vietnam was never all that ideologically communist," Pete Peterson, the former U.S. ambassador to Vietnam, told me. "It was always more socialist and nationalist. I told them they should stop calling themselves the Communist Party, but I didn't get anywhere with it. Everybody pays for everything over there, including health care. The government hardly provides anything. Sweden is more socialist than Vietnam."

I asked one Hanoi resident what the word *communism* even means anymore in Vietnam.

"Communism today just means we're run by one political party," he said. "Some people complain about that, but it doesn't matter to me as long as the government creates a good business and living environment, and it does. I don't want different political parties competing with each other and creating a crisis like in Thailand."

He may not have minded one-party rule, but plenty of Vietnamese did. The government created the conditions for the same kind of middle-class revolt that erupted in Taiwan and South Korea before they finally matured into multiparty democracies.

Vietnam was enjoying a holiday from history when I got there, basking in the prosperous and relatively "free" post-totalitarian phase of its evolution. Amid all the economic and cultural dynamism, the state was a weirdly distant anachronism, its billboards and slogans as out of place as World War II posters would be in America now. The party still blasted "news" over a thundering public-address system onto the streets and into everyone's home each morning and evening, but every Vietnamese person I talked to about it contemptuously dismissed it as "just propaganda."

Not only the ideology but also the state itself felt almost irrelevant to anyone who wasn't an outspoken dissident. Controlling Vietnam's people and imposing order on the nation's natural freewheeling chaos was an exercise in futility. No-honking signs and traffic regulations were utterly flouted, as were parking restrictions. I saw two police officers pull up in a car across the street from my hotel and yell at a bunch of people through a bullhorn to move their motorbikes off the sidewalk. They complied, but less than five minutes after the policemen drove off, the space filled up again.

The most striking example of the state's remoteness from reality that I encountered was inside an electronics store, where a vast selection of the most cutting-edge technology for sale compared with that of the best outlets in Silicon Valley. It sold the usual selection of smart phones and tablets, of course, and also "smart" rice cookers with options Americans have never even heard of. I saw an 82-inch Ultra HD TV with clarity so sharp, it stopped me dead in my tracks. The price tag read $15,000. Just down the same aisle was a small TV tuned to an official government "news" channel. It showed elderly men in army uniforms lecturing a room full of grandmothers old enough to remember the war and the great socialist revolution, who were sitting in metal chairs with their hands folded in their laps and listening like well-behaved children in class. The program's production values were no better than home movies made on a camcorder in 1986, which made the TV itself seem decades out of date, even though it had just come off an assembly line in Japan. I stood there and stared at it, fascinated by the dismal 1970s feel of it all in a room full of eye-popping technology. None of the Vietnamese shoppers paid the slightest bit of attention to it, seeming to recognize as I did that the regime is an undead relic from another era, overwhelmed and made irrelevant by its own country's prosperity and its younger plugged-in generations who refuse to take seriously the old men in uniforms who have no idea what century they're living in.

Vietnamese anti-Americanism scarcely existed. What we call the Vietnam War, and what they call the American War, cast no shadow—especially not in the south, which fought on the American side, but not even in Hanoi, a city that was heavily bombed by the United States.

I saw no evidence anywhere that the U.S. or anyone else ever dropped a single bomb on Hanoi. All the damage had apparently been repaired, and most Vietnamese are too young to remember it anyway.

That war was just one in a long history of conflicts that exists now only in textbooks, and it isn't even the most recent. After the U.S. withdrawal, the Vietnamese continued fighting *themselves*. "Open your eyes and turn over the enemy corpses," wrote poet Trinh Cong Son. "Those are Vietnamese faces upon them." They mounted a full-scale invasion of Cambodia in 1978 and dished out a long-overdue regime change against Pol Pot and his legions of genocidaires. China invaded Vietnam in 1979. Before its 20th century conflicts, the Vietnamese fought the Chinese on and off for more than a thousand years. The war we Americans know so well and mourn is a mere blip in their history, a blip that everyone in both countries knows will not be repeated.

Perhaps it's not so remarkable that the Vietnamese didn't hold any grudges. Americans likewise don't hold grudges for long after the furies of war have subsided. Hardly any of us hate the Japanese, the Germans or the Vietnamese. We rightly despise the Taliban but not the everyday people of Afghanistan. So the Vietnamese aren't unique for being emotionally mature about history, but they are unlike some, especially in the Middle East, who can't get past even the most ancient of grievances. George Santayana once said that those who can't remember the past are condemned to repeat it, to which P.J. O'Rourke added, with the Arab-Israeli conflict in mind, that "it goes double for those who can't remember anything else."

Both the Vietnamese people and government—in the *north* as well as the south—viewed Americans as allies. The leaders were communists who voluntarily embarked on a journey of economic dynamism and friendship with the United States. In doing so, they first abandoned and then reversed everything they once fought and died for. And they prospered as a result.

The city exhausted me after a while, so I took a brief break on the coast of the Gulf of Tonkin.

I did not drive there. Vietnam was so far the one country I'd visited where driving *must* be left to the professionals.

The near ubiquitous nice housing of the city continued into the countryside. Where was the poverty? Surely there must have been poverty somewhere out in the country. In the mountains, perhaps, or along the Cambodian border. But while the rural areas along the highway between the capital and the coast were less cosmopolitan and fashionable, they were not destitute. At least the ones along the main highway weren't destitute. I saw water buffalo and women with conical hats in the fields and three-story houses with balconies. The whole scene looked bucolic, though field work in that climate had to be brutal.

And the coast was spectacular, especially Halong Bay, roughly 30 miles south of the border with China. Hundreds of islands, most of them karst towers and cones topped with a riot of vegetation, spread out in a vast panorama that went on for miles.

Hạ Long means "descending dragon" in Vietnamese. The bay is a UNESCO World Heritage site and is considered one of the natural wonders of Asia.

Boat tours were startlingly cheap, so I booked one and set out. The air temperature dropped 10 degrees the minute the captain pushed us away from the shoreline.

Every direction looked like the setting for an Asian fairy tale. The land formations were wondrous, even surreal, and they were crawling with screaming insects that in concert sounded like a huge whirring bone saw. There was no other sound on the water.

Sadly, though, there was trash in the bay. Vietnam was not trashy in general, but I saw a heartbreaking amount of plastic bottles, beer cans, potato-chip wrappers and chunks of Styrofoam floating by in the water—along with jellyfish with heads the size of basketballs.

"How dangerous are those jellyfish?" I asked the captain. "What happens if they sting a person?"

"Pain," he said. "No die, but great pain."

The water was calm and refreshing, but swimming there at night would have been spectacularly foolish.

Much of the trash was generated by people who lived in floating villages made of clapboard houses on Styrofoam platforms far from the mainland. They had no electricity or modern amenities. Those villages were objectively poor. None of Vietnam's newfound prosperity had reached these people, but fewer than 200 still lived out there. The captain told me they lived in caves on the islands until the mid-1990s, when the government ordered them out and told them to live in floating houses instead. But they started polluting the water, so the government was phasing out the villages and relocating everyone to the mainland. Hanoi hoped to have everyone off the islands within the next couple of years. Whether they'd prosper after relocating or resent the state for moving them, I had no idea.

The coast was a pleasant diversion, but I found little grist for my writing mill there. It was beautiful and relaxing, but it was a place for tourists and poets, not journalists. So back to the city I went.

When I returned to Hanoi, I came back to familiar restaurants, cafés, narrow storefronts, traffic and noise. The hotel staff welcomed me back. It was like a tiny homecoming of sorts, and it triggered a question I often pondered when traveling abroad. Could I live there?

Lots of Westerners did. Even I could separate them from the tourists. Their motorbike helmets sometimes gave them away, but I could also tell by their ease in navigating the place, how they crossed the street with the confidence of a local and settled into cafés and restaurants as though they were regulars.

I found a cheap but pleasant-enough-looking restaurant, ordered a beer and some seafood and pretended in my own mind that I lived there. I wanted to know how I felt about that, partly to satisfy my own curiosity but also because it was an important question for me as a writer. It forced me to think seriously about how distressed a place was or wasn't, about the quality of life for the average person and about the political system.

I wasn't initially sure of the answer.

So I kept at it. I tried to look like I lived there by pretending I knew the waitress, drinking my beer with a bored confidence and not fiddling with my chopsticks like an amateur. Whether or not I actually looked like a resident expat, I was starting to feel like one. The only air-conditioning in that particular restaurant was a fan blowing the hot air around, and I didn't mind. My body had recalibrated its thermostat. Full-on air-conditioning made me feel cold. I later got into a taxi that felt like a refrigerator and laughed at myself when I almost asked the driver to turn up the heat.

But could I live there, at least for a while? I had to know. Most places I've traveled, it's an easy question to answer, but in Vietnam it was not.

Could I live in Cairo? No. Baghdad? Hell no. Havana? No chance. Not while it's under the boot heel of the Castros. Rabat? Perhaps. Beirut? I have already lived in Beirut and theoretically could do so again. But what about Hanoi?

Vietnam was a pleasant destination for tourists, for sure, but it was also a one-party, nominally communist state. I have viscerally detested communism since the first moment I learned about it as a child. No political system in the history of the human race has killed such a vast number of people. The fall of the Berlin Wall and the collapse of the Soviet Union were the greatest geopolitical events of my lifetime. Every cell in my body rebelled at the existential heaviness of the state in Cuba on my previous long trip abroad, and after a week I couldn't wait to get out of there.

I had to look it squarely in the eye in Vietnam without flinching.
Could I live there, despite it?
Yes. I believed so.
As long as I stayed out of politics.

Eleven

In the Land of the Brother Leader

Tripoli, Libya 2004

When you visit another country, it's hard to get a feel for what it's actually like until you leave your hotel room, go for a walk, take a look around and hang out while soaking it in. Not so in Libya. All you have to do is show up. It will impose itself on you at once.

My Air Afriqiyah flight touched down on the runway next to a junkyard of filthy, gutted and broken-down aircraft in an airport otherwise empty of planes. When I stepped out of the hatch into the Jetway, I came face-to-face with three uniformed military goons who scrutinized me and everyone else from behind oversize reflective sunglasses.

Colonel Muammar Qaddafi, mastermind of the 1969 al-Fateh Revolution (a euphemism for his military coup), Brother Leader of the Great Socialist People's Libyan Arab Jamahiriya, greeted arrivals in the passport-control room from a menacing, almost snarling gold-gilded portrait. A translated overhead sign (rare in Libya) said, "Partners Not Wage Earners." In other words: Don't expect to be paid.

A bored official glanced at my visa, rubbed his face, stamped my passport and pointed me toward my first Libyan checkpoint. A man in an untucked button-up shirt, with a cigarette jutting out the side of his mouth, waved me toward a metal detector. He hadn't shaved in two days. I walked through. The alarm screamed, and I braced for a pat-down. He just stood there, took a long drag on his cigarette and stared bleary-eyed into space over my shoulder. I guessed that meant I could go. So I did.

There were no other planes coming or going, so it was easy to find my ride. His name was Abdul. He wore a snazzy black leather jacket and a Western-style goatee.

"Welcome to Libya!" he said as he led me into a parking lot the size of an Applebee's.

"We're really busy right now. This is Libya's high season."

They must have shut down the airport entirely during the low season.

The capital city of Tripoli was an asteroid belt of monolithic apartment towers. The streets were mostly empty of cars, the sidewalks empty of people. I saw no restaurants, no cafés, no clubs, no bars and no malls. Nor did I see anywhere else to hang out. Libya, so far, looked depopulated.

We drove past a shattered former government compound surrounded by a lagoon of pulverized concrete that once was a parking lot. It was obvious when that thing was built. The 1970s were the 1970s everywhere, even in Libya.

Only as we approached the center of Tripoli did traffic pick up. Hardly anyone walked around, and it was no wonder: a mile-long pit on the side of the road appeared to be the place to give juice bottles, plastic wrappers, garbage bags and worn-out tires the heave-ho.

I saw no corporate advertising: no Pepsi signs, no movie posters and no cute girls flashing milk-mustache smiles for the dairy industry. I did, however, see one hysterical propaganda billboard after another. They were socialist-realist cartoons from the Soviet era, the same kinds of living museum pieces still on display in North Korea and other wonderful places where starving proles live in glorious jackbooted paradise.

The happy-worker theme was a common one; smiling construction workers wore hard hats, and Bedouins turned widgetmakers basked in the glory of assembly-line work. One poster showed two hands chained together at the wrist below an image of Qaddafi's sinister *Green Book* descending from heaven.

At the hotel I ran into my second Libyan checkpoint. A metal detector was set up at the entrance. A young security agent sat at a metal desk and showed off his open copy of the *Green Book*. He propped it at such an angle that I could read the cover, but he couldn't possibly read what was inside.

I stepped through. The alarm screamed, detecting (perhaps) my dental fillings or zipper. He looked up, gave me a nodding "What's up, dude" smile and went back to pretending to read.

I poked around the lobby while Abdul checked me in at the desk.

The gift shop offered a wide range of totalitarian propaganda books and pamphlets in multiple languages. A fantastic selection of Qaddafi watches ranged in price from $25 to $600. I bought one for $25. Qaddafi is shown wearing his military uniform, officer's hat and sunglasses like a swaggering Latin American generalissimo. It was busted right out of the box, the hour hand stuck forever at nine o'clock.

The lobby was plastered with portraits of the boss in various poses. He wore shades in most of them, but in some pictures from his early days, he wore a buffoonish 1970s haircut instead.

I had to suck down my giggles. God, was this guy for real? His inexportable Third Universal Theory was internationalist insofar as it obliterated any sense that Tripoli was Middle Eastern or African—at least from the point of view of the backseat of the car. I could have been in any Soviet-era republic, or even in some parts of the Bronx. But look at those portraits! Now there was something exotic.

Most of the other men in the lobby (I hadn't seen any women since I landed) looked like Arab businessmen who bought their suits from Turkish remainder bins. The only expensively dressed man sat at a shiny wooden desk, the kind you'd expect to see at a law firm. He had no work in front of him, not even papers to shuffle. His job was to stare holes through everyone who stepped into and out of the elevator.

There were no towels in my room. The bathroom was, however, generously stocked with products, all of them packaged in green—the color of Islam and Qaddafi's so-called revolution. The hotel gave me green shampoo, green soap, green bath gel, green toothpaste and even a green shoehorn and comb. All were clearly (and, I must say, unnecessarily) marked "Made in the Great Socialist People's Libyan Arab Jamahiriya." There was no booze (it's banned), no soda, no water, no juice in the minibar. A burn the size and shape of a deflated basketball was seared into the carpet.

I switched on the TV: nothing but hysterical state-run propaganda. I couldn't lower the volume (the knob was broken), but at least I could change the channel and choose whether I wanted to be droned at or screeched at in Arabic.

My window overlooked the Mediterranean Sea and, closer in, a drained and stained swimming pool. There was a forlorn rocky beach down there, cut off from the hotel and everything else by a blank gray slab of a wall. The cold wind whistling into the room from the patio sounded like moaning ghosts trapped in a well.

Until the middle of 2004, Americans were banned from Libya, not by Qaddafi but by our own government. The travel ban has been lifted, but tourists are still required to book their trip through a Libyan agency. The regime won't tolerate tourists running around loose on their own. You can make your own trip—you don't have to be a part of a tour group—but you'll still be babysat by a guide.

I didn't go to Libya to see the sights, such as they are. I wanted to see a once forbidden country as it really was. So I set out on foot on my own while I had a brief chance.

It was a jarring experience.

The main drag along the sea into the city was one straw short of a freeway. There were no houses, businesses, restaurants or shops along the way—only clusters of vertical human-storage units surrounded by empty lots the size of a Walmart. Trash was smeared on the sidewalks. It clogged all the street gutters. Almost every available blank space (and, oh, were there plenty of those) was a dump site.

I got agoraphobia walking around. The streets were too wide, the buildings too far apart, the landscape barren.

The traffic was too fast, too close and too hectic. I was pinned on a thin ribbon of sidewalk between the Mediterranean and the freeway.

There was no way I could cross that river of mayhem and steel unless I found a traffic light and a crosswalk—an unlikely event, from the look of the place. There wasn't much worth seeing on the other side anyway. Those towers and the empty lots strewn with soda cans, candy-bar wrappers and billowing plastic bags didn't get any prettier as they got closer.

The sea was all but boarded up behind blank white walls and a decayed postindustrial concrete catastrophe of a "waterfront." In the few places I could get a glimpse of the shoreline, it didn't have the look and feel of the familiar Mediterranean but rather an inland sea in a Central Asian republic. The city felt harsh and jagged, and the close but unreachable sea could not take the edge off.

Three young boys crouched next to the dry side of the seawall. They ran up when they saw me and asked for cigarettes. Those kids could not have been older than 10. I had two choices—corrupt Libya's youth or be a stuffy, uptight naysaying American. I chose to corrupt the children. When I handed over the smokes, each slapped his fist on his heart and cried, *"Allahu akbar!"*

The freeway continued as far as I could see without any way for me to cross it. Traffic was relentless, and I didn't dare wade into it without knowing the rules. I could have just bolted in front of the cars and they would have stopped. But I hadn't been in the country for even two hours. I didn't know how anything worked yet. So I went back to the hotel and ordered some dinner.

I'd say that was my mistake, but I did have to eat.

At the restaurant, there was no sign that said "Please Wait to Be Seated." Should I seat myself? Who knew? I felt ridiculous just standing at the entrance. So I found a table.

A waiter finally came over.

"Are you a tourist?" he said.

"Yes," I lied. Libya is a total-surveillance police state. One person in six works for the secret police. Best, I thought, to keep my journalistic intentions to myself.

"For tourists we have fish," he said. He did not give me a menu. I didn't see a single menu anywhere in the country. In Libyan restaurants, you sit down and eat whatever they give you.

"What kind of fish?"

"Eh," he said, taken aback by the question. "Fish. Fish. You know, fish."

"Great," I said. "I'll have the fish."

He brought me two small fish the size of my hand, each fried in a pan. Heads, fins and eyeballs were still attached. Bones and guts were inside. They tasted bad and smelled worse. The businessmen at the tables around me drank nonalcoholic Beck's "beer." But all I got was a bottle of water.

Abdul picked me up again in the morning. His job was to show me Tripoli's sights. There weren't many: Green Square, the museum and an old city smaller than downtown Boise. That's it. That's all there is.

We started with the museum. Phoenician and Roman artifacts were on the first floor. Upstairs was the "Islamic period." The top floor was entirely dedicated to the glorification of Qaddafi.

One room displayed gifts to the colonel from foreign officials and heads of state—swords, jeweled boxes, a crystal map of "Palestine" that included Tel Aviv. A living-room set upholstered with a tacky floral print was roped off in a corner.

"That's where Qaddafi sits with foreign guests he wants to impress," Abdul said.

Right outside the museum was Qaddafi's Green Square—which isn't green, by the way. It's famous, but it shouldn't be. This is no Italian piazza we're talking about. It's an asphalt parking lot ringed by a six-lane urban speedway.

The nice thing about Green Square is that it's central. The Italian

Quarter, built by Italy during Mussolini's fascist-imperialist period, is on one side. The old city is on the other.

The old city was the only neighborhood that looked Middle Eastern. Too bad much of it also looked like the backstreet slums of Havana. Not all of it, though. A few buildings—like the old mosques, a soaring clock tower and the Arch of Marcus Aurelius—were stunning.

It was a pleasant place, actually. Ancient buildings with handcrafted details on them are dignified even in squalor. Rotting grandeur is still grand, after all.

The streets were too narrow for cars. Not one of the shopkeepers harangued me when I walked by as they did constantly in Tunisia when I visited there a few months earlier. There were hardly any cheap tourist gimcracks for sale. I could walk the old city in peace.

Almost everything was solely for local consumption: clothes, fabrics, jewelry, shoes, batteries and so on. One of the narrower streets was lined with almost medieval metal forges, where copper pots and crescent moons for the tops of minarets were banged into shape with hammers and tongs over fires.

I didn't see theaters, clubs or any other places of diversion or entertainment. "Until two years ago," Abdul said, "there was nothing to do in Libya but sleep. Things are better now."

Things weren't much better, though. Libya's economy was still mostly socialist. There will be no fun without capitalism. Sorry. The state just isn't gonna provide it, especially not a state that can't even pick up the garbage.

"So, Abdul," I said as we walked through the souk. "How many Libyans wear a Qaddafi watch?"

"Um," he said and laughed grimly. "Not very many. There are, you know, enough pictures around." He leaned in and whispered, "I don't like him much, to be honest."

I had imagined not.

"Look over there," he said and pointed with his eyes. "You see those two?"

I saw a couple in their mid-20s chatting next to one of the gates to the old city. He wore a black leather jacket, she a long brown overcoat and a headscarf over her hair. They stood close together but didn't touch. They looked soft, comfortable and content together as if they were married.

"Five, 10 years ago I never saw anything like that. It was absolutely forbidden."

He told me to take off my shoes as he led me into a mosque. Seeing the handmade carpets, high ceilings, marbled walls, Roman columns, intricate tile work and soft lighting was like slipping into a warm bath for the soul. The heart-stopping beauty and serenity of the mosque in this harsh urban parking garage of a landscape was a strong incentive for piety, I suspected. I'm not religious, but I could see why some sought refuge from the modern in God. Modernity in this oppressive dystopian city was a spectacular galactic-size failure.

He dropped me off at my hotel before dark. Now that I knew the layout of the city, I decided to return to Green Square alone. I wanted to know what the real Tripoli, the not-touristed Tripoli, looked like.

It was worse on foot than by car and exactly what I expected: all right angles and concrete. Almost everyone in this part of town lived in a low barracks-like compound or a Stalinist tower. Landscaping didn't exist. There were no smooth edges, no soft sights, nothing to sigh at. Tripoli's aesthetic brutality hurt me.

I walked parts of the city that hardly any foreigners ever bothered to see. It looked postapocalyptic, as if it had been evacuated in war or hit with a neutron bomb. The sound of machine-gun fire off in the distance wouldn't have seemed out of place.

Less than 1 percent of the people I saw were women. All those who did go outside wore headscarves. So much for Qaddafi's being a "feminist," as he claims. Tripoli had as many women out and about as a dust-blown village in the boondocks of Afghanistan.

The few men I did see walked or huddled together. They looked sullen, heavy, severe. I felt raw and exposed, wondering what on earth they must have thought when they saw an obvious foreigner wandering around the desolate streets.

So I did what I could to find out. I smiled at everyone who walked past. You can learn a lot about a people and a place by trying this out. In New York City, people ignore you. In Guatemala City, people will stare. In Libya, they all smiled back, every last one of them, no matter how grumpy or self-absorbed they looked two seconds before.

I never detected even a whiff of hostility, not from a single person. Libyans seemed a decent, gentle, welcoming people with terrible luck. It wasn't their fault the neighborhood stank of oppression.

Most apartment buildings were more or less equally dreary, but one did stand out. Architecturally it was just another modernist horror. But a 6-by-8-foot portrait of Qaddafi was bolted to the facade three stories up. It partially blocked the view from two of the balconies. The bastard couldn't even leave people alone when they were home.

The posters weren't funny anymore. There were too damn many of them, for one thing. And, besides, Qaddafi is ugly. He may earn a few charisma points for traveling to Brussels and pitching his Bedouin tent on the parliament lawn, but he's no Che Guevara in the *guapo* department.

I felt ashamed that I first found his portraits even slightly amusing. The novelty wore off in less than a day, and he'd been in power longer than I'd been alive. He was an abstraction when I first got there. But after walking around his outdoor laboratory and everywhere seeing his beady eyes and that arrogant jut of his mouth, it suddenly hit me. He isn't merely Libya's tyrant. He is a man who would be god.

His Mukhabarat, the secret police, are omniscient. His visage is omnipresent. His power is omnipotent.

And he is deranged. He says he's the sun of Africa. He threatens to ban money and schools. He vanquished beauty and art. He liquidates those who oppose him. He says he can't help it if the people of Libya love him so much, they plaster his portrait up everywhere. Fuck him. I wanted to rip his face from the walls.

If you go to Libya, you simply must visit Ghadamis. Known by travelers as the jewel of the Sahara, it's worth all the money and all the hassle you have to put up with to get there.

In the early 1980s, Qaddafi's regime emptied the ancient Berber Saharan city by decree. Everyone was shepherded into the modern concrete "new town," which begins right outside the mysterious tomblike adobe gates of the old.

The old city doesn't look like a city when you're inside. It looks like a vast underground system of tunnels and caves lit by skylights. It's not underground; it was built with a roof over the top to keep the infernal summer heat out and the meager winter warmth in. Some of the streets (which really are more like passages) are pitch black even at noon. There was no need for light. The inhabitants had memorized the walls.

It is not a small town. It's an enormous weatherproofed adobe mini metropolis. There are seven quarters and seven gates, one for each resident tribe. Everything you expect in a city is there—streets, homes, offices, markets, public squares and mosques, all made of painted mud and sparkling gypsum. The only thing missing from the old city is people.

If Libya were a normal country—and if Ghadamis were a normal city—the old city would be packed with hotels, coffee shops, restaurants, bookstores, Internet cafés and desert-adventure tour offices. But Libya is not a normal country, and Ghadamis is an unwilling ghost town.

My travel agency replaced Abdul with a second guide for the trip to Ghadamis and into the desert. "Yasir," I said to him. "Why were the people of Ghadamis forced out of their homes?"

I knew the answer already. It was part of Qaddafi's plot to Arabize the Berbers and to construct the New Man, a ludicrous ideal hatched in the Soviet Union. (Berbers are also forbidden to write anything publicly in their own language.) But I wanted to see if a local was permitted to say it. He couldn't—or at least didn't—answer my question. He only shook his head and laughed nervously. There were others around who could hear.

The old city was declared a World Heritage site by UNESCO. A few engineers were inside shoring up the foundations of an old mosque.

"It's astonishing," one of them said when I chatted him up. He was an Arab who had studied engineering at a Western university and spoke masterful English in fully formed paragraphs. "The sophistication and aesthetic perfection in the old city contrasts markedly with the failures in the new."

No kidding. I've never seen anything like it anywhere else in the world. Neither have you. Because there is nothing like it anywhere else in the world. And there never will be.

"We're here to make this place livable again because someday, you know . . ." He trailed off, but I knew what he wished he could say. Someday Qaddafi would die. When his bones pushed up date palms, the people of Ghadamis could abandon their compounds of concrete and move back into the city that's rightfully theirs.

I returned to the old city at night by myself and saw a single square of light in an upstairs room of an ancient house. The owners are forbidden to stay there at night. But it's nice to know that some of them still leave the lights on.

When you visit another country, it's inevitable: you are going to meet other travelers. And you'll almost certainly talk about other places you've been. Go to Costa Rica, and conversations will turn to Guatemala and Bolivia. If you hang out in Cancún, you'll meet people who like the Virgin Islands and Hawaii. In Paris you'll hear talk of London, Prague and Vienna.

So what happens when you bump into others in Libya? In Tripoli, I met a photographer who spends every summer in Darfur. Out in the dunes, I met a long-haired, goofy, bespectacled English guy named Felix. This was the first time he had ever set eyes on a desert. (He really went for it.) He had a thing for totalitarian countries. "I like to visit places based on ideas," he said. Then he checked himself. "That doesn't mean I like the ideas."

"Where to next, Felix?" I said.

"North Korea, if I can get in."

"I'd like to see North Korea," I said. "But after that, what's left?"

"Only the moon," he said and laughed. "This is great, meeting you here. It's nice to know someone else who's open to nuttiness."

You'll find nuttiness in Libya even out in the boonies. On the treacherous so-called road from Ghadamis into the dunes, someone used an enormous piece of ordnance that looked like a mini-Scud missile to mark a 3-foot chassis-busting hole in the ground.

Yasir couldn't take me on that road in his van. So we hired Bashir to come with us. He was a burly man with a turban and a beard who taught philosophy in school. We didn't hire him, though, for his brain. We wanted his Land Rover.

The three of us left Ghadamis and headed straight toward the Algerian gate only a couple of miles away.

Just beyond it, a 300-foot-tall mountain of sand was piled in layers.

"You see that sand," Bashir said and pointed. I could hardly take my eyes off it. "Two weeks ago I drove some Japanese tourists out here. The old guy asked me who built the dune." He chuckled and shook his head. "I told him, well, my grandfather worked for a while on that project, but now he's dead."

"We can't go there," Yasir said. "We must visit Libyan sand. Last month some German tourists were kidnapped right on the other side of the border."

More than 100,000 people were killed in Algeria during the 1990s and into the 2000s in a civil war between the military regime and Islamist fanatics.

"Have you ever been to Algeria?" I asked.

"No one here goes to Algeria," he said.

We drove over a hill and were surrounded on three sides by

dizzying, towering, impossibly sized dunes. We slogged our way to the top, gasping, with calves and thighs burning, not daring to look down, to watch the sunset.

The top was unreal. The desert floor was another world far below ours. If birds were in flight, I could have looked down on them. On the western horizon was the Grand Erg Oriental, a sea of dunes bigger than France that looked from the side like a distant Andes of sand. Bashir made bread and sticky mint tea.

I watched the sun go down and the sky go out.

By Libyan standards, this was radical freedom. Life goes on even in countries like this one. No government, no matter how oppressive, can control all the people all the time—especially not in the vast and empty Sahara.

We ran down the sand and climbed back into the Land Rover. Bashir hit the gas. He zigged us and zagged us up, down and across 300-foot-tall dunes along the border with Algeria. At one point—and I couldn't tell if he was joking or serious—he said we had actually crossed into Algeria.

The stars came out. A full moon rose, turning the sand into silver. We laughed like boys as we rode the dunes in the moonlight.

I didn't go back to Tripoli to hang out in Tripoli. Tourists use the city as a base to visit the spectacular nearby Roman ruins of Sabratha and Leptis Magna. I'm not exactly a ruins buff, but trips to these places came with the package. So I went. And I saw. And I was nearly alone. I shared Leptis Magna with only my guide and some goats. Sabratha would have been empty if the vice president of the Philippines hadn't dropped by at the same time.

But I was glad to be back in Tripoli. This time my hotel was in the Italian Quarter, just two blocks from Green Square. Not again would I have to walk through a swath of Stalinist blocks to get to a proper neighborhood.

My new hotel was more upscale than the first. The management (or was it the state?) pretended to have tighter security. The metal detector just inside the entrance wasn't being watched by a college kid. It was staffed by the military.

Okay, I thought. Now they're gonna be serious. I stepped through and the metal detector screamed. The soldiers ignored me, joked with each other and never looked up. The same thing happened every time I walked through it.

Libya is a totalitarian police state. But it's an awfully lethargic totalitarian police state. It's been a while, I thought, since anyone there drank the Kool-Aid.

The heater in my room sounded like a chopper over the jungles of 'Nam. It was broken and stuck forever on Cold, but the maid left it on anyway. So while it was 60 degrees and cloudy outside, it was a teeth-chattering 50 degrees in my room. I opened the window, and the cold wind off the Mediterranean actually warmed the place up.

A bath could have made me feel better, but the hot-water knob came off in my hand. The hotel had the outward appearance of spiffiness, so I'm sure there was hot water somewhere in the building behind the hole where the knob had come off in my hand. I just couldn't get to any of it.

The elite were downstairs in the lobby. Slick men in suits, mostly from Arab countries, all but ignored the French delegation that was in town while Jacques Chirac cut new oil deals with Qaddafi. There were no Americans, no tourists and no women. I felt underdressed and out of place in my khakis and sandals, but what could I do? I was in a hard-line, oily-sheened Arab police state. I couldn't have blended in if I tried—except, perhaps, in one little corner of the Italian Quarter.

If you were dropped from the sky onto the main street that ran through that district, you could be forgiven if you thought you were somewhere in the West. It was strung from one end to the other with hip, cutting-edge perfume and clothing stores. These places had bright lights, colored walls and fancy displays. They piped in Western music through sophisticated sound systems. The salespeople wore snappy, stylish clothes. The customers were young and cool. There were, amazingly, hardly any portraits of Qaddafi in this part of town. (Perhaps the warehouse was out of stock and the new stores had them on back order.)

There was far less commerce in Libya than in most countries, but this little micro-corner was bustling. I found French cheese (but not prohibited wine), Japanese DVD players, Belgian chocolate and Swiss instant coffee.

At first I thought the only coffee shops in the city could be found along a single block on one of the back streets. Old men sat out front in cheap plastic chairs and grumpily smoked hookahs. That didn't look like very much fun.

But then I found an Italian-style café fronting Green Square. I ordered a double macchiato and a cheese pastry and actually found a nice dainty table. I looked around and thought, Heck, this could be Italy or even Los Angeles if it weren't for the total lack of women around. Globalization penetrates even Arab socialist rogue states these days. And what a relief, really. You'd never know you were in the beating heart of a brutal dictatorship while sitting in that little place.

Both my guides, Abdul and Yasir, took me to dinner. We could have eaten in the Italian Quarter. But no. They had to take me out to the Parking Garage Quarter, which is to say, anywhere else but the old city.

I groaned silently to myself. I liked these guys—if not their taste in dining establishments—but I hated being schlepped around all the time and never being asked when or where I wanted to eat.

The only time I truly needed a guide was on the road between Tripoli and Ghadamis.

I couldn't read the Arabic road signs. Armed soldiers demanded papers at checkpoints. I was grateful my guides had the stacks of papers prepared. But in the city, I was perfectly capable of finding a place to eat on my own. It wasn't easy, but it could be done with effort and patience.

I appreciated the hospitality, even though it was bought and paid for. Abdul and Yasir seemed to enjoy "buying" my dinner, but I felt micromanaged and babysat. Come here, look at that, sit there, eat this. They were great guys. But I lusted for solitude. If I said so, they would have been offended.

They took me to a restaurant in a neighborhood that was downright North Korean, it was so chock-full of concrete.

"We really hope you like this place," Yasir said.

It wasn't quite as bad as a parking garage, but it was a near miss. The main floor was reserved for a wedding, so we were shepherded upstairs to a huge, dimly lit room mostly empty of tables. The wedding party hadn't arrived yet. There was no one else in the building.

I didn't know what to say in this gloomy warehouse of a restaurant. I felt like we were the only people out for dinner that night in all of Libya. Abdul and Yasir hoped I would like this place? Oh, the poor dears. I was embarrassed for them and wondered what tourist in his right mind would come to Libya when he could go to Tunisia, Morocco or Turkey instead.

Worlds can't meet worlds. But people can meet people. I forget who said that, but I like it, and I thought about it as I walked around inside Libya, hanging out and talking to regular folks.

In a nation where so many report to the secret police, where a sideways word can get you imprisoned or killed, walking around blue-eyed and pale-faced with an American accent has its advantages. I met one shopkeeper who opened right up when he and I found ourselves alone in his store.

"Do Americans know much about Libya?" he said.

"No," I said. "Not really."

He wanted to teach me something about his country, but he didn't know where to start. So he recited encyclopedia factoids.

He listed the principal resources while counting his fingers. I stifled a smirk when he named the border states. (I hardly needed a sixth grade geography lesson.) When he told me Arabic was the official language, I wondered if he thought I was stupid or deaf.

"And Qaddafi is our president," he said. "About him, no comment." He laughed, but I don't think he thought it was funny.

"Oh, come on," I said. "Comment away. I don't live here."

He thought about that. For a long drawn-out moment, he calculated the odds and weighed the consequences. Then the dam burst.

"We hate that fucking bastard—we have nothing to do with him. Nothing. We keep our heads down and our mouths shut. We do our jobs, we go home. If I talk, they will take me out of my house in the night and put me in prison."

"Qaddafi steals," he told me. "He steals from us." He spoke rapidly now, twice as fast as before, as though he had been holding back all his life. He wiped sweat off his forehead with trembling hands. "The oil money goes to his friends. Tunisians next door are richer and they don't even have any oil."

"I know," I said. "I'm sorry."

"We get three or four hundred dinars each month to live on. Our families are huge, we have five or six children. It is a really big problem. We don't make enough to take care of them. I want to live in Lebanon. Beirut is the second Paris. It is civilized! Women and men mix freely in Lebanon."

Almost everybody I know thought I was crazy to travel to Libya. The unspoken fear was that someone might kill me.

Well, no. Nobody killed me. Nobody even looked at me funny. I knew that's how it would be before I set out. Still, it's nice to have the old adage that "people are people" proved through experience.

Libyans are fed a steady diet of anti-Americanism, but it comes from a man who has kicked them in the stomach and stomped on their face for more than a third of a century. If they bought it, they sure didn't act like it.

I crossed paths with a middle-aged Englishman in the hallway.

"Is this a good hotel?" he asked.

It sure beat my last place in town. At least I wasn't stranded out by the towers.

"It's a good hotel," I said, not really believing it but grateful for what I had.

"I think it's bloody awful," he said.

I laughed. "Well, yes," I said. "I was just trying to be nice. You should see the place where I stayed when I first got here."

I heard footsteps behind me, turned around and faced two Arab men wearing coats and ties and carrying briefcases. One wore glasses. The other was bald.

"It has been a long time since I heard that accent," said the man with the glasses.

I smiled. "It's been a long time since this accent was here," I said. Until just a few months earlier, any American standing on Libyan soil was committing a felony.

"We went to college together," he said, and jerked his thumb toward his friend. "In Lawrence, Kansas, during the '70s."

"Yes," his friend said as he rubbed the bald spot on his head. The two were all smiles now as they remembered. "We took a long road trip up to Seattle."

"We stayed there for two weeks!" said the first. He sighed like a man recalling his first long-lost love. I watched both their faces soften as they recalled the memories of their youth and adventures abroad in America.

"What a wonderful time we had there," said the second.

They invited me out to dinner, but I was getting ready to leave. I didn't want to say no. They looked like they wanted to hug me.

We shook hands as we departed. And as I stepped into the elevator, the first man put his hand on his heart. "Give two big kisses to Americans when you get home," he said. "From two people in Libya who miss you so much."

ALSO BY MICHAEL J. TOTTEN

The Road to Fatima Gate
In the Wake of the Surge
Where the West Ends
Taken: A Novel
Resurrection: A Zombie Novel
Tower of the Sun

www.ingramcontent.com/pod-product-compliance
Lightning Source LLC
Chambersburg PA
CBHW021139090426
42740CB00008B/842